English Idioms in Use

Michael McCarthy
Felicity O'Dell

CAMBRIDGE
UNIVERSITY PRESS

PUBLISHED BY THE PRESS SYNDICATE OF THE UNIVERSITY OF CAMBRIDGE
The Pitt Building, Trumpington Street, Cambridge, United Kingdom

CAMBRIDGE UNIVERSITY PRESS
The Edinburgh Building, Cambridge CB2 2RU, UK
40 West 20th Street, New York, NY 10011–4211, USA
477 Williamstown Road, Port Melbourne, VIC 3207, Australia
Ruiz de Alarcón 13, 28014 Madrid, Spain
Dock House, The Waterfront, Cape Town 8001, South Africa

http://www.cambridge.org

First published 2002
Third printing 2003

Printed in Italy by G. Canale & C. S.p.A

Typeface Sabon 10/12pt.   *System* QuarkXPress® [OD&I]

A catalogue record for this book is available from the British Library

Library of Congress Cataloguing in Publication data

ISBN 0 521 78957 5 paperback

Contents

Learning about idioms

Idioms to talk about ...

Idioms from the topic area of ...

Idioms using these keywords:

Acknowledgements

This book, like all our other books in the *In Use* series, is the result of the work of many people. Cambridge University Press editors, reviewers, designers, marketing staff, sales and publicity staff have all contributed their advice and expertise, and there are just too many to name here. We have also received invaluable feedback and suggestions based on earlier versions of units from teachers, students, reviewers, Cambridge University Press sales representatives and conference audiences all over the world, and we thank you all for suggesting ways forward, praising our good ideas and pointing out our shortcomings, so that, we hope, this book reflects what we have gained and learnt from you, and what you feel you need for your teaching and learning situations.

In particular we would like to thank the following teachers, students and institutions from all over the world who reviewed and piloted the material during its development:

Kristi Alcouffe, Alcouffe Formation, Paris, France
Duncan Campbell, London, UK
Ian Chitty, Cambridge, UK
Olga Gasparova, Moscow, Russia
Carol M. Geppert, Tübingen, Germany
Ludmila Gorodetskaya, Moscow, Russia
Diann Gruber, Champs-sur-Marne, France
Elsa Lattey, Tübingen, Germany
David Matley, University of Stuttgart, Stuttgart, Germany
Ewa Modrzejewska, Gdansk, Poland
Terry Nelson, Sungkyunkwan University, Seoul, Korea
David Perry, Valencia, Spain
Gordon Robinson, Nanyang Technological University, Singapore, Republic of Singapore
Diane Slaouti, Manchester, UK
Brendan Smith, Madrid, Spain
Anita Trawinska, EMPiK, Warsaw, Poland
Arthur Tu, Taipei, Taiwan
Marilyn Woolff, The English Centre, Hampstead Garden Suburb Institute, London, UK
Eliane Zamboni, São Paulo, Brazil

In addition, particular thanks must go to the following people: Nóirín Burke of Cambridge University Press, whose expertise and vision as our commissioning editor continues to be inspirational; Martine Walsh, also of Cambridge University Press, who has guided the project from its outset through to fruition and who has offered encouragement and advice all the way along; and Liz Driscoll, whose careful editing work on the final manuscript has made the book into what you have before you now. Finally, as always, we would both like to thank our domestic partners and loved ones for their unfailing support during the long days when we were shackled to our computer keyboards.

Michael McCarthy and Felicity O'Dell, March 2002

Using this book

Why was this book written?

It was written to help you improve your knowledge of idioms in English. Idioms are fixed expressions whose meaning is not immediately obvious from looking at the individual words in the idiom. You will come across a great many idioms when you listen to and read English. So it is important that you learn about the meanings of idioms and about how they are used. You can use this book either with a teacher or for self-study.

We wanted to encourage language learners to have a balanced approach to idioms in English. Sometimes in the past, teachers used to argue that it was a waste of time for learners to study idioms as they might start using them in an inaccurate or unsuitable way. But idioms are in such widespread use that it is inappropriate to ignore them. This book focuses just on those idioms which the modern student needs to know and it aims to provide the information and practice which will help you understand and use them correctly.

How were the idioms in the book selected?

There are a great many idioms in English, but some of them sound rather old-fashioned or are not very widely used. The 1,000 or so idioms which are worked on in this book were all selected from those identified as significant based on computer searches of huge language databases: the CANCODE corpus of spoken English, developed at the University of Nottingham in association with Cambridge University Press and the Cambridge International Corpus of written English. These databases show us how the idioms have actually been used by native speakers of English in conversations, newspapers, novels, and many other contexts. The idioms selected are all also to be found in the *Cambridge International Dictionary of Idioms* where additional examples and usage notes will also be found. You can search this dictionary online by going to the following website: http://dictionary.cambridge.org

How is the book organised?

The book has 60 two-page units. The left-hand page presents the idioms that are worked on in the unit. You will usually find an explanation of the meaning of each idiom, an example of it in use and, where appropriate, any special notes about its usage. The right-hand page checks that you have understood the information on the left-hand page by giving you a series of exercises that practise the material just presented. The exercises pay particular attention to checking your understanding of the idioms and how they are used because this is more important for most learners than being able to actively use the idioms.

The units are organised in three sections:

Idioms to talk about ... which groups idioms according to the topic area that they are used to talk about. Thus, **to be snowed under** [to have an enormous amount of work to do] is included in Unit 25, Work.

Idioms from the topic area of ... which groups idioms according to the image they are based on. Thus, **hit the roof** [react in a very angry way] is included in Unit 41, Houses and household objects

Idioms using these keywords which groups idioms according to keywords in them. For example, Unit 48 deals with a set of idioms based on the word **head**.

The book also has a key to all the exercises and an index which lists the 1,000 idioms we deal with and indicates the units where they can each be found.

How should I use this book?

As well as the 60 main units, there are two introductory units: Unit i What are idioms? and Unit ii Using your dictionary. It is strongly recommended that you work through these units first. After that, you may work on the units in any order that suits you.

What else do I need in order to work with this book?

You need a notebook or file in which you can write down the idioms that you study in this book as well as any others that you come across elsewhere.

You also need to have access to a good dictionary. We strongly recommend the *Cambridge International Dictionary of Idioms* as this gives exactly the kind of information that you need to have about idioms. Your teacher, however, may also be able to recommend other dictionaries that you will find useful.

So, we hope that this book will 'shed light' on all you need to know about English idioms (see Unit 8) and that, by the time you finish the units, you'll be saying: 'English idioms? A piece of cake!' (see Unit 17).

i What are idioms?

Idioms and meaning

Idioms are expressions which have a meaning that is not obvious from the individual words. For example, the idiom **drive somebody round the bend** means *make somebody angry or frustrated*, but we cannot know this just by looking at the words.

The best way to understand an idiom is to see it in context. If someone says:
This tin opener's driving me round the bend! I think I'll throw it away and get a new one next time I'm in town.
then the context and common sense tells us that **drive round the bend** means something different from driving a car round a curve in the road. The context tells us the tin opener is not working properly and that it's having an effect on the person using it.

B **Types of idioms**

form	example	meaning
verb + object/complement (and/or adverbial)	**kill two birds with one stone**	produce two useful results by just doing one action
prepositional phrase	**in the blink of an eye**	in an extremely short time
compound	**a bone of contention**	something which people argue and disagree over
simile /'sɪmɪli/ (*as* + adjective + *as*, or *like* + noun)	**as dry as a bone**	very dry indeed
binomial (word + *and* + word)	**rough and ready**	crude and lacking sophistication
trinomial (word + word + *and* + word)	**cool, calm and collected**	relaxed, in control, not nervous
whole clause or sentence	**to cut a long story short**	to tell the main points, but not all the fine details

C **Fixed aspects of idioms**

Most idioms are fixed in their form, and cannot be changed or varied. Sometimes, however, the grammar or the vocabulary can be varied slightly. Where this book or a dictionary gives information on what can be varied, always note it in your Vocabulary notebook.

variation	example
Occasionally an idiom in the active voice can be used in the passive.	Government Ministers always **pass the buck** if they are challenged about poverty. [blame somebody else / refuse to accept responsibility] The **buck has been passed** from Minister to Minister. No one seems prepared to accept the responsibility.
Some verb-based idioms also have noun-compound forms.	There is too much **buck-passing** in government nowadays. No one accepts the blame for anything.
One or more words in the idiom can be varied.	Stop **acting the fool/goat**! [stop acting stupidly]

Exercises

i.1 How much can you guess about the meaning of these idioms just by looking at the context? Tick the boxes according to what you can understand about the words in bold.

1 I decided I was going to get a place at university **by hook or by crook**. It had always been my dream to study for a degree in history.

	YES	NO	DON'T KNOW/ CAN'T TELL	
means using illegal methods if necessary	☑	☐	☐	
means nothing will stop me	☐	☐	☐	
means I was very determined	☐	☐	☐	See Unit 17.

2 The government and the unions are **at loggerheads**; there may be a general strike.

	YES	NO	DON'T KNOW/ CAN'T TELL	
means have a good relationship	☐	☐	☐	
means hate each other	☐	☐	☐	
means disagree very strongly	☑	☐	☐	See Unit 22.

3 We had to **pay through the nose** to get our visas in five days instead of the usual 30 days.

	YES	NO	DON'T KNOW/ CAN'T TELL	
means suffer in some way	☐	☐	☐	
means pay a small sum of money	☐	☐	☐	
means pay a large sum of money	☑	☐	☐	See Unit 24.

i.2 Classify the idioms in the sentences below according to their grammatical type:

Type A verb + object/complement
    (and/or adverbial)
Type B prepositional phrase
Type C compound

Type D simile
Type E binomial or trinomial
Type F whole clause or sentence

1 Should we fly or go by train? What are the **pros and cons**?
Type: ....E.....   See Unit 10.
2 I'm **having second thoughts** about going on holiday with Jean. She can be a bit difficult.
Type: ....A.....   See Unit 5.
3 When I had finished all my exams, I felt **as free as a bird**.
Type: ....D.....   See Unit 60.
4 I don't know much about design, so I **gave the decorator a free hand** in my new flat.
Type: ....F.....   See Unit 45.
5 She comes from a rather **well-to-do** family. She's always had a comfortable life.
Type: ....C.....   See Unit 24.
6 My old school friend Harriet arrived **out of the blue**. I hadn't seen her for 15 years.
Type: ....B.....   See Unit 42.

i.3 Correct the mistakes in the idioms in these sentences. Use the clues in brackets. Use a good general dictionary or a dictionary of idioms if necessary.

1 My father's foot was put down when I said I wanted a car for my seventeenth birthday. He said I was too young. (grammar – voice)   See Unit 46.
2 Her words put the cat among the birds; Jim is furious. (vocabulary)   See Unit 37.
3 You'll be pleased to hear we arrived sound and safe in Peru. (binomial)   See Unit 16.
4 He was lying in his teeth when he said he had got a first-class grade in his exam; the truth is he failed. (grammar – small word)   See Unit 51.

ii   Using your dictionary

A   What do you look up?

As it can be difficult to work out what an
idiom means even when you know all the
individual words in the idiom, you will often
need to look up idioms in a dictionary. If you are
working with a dictionary on CD-Rom, then you
will have no problems finding the idiom in
question, but working with a traditional dictionary,
you have to find where the idiom is listed. As an idiom consists of several words, which of
these do you look up in your dictionary? For example, do you try to find **kill two birds with
one stone** under *kill, two, birds* or *stone*, or **let the cat out of the bag** under *let, cat* or *bag*?

If you are using either the *Cambridge
International Dictionary of Idioms* (CIDI) or the
Cambridge Advanced Learner's Dictionary (CALD),
then the easiest way of finding what you need is
to look in the alphabetical index at the back of
the book. This lists all the expressions included
in the dictionary with the word where an entry
for the expression will be found in the
dictionary highlighted in bold. This shows that in CIDI **kill two birds with one stone** will be
found under *two* and **let the cat out of the bag** will be found under *cat*. In CALD these two
idioms will be found under *kill* and *cat*.

If you are using a different dictionary, read its introductory notes now to see how it deals
with idioms. This will avoid the frustration you would otherwise feel on deciding to look up
the wrong element of the idiom first.

B   What information does your dictionary give you?

Your dictionary will tell you a lot of other things as well as the meaning of the idiom. As
idioms are used in such fixed ways, it is important to read the notes in your dictionary
carefully if you want to use idioms as well as to understand them.

You will find all these things in a good dictionary of idioms:

- information about words that are interchangeable, e.g. **drive/send sb round the bend**
- information about how the idiom is used – brackets, for example, show if any words in the
  idiom can be left out, e.g. **I (can) feel it in my bones.**
- notes about the grammar of the idiom – there may be notes, for example, to say that an idiom
  is usually used in a passive construction or in a continuous form or in a negative sentence
- examples of the idiom in use
- comments on register – the register labels used in CIDI are *informal, formal, very informal,
  old-fashioned, taboo, humorous* and *literary*
- notes about regional variations in use – this is important as many British idioms will sound
  very strange to an American and vice versa

TIP   It is not possible for this book to include as much information about each idiom as you will find in a
dictionary. So, look up the idioms that you particularly want to learn from this book in a dictionary as
well. In your Vocabulary notebook, write any further information or other examples of the idioms in the
context that you find in the dictionary.

Exercises

ii.1 Look up the idioms in these sentences in your dictionary. What word is each idiom listed under?

1 It's the person in the street who **picks up the bill** for the government's mistakes.
2 She had a wonderful trip to Australia, but now she's **come back down to earth with a bump**.
3 John had a furious argument with his supervisor, but he managed to **stand his ground**.
4 He's feeling very miserable, so there's no need for you to **stick the knife in** too.
5 You're **banging your head against a brick wall** trying to get him to help you.
6 You **scared the living daylights out of** me by creeping up behind me like that.

ii.2 Which word(s) could be left out of the idioms in these sentences?

1 It's always hard when you have to **come back down to earth with a bump** after a holiday.
2 No one thought she could climb the mountain without oxygen, but she succeeded **against all the odds**.
3 She **hit him where it hurt most** by telling him that he had always been a disappointment to his parents.
4 The way he reacted **scared the living daylights out of** me!

ii.3 Which word in each idiom could be changed for another word?

1 Don't worry about a thing – I'm sure the company will **pick up the bill**.
2 I **came back down to earth with a bump** when I saw the pile of post waiting for me after the weekend.
3 The army had lost many of its men, but it managed to **stand its ground**.
4 Why do critics seem to enjoy **sticking the knife into** untalented actors and writers?
5 I feel as if **I'm banging my head against a brick wall** with him at the moment.
6 It's a terrifying film – it **scared the living daylights out of** me!

ii.4 What grammatical information does your dictionary give about these idioms? Read the information and then write a sentence with each idiom.

1 look a gift horse in the mouth
2 be pushing up the daisies
3 be on the brink of
4 tie yourself up in knots
5 be man enough

ii.5 Match the register labels in the box with the idioms in the sentences below.

A	B	C	D	E	F
formal	humorous	informal	literary	old-fashioned	very informal

1 I really don't like him – he's such **a slime ball**.
2 OK. I'll do the washing-up. **There's no peace for the wicked!**
3 Her family has lived in that village **from time immemorial**.
4 My grandma always used to say that **an apple a day keeps the doctor away**.
5 The food was so delicious – we **stuffed our faces**.
6 I hope that what I have said will **give you pause for thought**.

1 Health

A Idioms describing health

Mark had been feeling **under the weather**[1] for weeks. One day he came into work **looking like death warmed up**[2] and so we told him to go away for a few days to **recharge his batteries**[3]. After one day beside the sea, he no longer **felt off-colour**[4] and by the second day he knew he was **on the road to recovery**[5]. He sent us a postcard and we were all glad to learn that he was **on the mend**[6]. By the end of the week, he returned to work **as fit as a fiddle**[7]. And he's been **as right as rain**[8] ever since.

[1] not very well
[2] looking extremely ill
[3] do something to gain fresh energy and enthusiasm
[4] felt unwell

[5] getting better
[6] getting better
[7] perfectly well
[8] perfectly well

as fit as a fiddle

B Informal idioms for mad

There are many informal idioms which are used to say that someone is mad:

He's **not all there.**   She's **a basket case.**

She's **off her trolley.**   He's **off his rocker.**

He's **not right in the head.**   She's **one sandwich short of a picnic.**

She's got **a screw loose.**   He's **as nutty as a fruitcake.**

screw

rocker   *trolley*

C Informal idioms for die

There are also a lot of very informal idioms meaning *die*, for example:

She's **popped her clogs.**   She's **given up the ghost.**   She's **kicked the bucket.**

He's **bitten the dust.**   He's **fallen off his perch.**

D Idioms based on medical images

idiom	meaning	example
a sore point/spot	a subject which someone would prefer not to talk about because it makes them angry or embarrassed	Try not to mention baldness while he's here – it's a sore spot for him.
give someone a taste/dose of their own medicine	do the same bad thing to someone that they have done to you in order to show them how unpleasant it is	Refusing to lend him money now would give him a taste of his own medicine – he's never lent you any.
a bitter pill to swallow	unpleasant, but has to be accepted	Losing my job was initially a bitter pill to swallow.
sugar the pill	do something to make something unpleasant more acceptable	The boss has sugared the overtime pill by offering a large extra payment.
have itchy feet	want to travel or move on	I can't stay in one place for more than a year without getting itchy feet.

menni
akar

Exercises

1.1 Put these expressions into four groups of idioms that share the same meaning. (There are two groups of two idioms and two groups of four.) Explain the meaning in each case.

> give up the ghost   be on the road to recovery   bite the dust   be on the mend
> be as nutty as a fruitcake   feel off-colour   be not all there   feel under the weather
> pop your clogs   be off your trolley   fall off your perch   be a basket case

1.2 Complete each of these idioms.
1 Don't mention the merger to him – it's a bit of a _a sore_ spot for him.
2 Telling Joe what you feel may be a _a bitter_ pill for him to swallow, but you owe it to him nevertheless.
3 Watching travel programmes on TV always gives me _ea itchy_ feet.
4 I wonder what's happened to Stan – he looks like death _warmed_ up!
5 Plans to put increased funds into education are supposed to sugar the _pill_ of increased taxation.
6 Imagine someone as unfit as Ruth going on holiday in the Himalayas. She must have a _screw_ loose.
7 A good game of golf at the weekend always helps to _recharge_ my father's batteries.
8 Tom was quite ill for a while last year, but he's as fit as a _fiddle_ now.
9 I was exhausted when I got home from work, but, after a nice cup of tea, I'm as _right_ as rain.
10 Helen won't understand the problem – she's one _sandwich_ short of a picnic.

1.3 Which of the idioms meaning *die* do these pictures make you think of?

1.4 Match each statement on the left with the most likely response on the right.

1 I've got itchy feet.   Oh dear, I hope he's OK tomorrow. 5
2 He's as right as rain now.   Yes, but she'll soon get over it. 6
3 He's not right in the head.   Where would you like to go? 1
4 I'm going to tell him what I think of him.   That is a relief! 2
5 Dad's a bit off-colour today.   Good. Give him a dose of his own medicine. 4
6 Failing the exam was a bitter pill   I know, Jane told me he was off his rocker. 3
  to swallow.

Why do you think there are so many idiomatic expressions meaning *mad* and *die*? Is it the same in your language? Do you think it would ever be appropriate for you to use any of these English idioms for *mad* or *die*? If so, in what circumstances? If not, why not?

2 Happiness and sadness

Extreme happiness

There are many informal idioms
which mean *extremely happy*.

I'm thrilled to bits.

I am/feel on top of the world.

I'm on cloud nine.

I'm over the moon.

I'm in seventh heaven.

B **Other happiness idioms**

idiom	meaning	example
get a (real) kick out of something	very much enjoy doing something (informal)	I get a (real) kick out of going for a run first thing in the morning before anyone else is up.
do something for kicks	do something because it is exciting, usually something dangerous (informal)	Sandra is keen to have a go at bungee-jumping – just for kicks.
jump for joy	be very happy and excited about something that has happened	Rowena jumped for joy when she heard that she'd won first prize.
be floating/ walking on air	be very happy about something good that has happened	I've been walking on air ever since Chris and I started going out together.
something makes your day	something makes you feel very happy	It's great to hear from you. It's really made my day.

C **Sadness**

Dear Louise,
Hope all goes well with you. Unfortunately, everyone here is out of sorts[1]. Will is down in the dumps[2] because he doesn't like his teacher this year. I've told him that it's not the end of the world[3] and that he'd better just grin and bear it[4], but I think he likes being a misery guts[5] and so he complains about her every night. Pat is also suffering from sour grapes[6] because I got the role in the school play that she wanted. This puts a damper on[7] every meal, so I'm really looking forward to staying with you at the weekend.
Love,
Karen

[1] slightly unhappy or slightly ill
[2] unhappy (informal)
[3] what has happened won't cause any serious problems
[4] accept a situation you don't like because you can't change it
[5] someone who complains all the time and is never happy (very informal)
[6] being jealous about something you can't have
[7] stop an occasion from being enjoyable (sometimes *dampener* is used instead of *damper*)

Exercises

2.1 Combine the words in the box in order to make five expressions meaning *extremely happy*.
Use each word once only.

bits	cloud	heaven	in	moon	nine	of	on	on	over	seventh	the
the	thrilled	to	top	world							

2.2 Which idioms do these pictures make you think of?

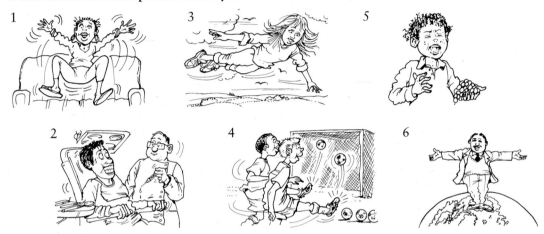

1   3   5

2   4   6

2.3 Correct the mistakes in these idioms.

1 The child was thrilled for *to* bits to have her photo in the paper.
2 I felt as if I was floating in *on* air as I ran down the hill into his arms.
3 Why does Marti look so out of sorts today?
4 Don't make such a fuss. It's not the finish of the world! *end*
5 Your telephone call has really done my day! *made*
6 Jill said she was on cloud seven and Jack agreed that he was in ninth heaven. *nine / seventh*
7 Why does Mark always have to be such a miserable guts? *misery*
8 Stereotypically, happy footballers say that they are over the sun. *moon*

2.4 Answer these questions.

1 Would a piece of good news or a piece of bad news be more likely to make your day?
2 If you got top marks in an exam, would you feel down in the dumps? *No*
3 Are people more likely to get a kick out of hot-air ballooning or cleaning their boots?
4 Do you have to grin and bear it when you are happy or unhappy about something that has happened?
5 If you are at someone's birthday party, what would be more likely to put a damper on the event – news of the illness of a close friend or a heavy shower of rain?
6 Do people usually enjoy or not enjoy being in the company of a misery guts?
7 You have a beautiful new sports car that a colleague is rather envious of. What is your colleague more likely to say out of sour grapes? 'I love its green colour!' or 'Of course, that model is very unreliable!'
8 A damper is literally a thing put on piano strings to make the sound less loud. How does knowing this help you to understand the idiom using the word *damper*?
9 Do you notice anything that a number of the images in the happiness idioms have in common?

3 Anger

Being angry

These informal idioms can be used either about yourself or about a third person.

I'm **fed up (to the back teeth)** with trying to live on such a small wage.

I'm **at my wits' end** trying to keep things in order. (wits = intelligence, brains)

I've **had it up to here** with this organisation!

These informal idioms are generally used about other people.

Your boss will **have/throw a fit** when he finds out you forgot to reply to those letters. (You can also say **go off the deep end / go spare / do his nut / blow a fuse**.)

These less informal idioms describe other people's anger and are based on the word *blood*.

If **someone's blood is up,** they are very angry or excited and may react in a violent way.

If you are **after someone's blood,** you want to catch them in order to hurt or punish them.

If you are **out for blood,** you are determined to find someone to attack or blame for something bad that has happened.

B Angry relationships

idiom	meaning	example
drive someone up the wall	make someone very angry (or sometimes very bored)	The neighbours' loud music every night is driving me up the wall.
drive/send someone round the bend/twist	make someone very angry (or sometimes very bored)	His lack of consideration is driving me round the twist.
rub someone up the wrong way	make someone annoyed	Jill always manages to say something to rub her father up the wrong way.
get/put someone's back up	make someone annoyed	Roger put his sister's back up by saying she would never be a good driver.
ruffle someone's feathers	make someone annoyed	Jo says what she thinks without worrying about whether she might be ruffling anyone's feathers.
put/send the cat among the pigeons	do or say something that makes a lot of people angry or worried	Danny put the cat among the pigeons by suggesting that the company might have to make some redundancies.
not be on speaking terms	be so angry with each other that they refuse to speak to each other	They haven't been on speaking terms for years although neither can remember what they first quarrelled about.
give someone an earful	tell someone how angry you are with them (informal)	The old lady gave the children an earful for nearly knocking her over.
give someone a piece of your mind	tell someone how angry you are with them	He'll give the boys a piece of his mind if he catches them in his garden.

Exercises

3.1 Put the expressions in the box into pairs that mean more or less the same.

went off the deep end	gave him an earful	drove him up the wall	gave him a piece of her mind
put his back up	did his nut	rubbed him up the wrong way	sent him round the bend

3.2 Complete each of these idioms.

1 Kevin has had it up to ....*here*........ with his work.
2 It's horrible living with two people who are not on speaking ....*terms*........ .
3 It'll really put the ....*cat*........ among the pigeons if you try to bring that up at the meeting.
4 My sister ....*goes*........ spare when she found out I'd burnt her new top.
5 Jez is ....*after*........ your blood now he knows it was you who told the police.
6 The demonstrators are furious and ....*out*........ for blood.
7 Your father will throw a ....*fit*........ if you go out dressed like that.
8 The baby hardly sleeps at night and her mother is at her ....*wits'*........ end.

3.3 Correct eight mistakes in this paragraph.

Yesterday I had terrible toothache. It hurt a lot and I guess that's why I was in a bad temper all day. Everything anyone said seemed to put the *my* back up and, in the end, I threw a fuse with the *blew* person I share my office with. Even when I'm in a good mood, she sends me up the twist with her *round* constant chatter and yesterday I had had it off to *up* here with her after only ten minutes. I really gave her an eyeful and the result is that we are no *earful* longer in speaking terms. I know I'll have to *on* apologise for doing my nuts like that, but perhaps *nut* I'll wait a while. It's much easier to work when she isn't talking to me! Perhaps I should give her a peace of my mind more often. *piece*

3.4 Answer these questions.

1 Name one thing that drives you up the wall. *Lloyd*
2 Find two idioms on the left-hand page that conjure up images of birds.
3 Can you remember a teacher ever going off the deep end? If so, what caused it?
4 Find seven idioms on the left-hand page that are based on parts of the body.
5 Has anyone recently rubbed you up the wrong way? If so, how did they do this?
6 Which idiom in A on the left-hand page do you think is usually accompanied by a gesture?
7 Have you ever given someone a piece of your mind? If so, what about?
8 Find an idiom on the left-hand page connected with electricity.

to) ruffle sb's feathers
to) put the cat among the pigeons

4 Knowing and understanding

A ## A Knowing and not knowing

knowing	meaning
She **knows** the system **inside out**.	She knows every detail of it.
When it comes to geography, he certainly **knows his stuff**.	He has a very good knowledge of it.
That book title **has a familiar ring to it**. I think I read it a long time ago.	It sounds familiar / I think I've heard it before.
I'm not sure if I know her, but the name **rings a bell**. (very commonly used with *name*)	I have a vague memory of someone with that name, but can't remember exactly.

not knowing	meaning
I **haven't (got) / don't have a clue** how to use this camera.	I don't know at all.
I **haven't (got) / don't have the faintest idea** where she lives.	I really don't know at all.
I **haven't (got) / don't have the foggiest (idea)** what this switch is for.	I absolutely don't know at all.
I **can't for the life of me** remember her first name.	I can't remember at all.
I'm a bit **out of touch** with computers these days.	I used to know about them, but don't know the latest developments.
I'm sorry, that name **doesn't ring any bells with me**. (very commonly used with *name*)	I don't think I've ever heard it before; it is unfamiliar.

B Coming to conclusions

I didn't actually know where you were staying, but Mark said you were with a relative. So I **put two and two together** and guessed it was that aunt of yours in Manchester. [concluded from the facts I knew]

I'm sorry, I **got (hold of) the wrong end of the stick**. I thought you were complaining about something. [came to the wrong conclusion]

'I think he's got hold of the wrong end of the stick.'

Exercises

4.1 **Correct the mistakes in these idioms.**

1 I don't have even a faint^{est} idea where he is today; you'll have to ask somebody else. *[handwritten: est above "faint"]*
2 The title of the CD has familiar rings to it, but I don't think I've ever heard it.
3 My cousin knows the tax laws ~~outside and in~~, so if you want advice on your tax, he'll help you. *[handwritten: inside out]*
4 I can't for ~~the of me~~ life think what it was I came into the kitchen for. *[handwritten: the of me]*
5 I saw Tom and Lily together in a restaurant looking adoringly into each other's eyes. I ~~added up~~ two and two, and decided they must be madly in love. *[handwritten: put]*

4.2 **Use the corrected idioms from exercise 4.1 to rewrite the underlined parts of this paragraph. Use each idiom once only.**

I always thought I knew my computer <u>in every detail</u>, but the other day it started to crash every time I opened a certain program. I could not <u>in any way</u> understand why it was doing this, and I didn't have <u>any idea at all</u> about what to do to fix it. I rang the helpline which I had used in the past, and after about 20 minutes I spoke to someone who said his name was Patrick, and that he was there to help me. He gave me some advice <u>which sounded quite familiar to me</u> from previous calls I had made to the same helpline. I <u>thought about all this</u>, <u>put the facts together</u>, and concluded that they give the same advice to everybody, and that it's just a way of getting rid of you. The computer still crashes every time I open the program. *[handwritten: inside out above "in every detail"]*

4.3 **Write sentences that mean the opposite of these sentences. Use idioms from the left-hand page and make any other necessary changes.**

1 Yes, that name is very familiar to me. I think I've met her several times.
2 I'm really up to date with TV soap operas these days. I watch them every day.
3 She knows absolutely nothing when it comes to the history of this area.
4 I correctly interpreted what she was trying to tell me and it solved a big problem.
5 No, sorry, her name means nothing to me. I may have met her, I just can't remember.

4.4 **Complete each sentence with a different idiom which refers to 'not knowing'.**

1 I don't have a clue .... how to use the photocopier. Do you think you could help me? (weakest of the three) *[handwritten: don't have a clue]*
2 I don't have the faintest idea .... where I left that letter I brought for you. I'm really sorry. (stronger than 1) *[handwritten: don't have the faintest idea]*
3 I haven't got the foggiest idea .... what she's talking about. She's crazy! (even stronger than 2) *[handwritten: haven't got the foggiest idea]*

FOLLOW UP
If you have access to the Internet, go to the *Cambridge International Dictionary of Idioms* website at dictionary.cambridge.org/idioms and do a search under the word *know*. You will get a list of all the idioms containing the word *know*. Choose any three of these that you have not seen before or which look interesting, click on each one to get their meanings and make a note of them in your Vocabulary notebook.

5 Experience and perception

A Learning from experiences

If ...	you can say ...
something bad has happened, but you decide to learn from it instead of being upset by it,	I've decided to **put it down to experience**.
you don't know what your position is or what your situation is with someone, and it's worrying you,	I just want to **know where I stand**, that's all.
something happens or someone says something that makes you think very seriously about it,	the events / your suggestions have certainly **given me food for thought**.
something bad happens to you and you decide you will never let it happen again,	I've **learnt my lesson**.
someone does something stupid which affects them in a way that they'll never want to do it again,	that will **teach him/her a lesson!**
someone finally becomes aware of a fact (often used with unpleasant facts),	I think he/she's **got the message**.
you tell the true facts to someone who has believed a different set of facts up to that moment,	I just want to **set/put the record straight**.

B Other common idioms connected with perceiving situations

I **heard it on/through the grapevine** that you're thinking of leaving the company. Is it true? [heard it from someone who had heard it from someone else]

He doesn't hate you at all. It's completely untrue. It's just **a figment of your imagination**. [something you have imagined which is not true]

The Prime Minister seems to have **lost sight of** why she was elected. She's broken all her promises to the people. [forgotten a central, important fact or truth about something]

What beats me is why people are prepared to sit in a traffic jam every morning for half an hour just to get to work. [what I cannot understand]

I'm **having second thoughts about** moving house. I like this part of the city and I'm not sure I'd be happy anywhere else. [I decided something, but now I am no longer sure about it]

I don't know all **the ins and outs of** the situation, but it seems that David has decided to move out of the flat he shares with Ruth and Monica. [the details of]

> **TIP**
>
> If an idiom has a preposition associated with it, e.g. *ins and outs **of***, *second thoughts **about***, always write the preposition with the idiom in your Vocabulary notebook, as well as any other important structural information.

Exercises

5.1 In each of these conversations, the second speaker uses an idiom to repeat what the first speaker says. Complete the idioms.

1 Martin: Well, Luke has finally learnt that he can't expect everyone else to pay for him.
  Philip: Yes, I think he's _got the message_ .
2 Anne: Well, Sheila will certainly learn never to do that again!
  Gerry: Yes, that should definitely _taught her a lesson_ .
3 Frances: His suggestions are worth taking seriously, aren't they?
  Brad: Yes, they've certainly given us _food for thought_ .
4 Will: Joe's convinced himself that his neighbours are drug smugglers. He's just crazy!
  Nick: Yes, I'm sure the whole thing is a _figment of their imagination_
5 Carol: Well, I think we were right to tell her what really happened, don't you?
  Steve: Yes, it was important to _set the records straight_ .

5.2 Complete the crossword.

				1 S					2 B
3 G	R	A	P	E	W	I	N	E	E
				C		N			A
				O		5 S	I	G	H	T
				N					S
			6 D	O	W	N			

Across
3 You can hear news through it.
5 Don't lose it.
6 Put it _down_ to experience.

Down
1 They're not your first thoughts.
2 Usually means *hits*, but is used in an idiom about not understanding something.
4 They go with 'outs'.

5.3 Complete each of these idioms.

1 I want to know _where_ I _stand_ . One day you say you love me, the next day you say I'm just a friend. It's driving me crazy.
2 He spent £500 of my money. I'll never lend him my credit card again. I've _learnt_ my _lesson_ .
3 I don't know all the _ins_ and _outs_ of the situation, but I think one of the directors is going to resign. There must be a big problem.
4 I can understand that she needed help, but _what beats_ me is that she should ask someone as stupid as Simon to help her!

5.4 Answer these questions.

1 Think of an occasion when you learnt your lesson.
2 Think of something which happened to you that you decided to put down to experience.
3 Have you ever decided to do something, then had second thoughts about it? What was it?
4 Think of something you heard recently on the grapevine. What was it?
5 Have you ever been in a friendship or relationship where you had to say 'I need to know where I stand'? What was the situation?

I am now!

Not to trust anyone.

6 Success and failure

A When things go well

If something ...	then it ...
makes all the difference (to something)	has a very good effect on a situation or a thing
works/goes/runs like a dream	works/goes/runs very well indeed
works like magic	works immediately and very well indeed
goes from strength to strength	gets better and better
does the trick	solves a problem very well
is the be-all-and-end-all (of something)	is the most important thing (often used in the negative: *not the be-all-and-end-all*)
is / turns out to be a blessing in disguise	has a good effect even though at first it seemed it would be bad

B ... and when they don't

If ...	then ...
someone/something is a victim of their/its own success	their/its success has negative effects as well as or instead of positive ones
someone doesn't have the ghost of a chance (of doing something)	they have no chance at all
someone/something gives up the ghost	they/it stop(s) working or they stop trying to succeed because they know they will not
someone/something leaves their/its mark (on someone/something)	they have / it has an effect (usually negative) that changes someone or something for ever

C Other useful idioms connected with success and failure

I always knew Ahmed **would go places**. He's been an excellent athlete since he was a teenager. [would be successful (*go places* is not used in the simple tense forms)]

He's a good writer, but he hasn't really ever **hit the big time**. [been successful nationally or internationally and made lots of money]

He's really **made a go of** that restaurant he bought. He's extended it and he employs about ten people now. [been very successful with]

> **TIP**
> If a dictionary or your teacher tells you an idiom is not used with a particular tense or has other grammatical restrictions, e.g. *go places* in C above, always make a note about the grammar in your notebook.

Exercises

6.1 Complete these idioms with prepositions.

1 His Internet company has gone .... strength .... strength in the last six months. He's making a lot of money now.
2 The flood ruined our old kitchen, but it was a blessing .... disguise, because the insurance company paid for a completely new one.
3 This new model is not the be-all-and-end-all .... digital cameras, but it certainly has many technical features that others do not have.
4 Your offer to drive us to the airport makes all the difference .... our travel plans.
5 Your plan to persuade Lela to join the committee worked .... magic.

6.2 Use the idioms from exercise 6.1 to rewrite the underlined parts of the sentences.

1 At first we thought the new road would spoil our village, but in fact it <u>was a positive development</u> and the village shops are doing more business.
2 I sprayed the stain remover onto my jacket and it <u>had an immediate positive result</u>. (Give two answers.)
3 This is not <u>the absolute best and most complete</u> cookery book, but it does have recipes from 100 different countries.
4 The school <u>has got better and better</u> since the new head teacher took over.
5 Getting new curtains has <u>changed</u> my flat <u>in a positive way</u>. It feels like a new one.

6.3 Who would be most likely to say these remarks? Choose the correct answer.

1 It left its mark on me.
   a) someone who had just spilt red wine over themselves
   b) someone who taught in a very bad school for ten years
   c) someone who had a wonderful birthday party

2 I'm a victim of my own success.
   a) someone who won a lot of money then spent it all
   b) a student who always passes every exam they take
   c) a popular teacher whose class everyone wants to be in

3 I don't think I'll ever hit the big time.
   a) a rock musician who is popular in local clubs
   b) an athlete who has just got a place in an Olympic team
   c) a dentist with a very heavy schedule of appointments

4 Work isn't the be-all-and-end-all in my life.
   a) someone who is unemployed
   b) someone who has a lot of interesting hobbies
   c) someone who never finishes a job they start

6.4 Complete each of these idioms.

1 The photocopier has completely .... the ghost. We need a new one.
2 I didn't think I .... ghost of a .... of passing the exam, but I did.
3 My new motorbike .... a dream; it's fast, but so smooth and quiet.

6.5 Answer these questions.

1 If you make a go of something, do you succeed or fail?
2 What should you remember about the grammar of the idiom *go places*?
3 What could you write in your Vocabulary notebook about the use of *be-all-and-end-all*?

7 Having problems

A Describing the problem

I've come up against a brick wall.
[something is blocking me from doing what I want to do]

I've been left holding the baby.
[others have left me to deal with a problem alone]

I put my foot in it.
[said something tactless and embarrassing]

They've got me over a barrel.
[have put me in a situation where I have no choice over what I can do]

I'm in dire straits.
[in a very difficult or dangerous situation]

I've come up against a stumbling block.
[a problem which stops me from achieving something]

I've dug myself into a hole.
[have myself caused a problem that will be difficult to escape from (informal)]

I'm clutching at straws now.
[am in such a difficult situation that I will try anything]

I've drawn a blank.
[am unable to find information or to achieve something I'd hoped for]

I've spread myself too thin.
[am trying to do too many things at the same time, with the result that I can't give any of them the attention they need]

So now we are all going to have to face the music.
[accept criticism or punishment for what you have done]

B Fact of life

Taxes are, unfortunately, **a fact of life**. [an unpleasant situation which has to be accepted because it cannot be changed]

A fact of life must not be confused with the phrase *the facts of life*, which is a slightly indirect (humorous) way of referring to information about sexual reproduction. Another humorous idiom for *the facts of life* is **the birds and the bees**.

C Easier said than done

Why don't you take the train to work? Then you'd avoid all the traffic jams.
Easier said than done! There are no trains at the right time. [something you say when something seems like a good idea, but is difficult to actually do]

> **TIP**
> Make a 'problems' idioms page in your Vocabulary notebook. You will find examples of other idioms that can be used for talking about problems in other units of this book too. As you find them, add them to this page of your notebook.

Exercises

7.1 Match the beginning of each idiom on the left with its ending on the right.

1 left holding the   wall
2 brick   block
3 stumbling   music
4 dire   baby
5 draw a   barrel
6 have you over a   straits
7 face the   blank

7.2 Put the words in the right order and make sentences.

1 done / said / Easier / than   *Easier said than done.*
2 too / to / Try / spread / thin / not / yourself   *Try not to spread yourself too thin.*
3 I / I / foot / it / wish / my / put / hadn't / in   *I wish I hadn't put my foot in it.*
4 a / life / older / of / Getting / fact / is   *Getting older is a fact of life.*
5 mother / tell / and / was / to / the / it / the / about / bees / Sarah's / decided / time / her / birds   *Sarah's mother decided it was time to tell her about birds and bees.*
6 life / primary / facts / of / the / Children / taught / in / school / are   *Children are taught in primary school the facts of life.*

7.3 Which idioms do these pictures make you think of?

I've dug myself into a hole.

I've been left holding the baby.

I've come up against a brick wall.

Face the music

7.4 Complete each of these idioms with one word.

1 You'd better stop talking or you'll dig yourself into a deeper _hole_ .
2 I hoped I'd find the address I needed in the library, but I drew a _blank_ .
3 If you take on any more work, you'll be spreading yourself far too _thin_ .
4 Stranded on the island with no money and no luggage, we were well aware that we were in dire _straits_ .
5 The police explored a number of leads, but each time they came up against a brick _wall_ .
6 Not having enough savings to set up a business was a major stumbling _block_ .
7 I wish I could leave my job, but they've got me over a _barrel_ .

FOLLOW UP Magazines often have articles about people's problems or question and answer pages dealing with problems of different kinds. Find an article or a question and answer page like this and make a note of any idioms that you find there.

8 Dealing with problems

A Trying to solve a problem

Ray needed a bookcase. He had been **making do**[1] with planks of wood on bricks, but he wanted something nicer now. His sister, Sandy, suggested buying a self-assembly bookcase where the pieces came in a flat pack for him to put together himself. Ray knew he wasn't much good at that sort of thing, but he decided to **give it a shot/whirl**[2]. When he opened the pack, it all looked very confusing, but he was determined to **get to grips with**[3] it. After a couple of hours, he had something that looked a bit like a bookcase but was rather wobbly. **To be on the safe side**[4], he asked Sandy to check it for him. 'There's something not quite right about this,' she said. 'I think we'd better **get to the bottom of**[5] it before you put your books on it.'

[1] managing with something that isn't as good as you would like
[2] give something a try (informal)
[3] make an effort to understand or to deal with a problem or situation
[4] to protect himself even though it might not be necessary
[5] try to discover the truth about something

B Light and understanding

The recent release of fifty-year-old documents has **shed a great deal of light** on the political crises of the 1950s. Some unexpected information about the government of the day has been **brought to light** and some surprising facts about the politicians of the time have also **come to light**.

The concept of *light* is often used to represent mental illumination or understanding. The idiom **bring something to light** (usually used in the passive – see above) means to discover facts that were previously unknown. Often, though not always, these facts are about something bad or illegal. **Come to light** gives a similar idea of unknown facts becoming known. **Shed/Throw light on something** means to help people understand a situation.

It's been a very difficult year, but at last I feel I can see the **light at the end of the tunnel**. [something makes you believe that a difficult and unpleasant situation is coming to an end]

C The problem's over

The Democratic Party is behaving as if victory was already **in the bag**. [certain to get or achieve something (informal)]

I was in despair until Chris turned up – **the answer to my prayers**. [something or someone that you have needed for a long time]

I want to **wave a magic wand** and make things better. [find an easy way to solve a problem]

I've got to **tie up a few loose ends** before I go on holiday. [deal with the last few things that need to be done before something is completed]

Once Sheila explains why she acted as she did, everything will **fall into place**. [you understand something that you did not understand before, or everything goes well]

After the flood, it took us some time to **pick up the pieces**. [try to return to normal]

Exercises

8.1 Match each idiom on the left with its definition on the right.

1 tie up loose ends — understand and deal with something
2 come to light — try something
3 give something a shot — find an easy solution
4 get to grips with something — just in case
5 make do — finish off final little tasks
6 to be on the safe side — uncover the truth
7 wave a magic wand — manage with something of worse quality
8 get to the bottom of something — be discovered

8.2 Complete each of these idioms with one word.

1 I've been busy at work, but I can see the light at the end of the ___tunnel___ now.
2 Sarah wanted to ___wave___ a magic wand and make her son happy again.
3 Just wait while I tie up these ___loose___ ends, then I'll go to the match with you.
4 When her parents gave her some money, it was like the answer to her ___prayers___ .
5 I've never tried yoga before, but I'd be happy to give ___it___ a shot.
6 The job isn't in the ___bag___ till you've had an offer in writing.
7 This research may shed fresh ___light___ on the causes of asthma in children.
8 As I listened to the evidence, everything began to ___fall___ into place.

8.3 Complete each sentence with an idiom from the box. Make any other necessary changes.

bring to light	come to light	fall into place	get to grips with	get to the bottom of
give it a whirl	pick up the pieces	shed light on		

1 I'd like to try that new bowling alley. Let's ___give it a whirl___ this evening.
2 I'm finding it quite hard _____ my new role at work.
3 When the business failed, Paul vanished, leaving his partner ___pick up the pieces___
4 Some important new evidence _____ in the last few days.
5 I hope that we'll be able ___get to the bottom of___ what's been going on.
6 New medical research _____ the causes of heart attacks.
7 As soon as I met Joshua's family, everything _____ .
8 In the investigation into their accounts, a number of errors _____ .

8.4 Match each statement on the left with the most likely response on the right.

1 I'll wash your car for you!   OK, just to be on the safe side.
2 Let's go home now.   If only I could wave a magic wand!
3 The job's in the bag!   You're the answer to my prayers!
4 We'd better take umbrellas.   Soon. I've still got some loose ends to tie up.
5 Can you make do with a pencil?   I hope you're right!
6 We just don't know what to do!   Sure, that'll do fine.

8.5 Which idioms do these pictures make you think of?

9 Power and authority

A Laws and rules

Note the idioms in this letter to the Editor of a newspaper.

Sir/Madam,

During the recent demonstrations in the city centre, we saw protesters **taking the law into their own hands**[1] and attacking the offices of the company responsible for the pollution of our beaches. While I can understand how angry these protesters must feel, it is clear that the most violent group of demonstrators, the so-called 'Nature's Commandos', **have become a law unto themselves**[2] and that the police are failing to control the situation. What we now need is a firm government that is prepared to **lay down the law**[3] to the big corporations which pollute our environment and to stop **bending the rules**[4] when it is a question of commercial interests. At the same time, the police must take firm action against the most violent groups. Only in this way can we solve the problems we now face.

Sincerely,
Laura Norder

[1] taking action which should be taken by the police or the courts
[2] are completely out of control and simply ignore the law
[3] be very firm and clear about the law, and enforce it
[4] making special exceptions; letting some people disobey the rules/laws

B Authority and responsibility

If you ...	then you ...
carry the can (for something which happens)	accept the blame/responsibility alone, even though other people were responsible
get / let someone off the hook	are free / leave someone free from all responsibility or from a difficult situation
leave someone to their own devices	allow them to decide how to act; do not control or supervise them
are at/on the receiving end (of something, for example, a person's anger/criticism)	suffer from / are the target of (the other person's anger/criticism, etc.)
are at someone's beck and call	do everything they tell you to do, whenever they tell you to do it
get your own way	persuade other people to let you do what you want

C Power and politics

The people of Sweden **go to the polls** next Sunday. [/pəʊlz/ vote in a general election]

The government's **spin doctors** always make sure the news is very positive. [public relations officers who meet the press/media and present events in a way that suits them]

I think there is **a hidden agenda** in the government's plans. [an attempt to hide their real intentions]

Exercises

9.1 Which of these people are in a good situation (from their point of view) and which are in a bad situation? The idioms all come from B on the left-hand page.

1 Tim has been let off the hook.
2 Sally has had to carry the can.
3 Carmen is at everyone's beck and call.
4 Fiona has got her own way.

9.2 Complete each of these idioms with a preposition.

1 It's wrong to take the law .... your own hands.
2 It's time I laid .... the law and made them do their duty.
3 I would not want to be .... the receiving end of his bad temper. (Give two answers.)
4 Old Bob seems to have become a law .... himself at work. He does just what he likes.
5 Nobody tells you what to do. You're just left .... your own devices.

9.3 Rewrite the underlined part of each sentence with an idiom.

1 I think there is <u>a reason she's not telling us about</u> that letter she sent to the boss.
2 I thought I was going to have to represent my class at the staff–student meeting, but <u>they've told me I don't have to</u>.
3 She's an awful boss to work for; the secretaries <u>have to do what she wants whenever she wants it</u>, eight hours a day, seven days a week.
4 He has <u>had to take</u> a lot of criticism from the press in recent weeks.
5 They cause all the trouble, and I always have to <u>take the blame</u>.
6 I don't want someone telling me what to do all the time. I'd rather be <u>allowed to make my own decisions about how to do things</u>.

9.4 Write a sentence or a couple of sentences for each of these idioms to show their meaning.

1 a hidden agenda
2 a spin doctor
3 bend the rules
4 go to the polls

'I think he must be one of those spin doctors.'

10 Structuring and talking about arguments

A Structuring arguments

> On the one hand[1], I don't think that schoolchildren should have mobile phones. No one knows what the health risks may be for young people's brains. On the other hand[2], they are a useful way for kids to get in touch with their parents when there is a crisis. Be that as it may[3], it is still a nuisance when phones go off in the middle of a lesson. To put it in a nutshell[4], there are a lot of pros and cons[5] with regard to kids and mobiles.

[1] and [2] these phrases are used to present two opposite facts or two different ways of looking at the same issue

[3] an expression which means you accept that something is true, but it still does not change your opinion

[4] indicates that you're describing something as briefly as you can

[5] advantages and disadvantages

B Noun phrases relating to arguments

She's caught in **a vicious circle**. She gets depressed, so she buys some new clothes, so she has no money, which makes her depressed again. [a problem that cannot be solved because it causes another problem that causes the first problem again]

Don't let's get onto corruption in the police. That would really be opening **a can of worms!** [a problem which you do not want to deal with because it will cause trouble (informal)]

The producer says critics love the film, but box-office takings will provide **the acid test**. [a key test which will prove the value, quality or truth of something]

Certainly, boarding school is hard for children. **The other side of the coin** is that they learn to be independent. [a different view, making something look either better or worse than before]

C Talking about arguments

idiom	meaning	example
tie yourself (up) in knots	become very confused when you are trying to explain something	Fiona tried to explain the problem, but she soon tied herself up in knots.
be brought/called to account	be forced to explain your actions and (probably) punished	The Ministers responsible should be called to account for their incompetence.
give someone the benefit of the doubt	believe something good about someone even though you could believe either good or bad	I'm not sure that David is telling the truth, but I'm giving him the benefit of the doubt.
go round in circles	make no progress in an argument or discussion	We're going round in circles. I wish you'd come up with a new idea!
won't budge/give an inch	won't modify an opinion or agree to even small changes that another person wants	I'm prepared to compromise, but Bert won't budge an inch.

Exercises

10.1 Match the beginning of each idiom on the left with its ending on the right.

1 a can of — circle
2 the acid — hand
3 a vicious — nutshell
4 in a — coin
5 on the other — inch
6 the other side of the — circles
7 tie yourself up in — worms
8 go round in — knots
9 be called to — test
10 won't give an — account

10.2 What are the situations describing? Match an idiom from the box with each situation.

> *a* a vicious circle   *b* going round in circles   *c* putting it in a nutshell   *d* the acid test
> *e* tying yourself up in knots   *f* the pros and cons of a situation

d 1 Trying out a new invention for the first time.
e 2 Trying to explain something complex that you do not really understand.
f 3 The advantages and disadvantages of moving to a different town.
c 4 Explaining a complicated situation in two minutes.
b 5 Trying to reach agreement when neither side is prepared to modify its position.
a 6 Getting rid of some books so you have space on your bookshelves, then buying more books because you now have space, so you now need to get rid of more books to clear a bit more space.

10.3 Complete each sentence with an idiom from the box.

> a can of worms   called to account   on the one hand   be that as it may
> give him the benefit of the doubt   the other side of the coin

1 In some ways it's glamorous being a pop star. But _the other side of the coin_ is that you no longer have any privacy.
2 It's time these petty criminals were _called to account_ for their irresponsible actions.
3 I know Bill's a nice friendly person, but, _on the one hand_, he still has to pull his weight in the office.
4 _Be that as it may_, I think Janna might have the best personality for the job, but, on the other, Mina has more experience.
5 If he's apologised, I think you should _give him the benefit of the doubt_
6 It would be opening _a can of worms_ to inquire about his finances.

10.4 Rewrite the underlined part of each sentence with an idiom.
1 I _tied myself in knots_ ~~got very confused~~ trying to explain to Karl how I felt about him.
2 I'd like you to write an essay on _the pros and cons_ the advantages and disadvantages of working abroad.
3 To put it briefly, James needs to produce better homework. _in a nutshell_
4 Natasha was prepared to compromise, but Alex wouldn't compromise at all. _be that as it may_
5 You need more money so you work more. You earn more so you spend more. So you need to work more. It never ends.
    Go round in circles.

11 Conversational responses

A Emphasis

possible stimulus	you say	you mean
You can borrow my car tonight.	**Thanks a million!**	Thank you very much indeed.
Did you get the job you wanted?	**No such luck!**	You're disappointed you were not able to do something.
Can I go skiing with you and your friends this weekend?	**The more, the merrier.**	You're happy for others to join your group or activity.
She's a great teacher!	**You can say that again!**	You totally agree with someone.
Come on the roller coaster with me!	**No way!**	You do not want to do something.
I don't know how you can drive a car in London traffic!	**There's nothing to it!**	You think something is easy.
You could become a model.	**Don't make me laugh!**	You think something is unlikely.
It's nearly the end of the holiday already.	**How time flies!**	You are surprised at how quickly time has passed.
We bumped into John's teacher in Venice!	**It's a small world.**	You are surprised at a coincidence, e.g. meeting someone unexpectedly or discovering mutual friends.

B Indifference

possible stimulus	you say	you mean
What do you think caused the problem?	**It's neither here nor there** what I think.	It is not very important.
Who do you think is to blame – the boss or the workers?	**It's six of one and half a dozen of the other.**	Two people or groups are equally responsible for a bad situation.
What do you think of Jed Hart's acting?	**I can take it or leave it.**	You do not hate something, but you don't particularly like it either.
Luke's got so many computer games.	I know. **You name it**, he's got it.	Anything you say or choose, e.g. *You name it, he's done it.*

C Life

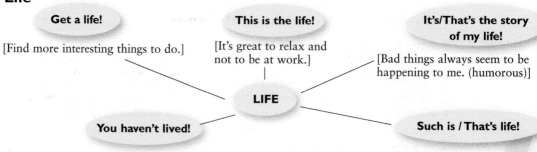

Get a life!

[Find more interesting things to do.]

This is the life!

[It's great to relax and not to be at work.]

It's/That's the story of my life!

[Bad things always seem to be happening to me. (humorous)]

LIFE

You haven't lived!

[Something someone has not experienced is very good or exciting and they should try it. (humorous)]

Such is / That's life!

[Bad things happen and you cannot prevent them.]

Exercises

11.1 Complete these dialogues with an idiom from A or B on the left-hand page.

1 A: My new neighbour was at school with you!
 B: *It's a small world.*

2 A: Is it OK if I bring Jeff to your party?
 B: *The more, the merrier.*

3 A: Do you think Anne or Brian is to blame for their break-up?
 B: *It's six of one and half a dozen of the other.*

4 A: Goodness! It's nearly midnight!
 B: *How time flies!*

5 A: Did you manage to get tickets for the concert in the end?
 B: *No such luck.*

6 A: Do you like caviar?
 B: *I can take it or leave it.*

7 A: He says he's going to be Prime Minister one day.
 B: *Don't make me laugh!*

8 A: Would you agree to do overtime for no extra pay?
 B: *No way.*

11.2 Complete these sentences with an idiom from C on the left-hand page.

1 A: I can't come out with you because I've got to wash my hair.
 B: *Get a life!*

2 A: I've never swum in the Mediterranean.
 B: *You haven't lived!* It really is wonderful!

3 A: Your new girlfriend has dropped you already!
 B: *It's the story of my life!*

4 A: As soon as I moved into my new flat, the roof started leaking.
 B: *Such is / That's life!*

5 A: It's wonderful being here on the river when everyone else is at work!
 B: You're right. *This is the life!*

11.3 Correct the mistakes in these idioms.

1 It's a lovely present. Thanks a ~~thousand~~. *million*
2 You won't find it difficult to learn to ski. There's really nothing to ~~that~~. *it*
3 It's either here or there which hotel you decide to stay in – they're both excellent.
4 Let's have a really big wedding. The more, the ~~merry~~. *merrier.*
5 You ~~may~~ say that again! I couldn't agree with you more! *can*
6 He's travelled a lot. You ~~say~~ it, he's been there. *name*

11.4 Which idioms do these pictures make you think of?

It's six of one and half of a dozen of the other   *It's a small world!*   *Time flies!*

12 Praise and criticism

A Praise and positive comments

In these conversations, the second speaker uses an idiom to repeat and sum up what the first speaker says.

Mieko: That little village was the most wonderful, beautiful place I've ever seen.
Tania: Yes, it really was **out of this world**, wasn't it?

Nora: Professor Breen is the best lecturer I've ever heard.
Alec: Yes, he's **second to none**, isn't he?

Lucy: I'm not looking forward to being group leader after John. He's so popular and successful.
Fergus: Yes, he's **a hard act to follow!**

Larry: Oh, I do like our new sofa. It looks just perfect here.
Susan: Yes, it's just **made for** this room, isn't it?

Kirsten: I admire William. He defended himself very well in the face of all the criticism and made some good points against his critics too.
Adrian: Yes, he **gave as good as he got**, didn't he?

Emilio: I don't think we'll get tickets for the cup final. They're all sold and we'd have to pay a huge sum of money to buy some on the black market.
Chris: Yes, they're **like gold dust**.

Mark: Dr Zasta's research is incredibly original and he has made some important new discoveries.
Nuria: Yes, he's done some really **ground-breaking** work.
(àtlò tš)

B Criticising people

Read Alice's account of some problems she had with a colleague at work. Note the idioms.

... Well, when I started working with her, at first she was all sweetness and light[1], but after a while she started getting/grating on my nerves[2], and we soon began to have arguments over stupid things. If I made even a small mistake with my work, she would give me a hard time[3], you know, and she would poke fun at[4] me if I smiled at or chatted with any of our male colleagues. To add insult to injury[5], she began to cast aspersions on[6] my honesty, and one day, when some money disappeared from someone's handbag, she told people she thought I'd stolen it. I don't think she was an out-and-out[7] evil person, but she was certainly asking for trouble[8], and one day I just lost my temper and, you know, told her exactly what I thought of her and how much I disliked her. She hasn't spoken to me since that day ...

[1] friendly and pleasant, but in a false way
[2] irritating/annoying me
[3] make me suffer / feel guilty
[4] tease/mock me (you can also say *make fun of* me)
[5] to make a bad situation even worse
[6] criticise my character; suggest that I was not honest (formal)
[7] completely/totally (for negative qualities of people)
[8] doing things that were certain to result in trouble (you can also say *asking for it*, which is more informal)

Exercises

12.1 Use an idiom in each sentence to repeat and sum up what the other person says.

1 A: Diana was very friendly and smiling after our quarrel, but in a really false way.
  B: Yes, I know. One minute she was angry, the next minute she was _all sweetness and light_ .

2 A: I tried to buy the new Madonna CD, but all the shops had already sold out.
  B: Yes, apparently they're _like gold dust_ .

3 A: If he continues to behave the way he is behaving, he's going to have big problems.
  B: Yes, I think he's just _asking for trouble_ . (Give two answers.)

4 A: Bridge Street College is the best school in the whole region.
  B: Yes, it's _second to none_ .

5 A: I enjoy being Chairperson, but I find it difficult coming after such a popular and successful Chairperson as Sarah.
  B: Yes, she's certainly _hard act to follow_ .

12.2 Correct the mistakes in these idioms.

1 She really gets ~~in~~ _on_ my nerve~~s~~ sometimes.
2 The last President was an ~~in-and-out~~ _out_ cruel monster, and the new one is not much better.
3 I don't think you should cast ~~aspirations~~ _aspersions_ on him. He's not here to defend himself.
4 The scientists did some ground-~~making~~ _breaking_ research on human genes.
5 She had already upset me, but to add ~~injuries~~ _insults_ to insults _injury_ she told me I was ugly.

ground-breaking work

12.3 Answer these questions.

1 What verb and preposition can be used instead of *make* and *of* in the idiom *make fun of somebody*?
2 What verb can be used instead of *get* in the idiom *get on someone's nerves*?

12.4 Complete each of these idioms.

1 They criticised her very strongly, but she _gave_ as good as she _got_ and made them shut up.
2 This dining table is just _made_ for this room. The wood matches the doors perfectly.
3 Why are you _giving_ me such a _hard_ time? I know I was wrong, but I said I'm sorry. I can't do any more.
4 We stayed at a luxurious five-star hotel. It was out of _this world_ .

13 Opinions on people and actions

A Evaluating people or things

It often helps to learn idioms by associating them with keywords.

keyword	idiom	example	meaning
answer	**have a lot to answer for**	Parents who don't control their children have a lot to answer for.	are the main cause of the problems
crack	something **is not all it's cracked up to be**	That restaurant is not all it's cracked up to be.	is not as good as people say it is
edge	someone/something **has the edge over** someone/something	This computer has the edge over other models because it has such a huge hard drive.	is slightly better than
desire	**leave a lot to be desired** (always in simple tense forms)	Her spoken English leaves a lot to be desired.	is not as good as it should be / as we might expect
make	**have all the makings of**	The recent events have all the makings of a big political scandal.	are likely to develop into
side	**on the big/expensive, etc. side**	This suitcase is a bit on the heavy side.	heavier than you want it to be
loss	**a dead loss**	This bottle-opener's a dead loss.	completely useless
ready	**rough and ready**	The accommodation was a bit rough and ready.	crude and lacking sophistication

B Commenting on people and their actions

If someone ...	then they ...
throws the baby out with the bathwater*	change things, but lose good things as well as bad
gets/jumps/leaps on the bandwagon	get involved in something already very successful
plays devil's advocate	pretend to be against an idea so that others discuss it
drives someone to distraction	make someone very angry or very bored
makes an exhibition of themselves	do things in public that make them look stupid
does something under false pretences	tell lies about who they are or what they're doing
never does anything by halves	always make a great effort and do things very well
is a laughing stock	are laughed at / mocked by everyone

* In former times, before people had bathrooms, all the family would bath in one bathtub. First the master of the house would bath, then his wife, then the children, and last of all the baby. By the time the baby was washed, the water was so dark and dirty there was a risk that no one would see the baby any more, and it would be thrown away with the dirty water!

Exercises

13.1 **Which idioms on the left-hand page have these keywords?**

	keyword	idiom
1	half	*never does anything by halves*
2	baby	*throws the baby out with the bathwater*
3	desire	*leave a lot to be desired*
4	bandwagon	*get/jump/leap on the bandwagon*
5	laugh	*is a laughing stock*

13.2 **Use the idioms from exercise 13.1 to rewrite the underlined parts of these sentences.**

1 The new documentary channel on TV <u>is not as good as it should be</u>. *is not all it's cracked up to be*
2 My brother <u>goes to enormous efforts to do everything perfectly</u>; he designed and built his own house, and designed most of the furniture too! *never does anything by halves*
3 He thinks everyone is afraid of him, but in fact <u>everyone laughs at him in secret</u>. *he is a laughing stock*
4 Yes, I think we should change the system, but I think we should <u>be careful to keep the good things about the old system</u>. *not throw the baby out with the bathwater*
5 Five years ago, there were not many companies selling on the Internet, but now everyone <u>has joined in because it's so successful</u>. *get on the bandwagon*

13.3 **Answer these questions.**

1 During the discussion, Kelly played devil's advocate. Did she agree or <u>disagree</u> with everyone else? In what way?
2 The buses that go from the airport to the city are a bit rough and ready. Are they nice to ride in? *No* Does the idiom mean they are usually ready to go when you arrive?
3 Walter was acting under false pretences when he worked as an electrician. What did Walter do which was wrong? *He wasn't an electrician*
4 Camford University is not all it's cracked up to be. Would you want to study there? Why? / Why not? *No*
5 Your friend has driven you to distraction. Do you say 'Thanks for the lift'? Are you happy with him/her? Why? / Why not? *He made me very angry*

13.4 **Complete each of these idioms. Use the clues in brackets.**

1 That new motorway project has ....*all*.... the ....*makings*.... of a disaster for the environment. It will go through the middle of a wildlife area. (is likely to become)
2 Zara ....*made*.... a real ....*exhibition*.... of ....*herself*.... in class the other day. It was so embarrassing! (behaved in a way that made her look stupid)
3 The Krona Hotel is a bit ....*on the*.... ....*the*.... expensive ....*side*..... Couldn't we stay somewhere cheaper? (more than I want to pay)
4 This new digital camera is a ....*dead*.... ....*loss*..... The batteries run out after about ten photos. (useless, no good)
5 I think Paris ....*has*.... the ....*edge*.... over other European cities as a place for a holiday. (slightly better)
6 The government has got a ....*lot*.... to ....*answer*.... for with regard to unemployment. (has caused a lot of problems)

14 Behaviour and attitudes

A Behaviour to yourself and others

idiom	meaning	example
look right/straight through someone	behave as if you do not see someone either because you do not notice them or because you are ignoring them	Ann often looks straight through you, but I think it may be because she's short-sighted.
leave someone in the lurch	leave someone at a time when they need you to stay and help them	I'm sorry I'm leaving you in the lurch, but I've got to get to a meeting by 10 a.m.
give someone a hard/ rough/tough time	make things difficult for someone	The teacher will give you a rough time if you don't finish the book.
keep a lid on something	control the level of something in order to stop it increasing	Rolf's been trying to keep a lid on his emotions, but every now and then his anger erupts.
let (yourself) go	either take less care of your appearance or relax completely and enjoy yourself	Sophie used to be so elegant, but now she's really let herself go.
blow something out of (all) proportion	behave as if something that has happened is much worse than it really is	The newspapers have blown the dispute out of all proportion.

B Attitudes towards events

When we got to our holiday destination, it was a very long climb up to the cottage that we were renting. John **thought nothing of**[1] it, but I found it quite difficult. However, when we got to the top, the view was so beautiful that it **brought a lump to my throat**[2]. We were only going to be there for two weeks, so we were determined to **make the most of**[3] it. Then my mother rang to say that my grandmother had been taken ill and her life was **hanging in the balance**[4]. Of course, everything else **faded/paled into insignificance**[5] then and we agreed that we **wouldn't dream of**[6] staying away in those circumstances. We caught the next plane home and spent the flight trying to **come to terms with**[7] the thought that she might die. However, thank goodness, when we got to the hospital, she was sitting up completely recovered and very apologetic that she had spoiled our holiday.

[1] did something that other people found difficult very easily
[2] found it so moving that I wanted to cry
[3] take full advantage of something because it may not last long
[4] no one knows what will happen to it in the future
[5] did not seem at all important when compared to something else
[6] would never do something because we think it is wrong
[7] start to accept emotionally and to deal with a difficult situation

TIP Idioms are frequently used for commenting on your own or others' behaviour and attitudes. Try to notice how idioms are used in this way when you are reading or listening to English. Note the context as well as the idiom in your Vocabulary notebook.

Exercises

14.1 Which of these sentences describe basically positive behaviour or attitudes and which describe behaviour or attitudes that are negative (at least from the speaker's point of view)?

N 1 Mark looked straight through me when I walked into the hall.
N 2 Rachel left me in the lurch as she usually does.
N 3 Sam has really let himself go since his wife died.
P 4 Let's make the most of this beautiful weather.
P 5 The boy's soprano ringing through the church brought a lump to my throat.
N 6 Rita's husband has blown the argument out of all proportion.
P 7 It'll be great to be able to let ourselves go once term ends.
P 8 They are gradually coming to terms with their loss.

14.2 Complete each of these idioms with one word.

1 The government has been quite successful at keeping a ____lid____ on inflation.
2 Her boss is still giving her a _hard / rough / tough_ time for forgetting to circulate his report. (Give three answers.)
3 In the light of what has happened since, our problems then have paled into _insignificance_ .
4 Jeremy thinks nothing ____of____ being interviewed on TV.
5 The newspapers often ____blow____ minor stories out of all proportion.
6 The beauty of the sunset brought a ____lump____ to my throat.
7 The fate of my application is hanging in the ____balance____ until my exam results come through.
8 I wouldn't ____dream____ of telling anyone your secret.

14.3 Answer these questions.

1 Have you ever been left in the lurch? If so, when? Yes
2 Has anyone ever given you a rough time? If so, why? Yes, my boss gives me every day
3 Is there anything difficult that you think nothing of doing? If so, what?
4 What do you think it is important to make the most of? One you'd luck in stg.
5 What was once a big problem for you that has now paled into insignificance? Had to leave England.
6 What sorts of things bring a lump to your throat? Romantic film/music
X 7 Can you think of something that you have had to come to terms with? If so, what?
8 What would you never dream of doing?

14.4 Which idioms do these pictures make you think of?

1 hanging in the balance

2 keep the lid on stg.

3 blow stg out of proportion

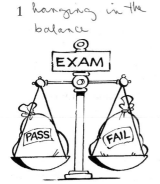

X The death of my grandparents.

15 Reacting to what others say

A Complete phrases

possible stimulus	response	meaning of response
I understood everything he said to me in French. I was just pretending not to.	Really? **You could've fooled me!**	You do not believe what someone says about something that you saw or experienced yourself.
Josh adores cowboy films!	**There's no accounting for taste(s)!**	You can't understand why someone likes or doesn't like something.
Are you prepared to hand in your notice to stop them going ahead with their plans?	Yes, **if all else fails**!	If all other plans do not work.
What do you think of the Labour candidate in the election?	**The lesser of two evils**, I suppose.	It is the less unpleasant of two bad options.
How did we get into this terrible position?	**One thing just led to another.**	A series of events happened, each caused by the previous one.
It was such a stupid thing to say to her.	I know. **I'll never live it down!**	You think that you have done something bad or embarrassing that people will never forget.
My boss just congratulated me on my report. Should I ask him for a pay rise now?	Yes, go on. **Strike while the iron is hot.**	Do something immediately while you have a good chance of success.
How are you going to live on such a small salary?	I don't know – **one way or another**.	You are not sure exactly how yet, but it will happen.

B Prepositional phrases

It's a bit **over the top!**
[more extreme than is necessary or appropriate]

Profits are falling. Do you think I should sack half the staff?

If I were **in your shoes,** I wouldn't do that!
[in your position]

It wouldn't be **at the top of my agenda!**
[the most important priority for me]

It's just **not on!**
[not an appropriate way of behaving]

Exercises

15.1 Match each idiom on the left with its definition on the right.

1 not on   somehow
2 one way or another   as a last resort
3 at the top of your agenda   exaggerated
4 over the top   now
5 if all else fails   important
6 strike while the iron is hot   inappropriate

15.2 Which of the idioms from A on the left-hand page might the second speaker use in these situations?

1 A: I love to put a bit of sugar on my lettuce.
   B: *There's no accounting for taste(s)!*
2 A: I really didn't mind at all that I didn't win the prize!
   B: *You ~~too~~ could've fooled me.*
3 A: Do you think I should go and speak to her now?
   B: Yes, *strike while the iron is hot.*
4 A: Would you rather have Smith or Jones as your boss?
   B: I suppose Smith's *the lesser of two evils.*
5 A: Will you walk to work if your car won't start tomorrow?
   B: *If all else fails.*

15.3 Correct the mistakes in these idioms.

1 If I were in your ~~boots~~ *shoes*, I'd take the job in New York.
2 Asking the Managing Director for his ID was a really stupid mistake to make. I'm sure my colleagues will never let me live it ~~off~~ *down*.
3 Improving office morale is said to be high on the new boss's ~~calendar~~. *agenda*
4 We hadn't intended to stay there so long, but one thing ~~took~~ to another. *just led*
5 Take your chance now. Strike while the ~~flame~~ is hot. *iron*
6 I can't understand what people see in the exhibition. There's no accounting for ~~likes~~. *tastes*
7 If all else ~~falls~~, I suppose I'll have to go and live somewhere else. *fails*
8 Given the choice between watching football or golf, I suppose football is the ~~less~~ of two evils. *lesser*

15.4 Complete these sentences in any way you like.

1 If I were in *your* shoes, I'd *leave that man immediately* .
2 *Prepare myself for my English exam* is at the top of my agenda at the moment.
3 *Speaking to me* is just not on, as far as I'm concerned.
4 I'm determined to *go and settle down in London* , one way or another.
5 I think that .... is/was over the top.
6 In my opinion, if you compare .... and .... , then .... is the lesser of two evils.

16 Danger

A Getting into danger

The soldiers **were caught napping** by the sudden attack. [got into trouble because they were not paying enough attention (napping = sleeping)]

The Health Minister risked his job by **going out on a limb** and criticising the proposals put forward by the Prime Minister. [stating an opinion or doing something different from anyone else. You can also be **out on a limb**, which means you are alone and lacking support from anyone else (limb = large branch of a tree)]

John was a weak man, easily **led astray** by others. [influenced so that he did bad things (astray = away from the main path)]

I'd **leave well alone** if I were you; Jack hates people to tidy his papers. [try not to change or improve something because this might make things worse]

Although it's always **panic stations** before the performance, everything goes smoothly as soon as the curtain goes up. [a time or situation where you feel very anxious and have to act quickly (informal)]

Taxes are **a necessary evil**. [something you do not like, but you agree that it must exist or happen]

Thank goodness, you're **safe and sound**. I was so worried about you when I heard about the accident. [this phrase simply emphasises the word *safe*]

B Being close to danger

idiom	meaning	example
have a narrow escape	just manage to avoid danger or trouble	The crew had a narrow escape when the pilot made a crash landing.
do something by the skin of your teeth	only just succeed in doing something	We won the match by the skin of our teeth.
rather/too close for comfort	so close in distance or similar in amount that you are worried or frightened	We won the election, but the results were rather close for comfort.
cut things fine	leave yourself only just enough time to do something	I prefer getting to the station early, but Lee always cuts things fine.
something sets alarm bells ringing	something worries you because it is a sign that there may be a problem	The strange look she gave me set alarm bells ringing.
take your life in(to) your hands	do something very risky	You're taking your life into your hands crossing the road here.
your life is in someone's hands	that person can affect whether you live or die	When you go into hospital, you put your life in the hands of strangers.
hanging by a thread	likely to fail in the near future	The economy is hanging by a thread.
on a knife-edge	in a very difficult situation and there are worries about the future	The business is on a financial knife-edge and may go bankrupt.

Exercises

16.1 Match the beginning of each idiom on the left with its ending on the right.

1 be caught ——— limb
2 have a narrow —— sound
3 safe and —— alone
4 be led —— escape
5 by the skin of your —— stations
6 be panic —— astray
7 leave well —— napping
8 go out on a —— teeth

16.2 Correct the mistakes in these idioms.

1 When David suggested they should come and stay for a weekend, it set alarm clocks *bells* ringing in my mind.
2 The patient's life is hanging by a string. *thread*
3 Having to go to work is an evil necessity. *necessary evil*
4 Why do some people always cut a thing fine?
5 They are on a knife-blade waiting for the results of Brian's medical tests. *edge*
6 As the building was on fire, he had no choice but to put his life in the firemen's hand and climb out of the window and onto their ladder.
7 You'll be taking the life in your hands if you make a speech like that to such an audience.
8 I think it would be more sensible to leave good alone. *~ well*

16.3 Which idioms do these pictures make you think of?

set alarms bells ringing

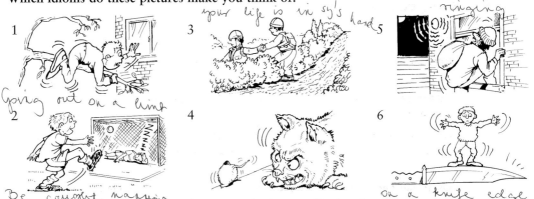

Going out on a limb

your life is in sy's hand

Be caught napping

on a knife edge

16.4 Rewrite each sentence with an idiom. Use the keyword in brackets.

1 I suppose that exams are just something that you have to do. (EVIL)
2 It was such a relief when Ralph arrived back from his Arctic expedition fit and healthy. (SOUND) *safe & sound*
3 You took an enormous risk by agreeing to go up in a helicopter with such an inexperienced pilot. (LIFE)
4 The hurricane seems to be getting a bit too near to our town and I'm beginning to feel rather nervous. (COMFORT)
5 If I were you, I wouldn't attempt to change things. (WELL) *d leave well alone*
6 We were in a state of chaos before the important visitors arrived, but we managed to get everything under control in time for their visit. (STATIONS) *panic station*
7 The Smiths almost missed the train. (TEETH) *just caught the train by the skin of*
8 I hope the other students won't distract our son from his studies. (LEAD) *their teeth*

17 Effort

A Making an effort

idiom	meaning	example
give something your all	use all your energy and effort to do something	I gave it my all, but only managed to come second in the race.
go all out	use a lot of energy and effort to do something	Jack is going all out to win the contract – I hope he'll succeed.
go out of your way to do something	try very hard to do something, usually something nice	Maggie always goes out of her way to put new employees at their ease.
pull your weight	work as hard as other people in a group	If Sarah pulled her weight, we would easily be able to complete the project on time.
by hook or by crook	using whatever methods are necessary	Our football team is determined to win the championship, by hook or by crook.
pull your finger out	make more of an effort (very informal)	If you don't pull your finger out, you'll get the sack.
at a push	probably possible, but it will be difficult	I could finish the report by Wednesday – at a push, Tuesday.

B Trying

You're not having much luck threading that needle, are you? Let me **have a go**. [try to do something]

I'll **have a bash** at painting the fence tomorrow if you like. [more informal way of saying *have a go*]

I **went through the motions** of tidying the house, but my thoughts were far away. [did something because you are expected to do it, not because you want to do it. In other words, you do it but without putting much effort or enthusiasm into it]

C Saying something is easy or difficult

child's play
[extremely easy]

How was your test?

as easy as falling off a log
[extremely easy (informal)]

a piece of cake
[extremely easy (informal)]

as easy as taking candy from a baby
[extremely easy]

a doddle
[extremely easy (informal)]

heavy-going
[difficult and needed a lot of effort]

Exercises

17.1 Match each idiom on the left with its definition on the right.

1 go all out — make an attempt
2 be a doddle — be difficult or tiresome to do
3 go through the motions — do your fair share
4 be heavy-going — do something without enthusiasm or effort
5 pull your weight — make a lot of effort
6 have a bash — be very easy to do

17.2 Correct the mistakes in these idioms.

1 I wish you'd pull your ~~hand~~ finger out and help me move the furniture.
2 Sam didn't like the exam, but I thought it was a ~~slice~~ of cake. piece
3 I'm going to get the job somehow, by hook ~~and~~ by crook. or
4 Sally could, in a ~~push~~, take over the project for you. at
5 The test was as easy as falling off a ~~tree~~. log
6 Don't worry if you don't win the game – just as long as you give ~~that~~ your all. it
7 Why don't you have ~~the~~ go at repairing the washing machine yourself? a
8 Persuading him to do what I wanted was like taking candy from a ~~child~~. baby
9 Max will always go out of his ~~road~~ to help others. way
10 I had no problems using the public transport system there – it was ~~a~~ child's play.

17.3 Complete the idioms in this paragraph with prepositions.

The students in my class have to hand in an assignment on Friday. Masako is going all
......out...... (1) to get a good mark. Marc usually just goes ...through.... (2) the motions of
writing an essay, but this time he's really pulled his finger ...out...... (3) and is going
...out of.. (4) ...of...... (5) his way to write something good. He says that he wants to
get an A ....by....... (6) hook or ....by......... (7) crook. Paul says he found the assignment
as easy as taking candy ......from....... (8) a baby, but Sandra says that, although she had a
good go .... (9) it, she found it quite heavy-going.

17.4 Rewrite each underlined idiom with another idiom which has the same meaning.

1 A: Do you think I'll be able to manage a snowboard?
   B: Course, you will. It's <u>as easy as taking candy from a baby</u>. as easy as falling off a log
2 A: I can't open this bottle.
   B: Let me <u>have a bash</u>. / have a go
3 A: How's John getting on with his new boss?
   B: He is going <u>all out</u> to make a good impression on her. to give it his all
4 A: Did you find it easy to make that dress?
   B: It was <u>child's play</u>. a doddle / a piece of cake

17.5 Which of the two speakers in each case is speaking in a more informal way?

1 Matt: I think I'll have a bash at making some bread this weekend.
   Alex: I think I'll have a go at making some bread this weekend.

2 Leah: I wish you'd pull your weight more with the project.
   Sam: I wish you'd pull your finger out and help more with the project.

3 Tom: Getting him to do what I want is child's play.
   Sonya: Getting him to do what I want is a piece of cake.

18 Necessity and desirability

A Necessity

> Return-Path: <g.bookworm@cup.cam.al.uk>
> Mon, 04 Sep 2000 05:37:33 2000
>
> Hi Gerry,
> Good to get your e-mail. Things are fine here
> and we're busy. Nothing to complain about,
> except that an extra computer **wouldn't go
> amiss**[1].

> Return-Path: <k.estrella@frolick.com>
> Thu, 31 Aug 2000 12:53:36 -0400
>
> Kate,
> I feel **duty bound**[4] to tell you that all is not
> well in the secretaries' office. Nothing to
> panic about right at the moment, but you
> know how

> Return-Path: <k.l.pod@greedroyd.hjnet.co.uk>
> Sun, 03 Sep 2000 14:25:55 -0400
>
> Hello Kim!
> Thanks for your e-mail. Your new job sounds
> great. Things are horrible here, and **if push
> comes to shove**[2], I'll just have to leave. **If
> need be**[3], I'll work in a fast food place just

> Return-Path: <l.t.sparks@dow.org>
> Tue, 05 Sep 2000 07:37:38 2000
>
> Dear Lorna,
> How are you? I'm fine, but I'm a bit angry
> today. The boss has asked me to go to London
> tomorrow, and **I need** a trip to London **like
> I need a hole in the head**.[5] I may pretend

[1] would be very useful/good; we need them
[2] if the situation becomes very bad, this is
what I can do
[3] if it is really necessary / if I have no choice
[4] I feel that it is my duty / that I really ought to
[5] I don't need it at all, and don't want it

B Wanting and desirability

In these pairs of sentences, the second sentence means more or less the same as the first.

I'm really really looking forward to meeting your cousin. **I'm dying to** say hello to her.
(Note: always continuous tense form)

Nothing would persuade me to ride a motorbike. I **wouldn't be seen dead** riding one.
(Note the -ing form when a verb follows)

I left home because I wanted to be independent. I just wanted to **do my own thing**.

I'd do anything for a chance to meet the President. I'd **give anything** to shake his hand.

His comments were just not appropriate. They were not **in keeping with** the tone of things.

I would never ever consider a job like that. I **wouldn't touch it with a barge pole.**
(barge pole = a long pole used to push forward a barge, which is a canal boat)

C Other useful related expressions

Customer: Have you got a copy of *Advanced English Grammar*?
Bookseller: You're **in luck**. We have just one copy left. [said when you get something good
that you were not expecting]

It's **not worth my while** buying a new car this month. They're always cheaper later in the
year. [I will not benefit from doing it]

You need a dictionary? **Take your pick.** There are three different ones over there on the
bookshelf. [choose whichever you want]

Exercises

18.1 Complete each of these idioms.

1 I wouldn't be .... working in a hamburger restaurant. All my friends would laugh at me. I just couldn't do it.
2 I feel duty .... to go home and see my parents at least once a month.
3 I've had enough coffee, thanks, but another one of those lovely cakes wouldn't go ....
4 I think that CD player he's trying to sell is stolen. If I were you, I wouldn't .... it with a ....
5 It's not .... my .... trying the exam again. I failed the first time, and I'll probably fail again.

18.2 Complete the crossword.

			¹T	²H	I	N	G
				O			
			³L	U	C	K	
⁴S	H	O	V	E			

Across
1 I want to do my own _thing_ .
3 You're in _luck_ ! She's just arrived.
4 If push comes to _shove_ .

Down
2 I don't want one in my head. ᵃhole

18.3 Now use the idioms from the crossword to rewrite these sentences.

If push comes to shove

1 You are very fortunate. We have just one room left for tonight. *You're in luck.*
2 If the situation really becomes bad enough, we'll just have to sell the apartment.
3 I don't want to go with a big group of people. I want to be independent. *To do my own thing*
4 I got a bill today for £700 for repairs to my car. I'm telling you, the last thing I need in this world is a bill for £700 right at this moment. *I needed it like I need a hole in the head.*

18.4 Answer these questions.

1 Which idiom containing the word *need* means 'if it is really necessary' / 'if we are forced to act'? *If need be*
2 What is another way of saying 'choose what you want from the available selection'? *Take ur pick!*
3 What should you remember about the grammar of the idiom with *die* that means 'want very much' / 'really look forward to'?
4 What idiom is based on the verb *keep*, and means 'suitable for' / 'in line with'?

18.5 Answer these questions for yourself.

1 Is there anyone that you would give anything to meet?
2 Is there something that you're dying to do in the next few days?

FOLLOW UP Idioms are usually most common in informal texts – like the e-mails in A on the left-hand page. Try to read as many informal English texts as you can, for example, letters to popular magazines from readers, Internet chat and newsgroup texts, tabloid newspaper editorials, etc., and note any idioms you find. If you would occasionally like to try out some of the idioms you have learnt in this book, then informal e-mails are a good, natural context for using them.

19 Probability and luck

A Probability

You try something **on the off-chance**[1] at work this week and achieve success **against all the odds**[2]. At home you must be careful not to **take someone** close to you **for granted**[3] as, if you do, it **is a foregone conclusion**[4] that you will regret it sooner rather than later. Others **have seen** changes in your love life **coming a mile off**[5] and it is **touch-and-go**[6] whether your current relationship will survive this week. **No prizes for guessing**[7] who is to blame for the problems. However, you may still be able to get back together. Do not listen to others when they say that **the cards are stacked against**[8] you. It is always worth **chancing your arm**[9]. Whether you succeed or not **is in the lap of the gods**[10].

1 because you hope you will do or find something or someone even if you do not think success is very likely
2 despite a lot of problems making it unlikely that you will succeed
3 you don't show you're grateful to someone because they are with you so often
4 the result is obvious to everyone even before it happens
5 have seen that something, usually something bad, is likely to happen (*a mile off* adds emphasis and is not always included in the expression)
6 not certain (often followed by *whether*)
7 it is very easy to guess (usually followed by a question word)
8 you are not likely to succeed because there are so many obstacles in your way
9 taking a risk to achieve what you want (informal)
10 not something that you can control yourself

B Luck

possible stimulus	you say	you mean
I got away with missing afternoon school last Friday, so I'm going to try taking all of Friday off next week.	**Don't push your luck!**	Don't try too hard to get what you want and risk losing what you have achieved.
Would you like to choose which hotel room you want?	**We'll take pot luck.**	We'll take whatever is available without knowing if it will be good or not.
Do you always get a good horse at the riding stables you go to?	**It's the luck of the draw.** (draw = competition where winners are chosen at random)	It's a matter of chance and you have no control over it.
You're playing against the best player in the competition!	**Just my luck!**	You say this, usually humorously, to mean that you are always unlucky.
Did you manage to persuade Jane to come on holiday with you?	**No such luck!**	You are disappointed you weren't able to do what you would have liked to do.
I dreamt that Elton John invited me to one of his parties last night!	**You should be so lucky!**	What someone wants to happen is unlikely to happen.

Exercises

19.1 Comment on each of these sentences. How likely or unlikely is it that the action referred to will happen?

1 Against all the odds Jack is attempting to climb the mountain without oxygen.
2 Will Molly get the job she wants? It's in the lap of the gods.
3 No prizes for guessing which role Tom's got in the play.
4 The cards are stacked against her completing her course.
5 It's a foregone conclusion that Beth will come top in the exam.
6 I think it's touch-and-go whether Rob will pass his driving test.
7 Let's go to the library on the off-chance that they'll have the book we need.
8 Green will lose his job in the Cabinet reshuffle – you can see it coming a mile off.

19.2 Match each response from the box with a statement.

> Don't push your luck!   I'll take pot luck.   It's the luck of the draw.   Just my luck!
> No such luck!   You should be so lucky!

1 A: Did you win anything in the lottery?
   B: _No such luck_
2 A: Your bike has a flat tyre, I'm afraid.
   B: _Just my luck._
3 A: We can't choose which team we play against first in the tournament.
   B: I know. ....
4 A: I've been getting the best sales results of anyone on the team. I'm going to ask the boss for more pay.
   B: ....
5 A: You're welcome to come for dinner, but I don't know what we're having.
   B: Don't worry. ....
6 A: I feel sure Dad's going to give me a car for my birthday.
   B: ....

19.3 Correct the mistakes in these idioms.

1 They've been married for so long that they take each other as granted.
2 We've done all we can. Now the results of the election are in the lap of gods.
3 Alex is chancing the arm a bit only applying to one university.
4 No prizes for guess who got the job in the end!
5 The cards were stacked on Bart being able to persuade him.
6 It was touch-or-go who would win the match.
7 We could all see Jan's collapse come.
8 Let's go down to the theatre off the on-chance that we can get some tickets that have been returned.

19.4 Choose six expressions that you would particularly like to learn – three from A and three from B on the left-hand page. Write sentences using the idioms in relation to a situation that is significant to you personally.

20 Social status

A Social status and how people see it

example	meaning
He's very nice and friendly, but his brother is very **toffee-nosed**.	thinks he is of a high social class and looks down on people of lower class (negative)
Don't try **putting on / giving yourself airs and graces**. Remember, I know that you come from a very ordinary family.	acting as if you were someone of a higher social class than you really are
Everyone was shocked to hear he was involved in crime. He was such **a pillar of society**.	a solid, respectable and respected member of society
Her new boyfriend's a bit of **a rough diamond**, but he's very nice really.	a person who seems impolite / of low education at first, but who is usually of good character
She's always giving money to **down-and-outs** and anyone who begs in the street.	people who have no home, no money and no job, who live on the streets
We can't really afford new furniture, but we have **to keep up appearances**, so we'll buy some.	continue to live at the same social standard we have lived at, even though we have money problems

B Social status and job/career

These clips from a magazine with stories about people in the news contain idioms that refer to success or status in their careers.

He was a **high-flyer**[1] in the world of computers in the 1990s, and went on to

She is one of several **up-and-coming**[4] actresses who have appeared in the new

He first made a name for himself[2] in the world of classical music, then

The company needed **new blood**[5] and she provided it. Within months, sales had gone

Kenneth Briggs is definitely **on his way up**[3] in the financial world. He has just joined the

[1] rose very quickly to a successful position
[2] became well-known
[3] rising to better and better positions
[4] becoming more and more popular/famous
[5] a new person from outside the company

C Other useful idioms connected with social status/situation

I prefer to **keep a low profile** at work. I'm not interested in promotion. [not draw attention to myself; be unnoticed]

Oh, you must come to the party! **Anybody who is anybody** will be there. [all the important people]

Harriet always seems to be **the odd one out**. She never seems to fit in socially. [different from everyone else]

You can't call someone 'unemployed' any more. The **politically correct** name is 'unwaged'. [acceptable and non-offensive way of talking about particular social groups; usually used in a mocking or negative way about people who insist on using politically correct language]

Exercises

20.1 **Correct the mistakes in these idioms.**

1 He is always the odd ~~out~~ one. [out] If all his friends do one sport, he does a different one.

2 When he lost all his money, he still tried to keep [up] appearances even though he could not afford his lifestyle.

3 Sometimes it's better to ~~give~~ [keep] a low profile at work. In that way, nobody asks you to do difficult jobs.

4 She ~~became~~ [made] a name for herself by being the first woman to climb Mount Everest.

5 He's always putting on air and grace, but everyone knows he's just an ordinary person with a very ordinary background. [himself]

20.2 **Rewrite the underlined part of each sentence with an idiom.**

1 <u>All the most important people</u> [Anybody who is anybody] will be at the concert on Friday, so don't miss it.

2 It's not <u>socially acceptable</u> to refer to 'underdeveloped' countries any more. If you don't want to offend people, you should say 'developing nations'. [politically correct]

3 He was voted 'Best actor <u>who is quickly becoming well-known</u>' of 2001. [made a name for himself]

4 They employed a lot of young people as they felt they needed <u>new people with fresh ideas</u>. [blood]

5 A lot of the people who live in those huge houses near the beach <u>think they're a better social class than other people and look down on them</u>. [toffee-nosed]

6 My boss <u>gives the impression of being rather rude and uneducated</u>, but he's a very nice guy in fact. [is a bit of a rough diamond]

7 She was <u>a very respectable member of society</u>, but then it turned out she was involved in the illegal drug trade. [a pillar of society]

20.3 **In your own words, say what it means if ...**

1 ... you're on your way up in your profession.

2 ... someone is down and out.

3 ... someone is a high-flyer in the computer industry.

4 ... someone is toffee-nosed.

20.4 **Which idioms do these pictures make you think of?**

1 [a pillar of society]

2 [rough diamond]

3 [high-flyer]

FOLLOW UP Look in your Vocabulary notebook or in other units in this book where there are no pictures and see how many idioms you could draw a picture of. Draw simple pictures that might help you to remember three idioms.

21 Feelings

A Feeling good, feeling bad

good/positive feelings		bad/negative feelings	
example	meaning	example	meaning
I am/feel **on top of the world** today. I've just passed all my exams.	very happy indeed	I've been (feeling) a bit **down in the dumps** lately.	depressed / in low spirits
She was **thrilled to bits** when I told her she had been picked for the team.	very happy and excited	She's been/felt **on edge** all day.	nervous, agitated, anxious
Jo was very **cool, calm and collected** just before the job interview.	relaxed, prepared, in control, not nervous	I just don't know what to do about the problem. I'm **at the end of my tether***.	am so tired or annoyed, I just can't deal with the situation any more
When I saw how happy Nancy was with the present we gave her, it **made my day**.	made me feel very happy/satisfied	I've **had my fill of** exams. I hope I never do another one for the rest of my life.	had enough (often in a negative sense)
I **jumped for joy** when they told me I didn't have to do the English test.	felt very glad/happy about something, often a reaction to good news	I'm **sick and tired of** studying. I just want to get a job and earn money.	have had enough (always negative, much stronger than *have your fill*)

* A *tether* is a rope used to limit an animal's movements and where it can feed. If the animal reaches the end of its tether, it can't find any more grass to eat, so becomes hungry and unhappy.

B More reactions to events

In this letter to the *Problems* page of a magazine, the context should give you a good idea of the meaning of the idioms in bold.

> Dear Paula, I'm 22 and work in an office in London. I have been going out with a boy for the last six months, but lately it has all gone wrong. When I first saw him, he just **took my breath away** – I could hardly speak, he was so attractive and intelligent. We started going out, and after a while he said he loved me. I think this gave me a false sense of security, and I never thought anything bad could happen. But then someone told me he was dating a good friend of mine. The news was so terrible I just **didn't know what had hit me**, and I was so embarrassed I **didn't know where to put myself**. I asked him about it, but he **didn't take kindly to** the idea that I was suspicious of him. He got a bit angry, and told me that that side of his life had nothing to do with me. I **have mixed feelings** about this news, sometimes I feel positive, sometimes very down, and I **don't know which way to turn**. What should I do? Should I finish with him, or should I accept his right to have other dates apart from me? I still love him.
>
> Yours,
>
> *Diana Noe*

> **TIP**
>
> Tables like the one in A can help you organise your vocabulary learning better. Wherever you can, make tables in your Vocabulary notebook. Use separate columns for positive and negative expressions, or for formal and informal ones.

Exercises

21.1 Complete each of these idioms with a preposition.

1 I've had my fill ___of___ meetings. I hope we never have another. They're so boring.
2 She jumped ___for___ joy when they told her she had won a trip to Paris.
3 Jane has been ___down___ ___in___ the dumps since her boyfriend went away.
4 He was thrilled ___to___ bits when I told him Sara was coming to stay.
5 I couldn't face all the problems any more. I was ___at___ the end of my tether.
6 I've been ___on___ edge lately, but I don't really know why. Sorry if I sound impatient.

21.2 Answer these questions.

1 Name something you are sick and tired of. My job
2 When was the last time you felt on top of the world? Why? When I was in Alan's bed.
3 Is there any place you have visited which is so beautiful it took your breath away? London
4 In what kinds of situations do you feel on edge? exams, job interviews
5 Have you ever been in a situation where you didn't know where to put yourself? What was it?

21.3 Look at these extracts from letters to the problem page of a magazine. Complete in your own words the sentence below each one.

1

> She told me she was leaving me. I didn't know what had hit me, I just

When she told me, I _____ .

3

> I'd always been cool, calm and collected in my job, but suddenly

I had always been _____ .

2

> Please help me. I don't know which way to turn. Would it be

I need help, I _____ .

4

> I'm writing to you because I'm at the end of my tether. Recently, a

I'm writing because _____ .

21.4 Complete each of these idioms. Use the keyword in brackets.

1 Meeting her there when I wasn't expecting to see her _it made my day_ . (DAY)
2 I'm not sure whether I want the job or not. I 've _mixed feelings about it_ . (MIXED)
3 The good news made me _jumped for joy_ . (JOY)
4 I got a chance to go to Canada for a week. I was _thrilled to bits_ . (BITS)
5 He doesn't like people using his computer, so he won't _take kindly to_ the idea of sharing one. (KINDLY)
6 If you're feeling _down in the dumps_ , why don't you come out with us tonight? (DUMPS)
7 I've _had my fill of_ job interviews – six in just two weeks! I never want another one. (FILL)

FOLLOW UP Watch an English-language talkshow on TV where people talk about their personal problems. Note any useful idioms, check their meaning, then think how they might relate to you personally.

22 Human relationships

A Good relationships

idiom	meaning	example
be in someone's good books	that person is pleased with you – possibly only temporarily	I'm in the teacher's good books – I helped her tidy the classroom.
get on like a house on fire	get on extremely well with someone	Fortunately, we got on like a house on fire from the start.
keep/get/be/stay in touch with someone	keep/get/be/stay in contact with someone	We must all keep in touch after our course is over.
make it up to someone	do something good for someone you have done something bad to in the past	I'm sorry I forgot your birthday. I promise I'll make it up to you.
take a shine to	like someone immediately (informal)	I could see from her smile that she had taken a shine to him.
have a soft spot for	feel a lot of affection for one particular person, often without knowing why	Nick was a naughty little boy, but I couldn't help having a soft spot for him.

B Difficult relationships

idiom	meaning	example
be at loggerheads (of two people or groups)	disagree strongly with each other	The council and local residents are at loggerheads over the plans for a new car park.
be (talking) at cross-purposes (of two people or groups)	not understand each other because they are trying to do or say different things	We're talking at cross-purposes. I was referring to my brother and you're talking about my father.
have it in for someone	be determined to criticise or harm someone	I can't understand why he has it in for me – I've never done anything to harm him.
have it out with someone	talk to someone about something they have done in order to solve the problem	I can't take Ben's selfishness any longer – I'm going to have it out with him this evening.
rub someone up the wrong way	irritate someone	She seems to always rub her boss up the wrong way.
two-time someone	have a romantic or sexual relationship with two people at the same time	She refused to believe he was two-timing her until she saw him with another girl.
keep someone/something at bay	prevent someone/something from coming near or harming you	So far this year, I've managed to keep the flu at bay.
keep yourself to yourself	prefer to be on your own and avoid talking with or doing things with other people	Judy seems nice. But she keeps herself to herself, so I don't know much about her.

Exercises

22.1 Which of the neighbours referred to does the speaker have a good relationship with and which does he have a bad relationship with?

> I get on well with some of my neighbours but not with others. I get on like a house on fire with Anna who lives next door, but Rob on the other side has it in for me for some reason. I'm always at cross-purposes with Jane from over the road, but I'm in her husband Pat's good books. I used to be at loggerheads with the Browns, but we had it out and now things are OK. I prefer to keep the dog from number 22 at bay and its owner, Jack, and I always seem to rub each other up the wrong way. However, I've got a soft spot for his son, Jimmy.

22.2 Correct the mistakes in these idioms.

1 I would immediately drop any boyfriend that tried to two-times me.
2 Susie has taken the shine to her new teacher.
3 Please stay into touch with me once you go home.
4 Nita's boyfriend promised to make up it to her for forgetting her birthday.
5 There's something about him that always rubs me down the wrong way.
6 We try to be friendly, but the Smith family prefer to keep them to themselves.
7 If you want to leave early, you'd better try and stay in the boss's good book.
8 Rana really seems to have it out for me today – I don't know how I've upset him.

22.3 Choose the correct answer.

1 The neighbour's pet rat is supposed to be friendly, but I'd rather … .
  a) not keep in touch with him   b) keep him at bay
2 The union and management have been … ever since management proposed issuing new contracts.
  a) at loggerheads   b) at cross-purposes
3 If you feel so strongly that he is wrong, wouldn't it be better to … ?
  a) have it in for him   b) have it out with him
4 Her habit of finishing every sentence of mine really … .
  a) rubs me up the wrong way   b) makes it up to me
5 Why don't you … with my aunt when you go to New York?
  a) get on like a house on fire   b) get in touch

22.4 Answer these questions.

1 What might a young child do to try to get in the teacher's good books?
2 If you are at cross-purposes with someone, are you angry or confused?
3 How might you try to make it up to a friend whose car you've scratched?
4 What are three different ways in which you can keep in touch with distant friends? Which way do you like best?
5 Are there any things that people say that really rub you up the wrong way?
6 What do you think should happen to someone who two-times a boyfriend or girlfriend?
7 If you keep yourself to yourself, are you lonely?
8 If you take a shine to someone or have a soft spot for them, is the feeling mutual?

23 Size and position

A Big and large

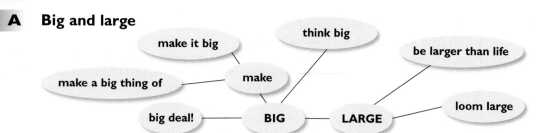

example	meaning
She's a great singer. She'll **make it big** one day.	succeed; become famous
It's my birthday on Saturday, but I don't want to **make a big thing of** it, so don't tell anyone.	make it a special occasion; have a big celebration
If you're going to invest your money, you should **think big**. Put twenty thousand into oil shares.	have ambitious plans and ideas, and be keen to achieve a lot
So? You won ten pounds on the lottery. **Big deal!**	said when something happens but you are not impressed/excited, even if others are
The characters in his films are always **larger than life**.	much more exciting and interesting than average people
The threat of an earthquake **looms large** in the lives of the city's inhabitants.	something which could happen and which is a huge worry for people

B *Inch, mile* and distance

Note: Although British people now use metric measurements, many expressions are still used which include old measurements. An inch is 2.54 centimetres, a mile is 1.6 kilometres.

Mary: Is she willing to change her mind?
Tony: No, she refuses to **budge an inch.**
[refuses to change her position even a little bit]

Luke: Are you listening to me?
Anne: Sorry, I was **miles away!**
[not concentrating, but thinking about something else]

Tom: It's obvious Ruth really likes Jack.
Noel: Yes, you can **see/spot** that **a mile off!**
Or It **sticks/stands out a mile.**
[it's very easy to see / obvious]

Dave: It's a very ugly hotel and the food's awful.
Fran: Yes, it's **a far cry from** that lovely hotel we stayed in last year.
[very different from]

C Other related expressions

Relatives are nice **in small doses**, but can be very boring if they stay a long time. [you like them only for short periods]

His new house cost **a small fortune**. [a huge amount of money]

You can buy sunglasses in **all shapes and sizes** these days. [in a wide variety of types/sizes, etc.]

Joss is **an unknown quantity**. We'll have to be careful with him. [we know very little about him]

 Networks can sometimes help you to visualise and remember a lot of information more easily than memorising a list. Try making networks for groups of idioms from different units in this book.

Exercises

23.1 **Answer these questions.**

1 In which idiom does *small* mean big/huge? (clue: money) *small fortune*
2 In which idiom does *big* really mean small/insignificant? (clue: not impressed) *Big deal!*
3 Which idiom means someone is more exciting/interesting than the average human being?
4 Which idiom with *big* means to become famous? *make it big* / *larger than life*

23.2 **Use an idiom in each sentence to summarise the situation.**

1 Maria is not listening to what Eddie is saying. Her mind is on something else.
   Maria is ___*miles away*___ .
2 There are big chairs and small chairs, armchairs, garden chairs and office chairs.
   Chairs are sold in ___*all shapes & sizes.*___ .
3 Our old school was dark and depressing. Our new school is light and pleasant.
   The new school is a ___*far cry from our old one*___ .
4 Jerry looks at Jenny with a romantic look in his eyes. He always wants to sit next to her,
   and always wants to talk about her.
   You can see he's in love. It ___*sticks/stands out a mile*___ .
   Or: He's in love. You can see/spot it ___*that a mile off*___ .

23.3 **Complete each of these idioms.**

1 She's 40 next week, but she doesn't want to ___*make a big thing of it*___ . She'd prefer
   just to go out for a meal with her husband rather than have a big party with lots of people.
2 For any person in a temporary job, the possibility of unemployment
   ___*looms large*___ , especially in a time of economic recession.
3 The unions are prepared to discuss the problem, but the employers will not
   ___*think big*___ . They say they have made their final offer, and
   that's that.
4 We have a new boss starting next week. He's a bit of ___*an unknown quantity*___
   – nobody has met him or knows much about him.
5 I like having friends to stay in my flat, but only for a couple of days. In general, friends
   are nice ___*in small doses*___ ; if they stay too long, they always irritate me.
6 We should think ___*larger than life*___ when we come to plan the new
   website. There's no point in having one single, dull page; we should have lots of links and
   video clips, and as many colour pictures as possible, and sound.

23.4 **Use a dictionary to check the meaning of these idioms and then write a sentence for each one.**

the middle ground   the middle of nowhere   be caught in the middle

Well, I wanted a pet, and
you're always telling me I should
think big when I make decisions
for the future.

24 Money

A People's financial circumstances

idiom	meaning	example
be on the breadline	be very poor	More people in Britain are on the breadline now than thirty years ago.
live in the lap of luxury	live an extremely comfortable life, because you have a lot of money	We live simply during the year, but enjoy living in the lap of luxury in a nice hotel for our summer holiday.
well off / well-to-do / well-heeled	having plenty of money	Most of the people living here are clearly very well-to-do, but there are a few poorer families.
spend money like water	spend too much, often without thinking about it	He spends money like water – I wonder where he gets it all from.
tighten your belt	spend less than you did before, because you have less money	I'm afraid we'll have to tighten our belts now there's another mouth to feed.
make a killing	earn a lot of money very easily	The new Internet companies have made an instant killing.
be a money spinner	be a successful way of making money	My dog-walking business was quite a money spinner when I was at college.

B Costs

We had to **pay through the nose** to get our car repaired, but at least it's working now. [pay a lot of money]

If you say that something **is a rip-off** (informal), you mean that it is not worth the money that you paid for it.

We had to spend **a small fortune** on getting everything we needed for our holiday. [a lot of money. (You can also say that something **cost a small fortune**)]

Someone can also **make a small fortune** out of a business or they can **lose a small fortune**.

C Idioms based on the money metaphor

Bill is a generous man who is happy to **pick up the tab/bill**[1] for anything. He managed to rise to the top of his profession in the police force, but it was **at a considerable price**[2]. His marriage suffered as a result. This was largely because his dedication to his work **put paid to**[3] his wife's career as a nurse as soon as their first child came along. Unfortunately, Bill is **paying the price for**[4] his ambitiousness now as his wife has left him and taken their son.

[1] pay for something, often something that is not your responsibility (informal)
[2] by sacrificing a lot or by doing something unpleasant in order to get it
[3] stopped someone from doing something that they were planning to do
[4] experiencing the unpleasant consequences of

TIP

Help yourself to remember idioms by making a picture of their literal meaning in your mind (or on a piece of paper if you like drawing) as you learn them. To help you remember *well-heeled*, for instance, you might imagine or draw a pair of smart high-heeled shoes.

Exercises

24.1 Put these expressions describing how much money someone has on a scale from poor on the left to rich on the right.

1.   2.   2.

3.
| living in the lap of luxury | on the breadline | well-to-do | well-heeled |

24.2 Which person in each pair of speakers is probably more satisfied?

1 Anne: Our new business venture means we're going to have to tighten our belts.
 *Bob: We're making a killing with our new business venture.

2 *Colin: Our new car cost a small fortune.
  Daisy: Our new car was a rip-off.

3 Ed: My daughter spends money like water.
 *Fred: My daughter's quite well off.

4 *Gill: This business venture has put paid to our hopes of success.
  Harry: This business venture has brought success, but at a considerable price.

24.3 Complete each of these idioms with one word.

1 Gina is ...._making_.... a killing in her new job.
2 I was put in the position where I had no choice but to ...._pick_.... up the tab.
3 We spent a weekend at the hotel living in the ...._lap_.... of luxury.
4 Our neighbours spent a small ...._fortune_.... on their new conservatory.
5 The first book Marvin wrote turned out to be more of a ...._money_.... spinner than anything he has written since then.
6 As Zak has lost his job, we're going to have to ...._tighten_.... our belts for a while.
7 We had to pay through the ...._nose_.... to get tickets for the match.
8 If you don't study now, you'll .... the price later on in the year.
9 Another expression that means *spend money like* ...._water_.... is *spend money like there was no tomorrow*.
10 He started his own business after ...._make_.... a small fortune on the stock exchange and deciding that he should put his luck to good use.

24.4 Which idioms do these pictures make you think of?

pay through the nose

be a money spinner

well off

rip off

tighten ur belt

25 Work

A One man's career

When Simon started work, he was at the very bottom of the career ladder[1]. He had quite a dead-end job[2] doing run-of-the-mill[3] tasks. He stayed there for a couple of years, but then decided he had to get out of a rut[4]. He pulled out all the stops[5] and managed to persuade his manager that he should be given more responsibility. The deputy manager got the sack[6] for incompetence and Simon stepped into his shoes[7]. For several months he was rushed off his feet[8] and he had his work cut out[9] to keep on top of things. But he was soon recognised as an up-and-coming[10] young businessman and he was headhunted[11] by a rival company for one of their top jobs. Simon had climbed to the top of the career ladder[12].

[1] in a low position in a work organisation or hierarchy
[2] job without a good future
[3] boring, routine
[4] escape from a monotonous, boring situation (see picture of horse)
[5] made a great effort to do something well (see picture of organ; stops increase the sound of an organ)
[6] was dismissed from his job (also *be given the sack*)
[7] took over his job
[8] very busy
[9] had something very difficult to do
[10] becoming more and more successful
[11] invited to join a new workplace which had noticed his talents
[12] got to a top position in a work organisation or hierarchy

This is a rut.

These are called stops.

B Being busy

To be **rushed off your feet** is just one way of saying that you are very busy at work. Here are some other idioms which give the same idea.

Are you very busy at work at the moment?

Yes, I'm **snowed under.**

Yes, I've certainly **got my hands full.**

Yes, I'm **up to my eyes/ears** in work.

Yes, I'm **on the go** all the time.

C Other idioms connected with work

Plans for building the extension have been **put on hold** until our finances are in a better state. [left until a later date (usually used in the passive)]

The plans look great **on paper**, but you never know quite how things will turn out, of course. [when you read about it, but might not turn out to be so]

A lot of preparation has gone on **behind the scenes** for the opening ceremony for the Olympics. [in secret, often when something else is happening publicly]

Please don't **talk shop.** It's too boring for the rest of us. [talk about work when you are not at work]

Exercises

25.1 **Complete each of these idioms with one word.**

1 The job looks good on ....*paper*........., but the reality is quite different.
2 I'd hate to work in a run-of-the-....*mill*........ job.
3 Mary has been up to ......*her*...... eyes in work all day.
4 When John retires, his son will ....*step*......... into his shoes.
5 My cousin's an up-and-....*coming*....... musician.
6 I must try to get out of a ......*rut*....... at work.
7 I've been on the ......*go*...... all day.
8 Why did Kirsty's boss give her the ....*sack*...... ?
9 I wish you wouldn't talk ....*shop*..... all the time!
10 Rosie was very thrilled to be ......*head*.......hunted for her new job.

25.2 **Which idioms do these pictures make you think of?**

25.3 **Match each idiom on the left with its definition on the right.**

1 behind the scenes   very busy
2 dead-end   be dismissed
3 get the sack   make an effort
4 off the record   promising
5 on hold   hidden
6 pull out all the stops   unofficially
7 rushed off your feet   delayed
8 up-and-coming   without prospects

25.4 **Complete each of these idioms.**

We had a difficult day at work today. We were all (1) ....*snowed*..... under because we are having some important visitors next week and management has decided to pull out all the (2) ....*stops*.... to impress them. We are going to have our work (3) ....*cut*.... out to get everything done in time. Long-term tasks have been put on (4) ....*hold*.... so that everything is ready for our visitors. Anyone who objects has been told that they will (5) ....*get*.... the sack and everyone who wants to (6) ....*climb*.... the career ladder will have their (7) ....*hands*.... full until the week is over. The visitors would be horrified if they knew what was going on (8) ....*behind*.... the scenes!

25.5 **Write sentences using six of the idioms from the left-hand page about your own work at present and your hopes and plans for work in the future.**

26 Speed, distance and intensity

A Speed

idiom	meaning	example
by/in leaps and bounds	very quickly	Club membership has grown by leaps and bounds this year.
get a move on	hurry (often used as an order)	Get a move on! You'll be late for school.
be on the run	try to avoid being caught (especially by the police)	The bank robbers are still on the run ten years after the crime.
fast and furious	full of speed and excitement	The car chase at the end of the film was fast and furious.
step by step (**step-by-step** when used as an adjective before a noun)	slowly; gradually	Changes need to be introduced step by step, not all at once.
drag your feet/heels	deal with something slowly because you don't really want to do it	We mustn't drag our heels over implementing the new legislation.

B Distance and intensity

idiom	meaning	example
the word spread	the news went from one person to the next	I told only Joy about it, but the word quickly spread and soon everyone seemed to know.
keep track	continue to know what is happening to someone or something	The school likes to keep track of its former pupils.
get off to a flying start	start well	The evening got off to a flying start as everyone was very impressed by the restaurant.
on the spot (**on-the-spot** when used as an adjective before a noun)	immediately or in the place where something is happening or has just happened	The police can impose on-the-spot fines on people found drunk in the street.
all over the place	in or to many places	I looked for you all over the place.
left, right and centre	happening in a lot of places or to a lot of people	People have been coming down with flu left, right and centre.
reach / be at fever pitch	(used of emotions) to get so strong that people can't control them	By the end of the match, feelings had reached fever pitch.
be in full swing	to have been happening for a long time and there is a lot of activity	The party was in full swing by the time we arrived.
get/go beyond a joke	be/become extremely serious and worrying	The children's behaviour has gone beyond a joke this time.

Exercises

26.1 Put the idioms in the box into two groups: those focusing on time and those focusing on place. You can use one idiom for both.

> all over the place   by leaps and bounds   drag your feet   fast and furious   get a move on
> left, right and centre   on the spot   step by step   the word spread

26.2 Match the beginning of each sentence with its ending.

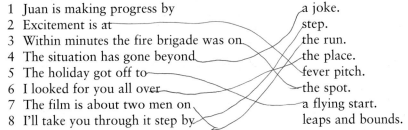

1 Juan is making progress by   a joke.
2 Excitement is at   step.
3 Within minutes the fire brigade was on   the run.
4 The situation has gone beyond   the place.
5 The holiday got off to   fever pitch.
6 I looked for you all over   the spot.
7 The film is about two men on   a flying start.
8 I'll take you through it step by   leaps and bounds.

26.3 Choose the correct answer.

1 Grandma is recovering ... .
   a) left, right and centre   b) step by step   c) all over the place
2 My first day at school ... .
   a) was at fever pitch   b) kept track   c) got off to a flying start
3 Why are you ... ?
   a) dragging your heels   b) getting a move on   c) going beyond a joke
4 When I arrived at Jane's house, preparations for the party were ... .
   a) in full swing   b) getting a move on   c) dragging their heels
5 The football match was ... .
   a) fast and furious   b) on the spot   c) in leaps and bounds

26.4 Answer these questions.

1 Would you be pleased if your English teacher said you were making progress by leaps and bounds? *Yes, I would*
2 Would you be pleased if you were told that your behaviour at work had gone beyond a joke? *Depends on the situation*
3 What would you be expected to do if you were told to get a move on? *Hurry up!*
4 Is it athletes who spend life on the run? *No*
5 Do you drag your feet when you are ill? *No*
6 What kind of films tend to be fast and furious? *Action films*
7 Would you be pleased if a party of yours got off to a flying start? *Yes, definately*
8 What can you do to help yourself keep track of all your appointments and other commitments?
9 If things are all over the place in a room, what does the room look like? *Messy*
10 If feelings reach fever pitch, how are people probably feeling? *very excited, uncontrollable*

27 Communication 1: commenting on language

A Commenting on things people say

In these remarks, the speaker uses an idiom to repeat or sum up the underlined part of what he/she has just said.

I knew everything Bella said was completely untrue. It was all **a pack of lies**.

I didn't say it seriously or even think about it. It was just an **off-the-cuff** remark.

I find it very hard to believe he was just hugging her because he thought she was feeling sad. **That's a likely story!**

I'm sorry. I said 'Iceland', but I meant 'Ireland'. It was just **a slip of the tongue**.

We didn't talk about any serious topics, you know, just the weather, holidays, that sort of thing. It was just **small talk** really.

He just said two completely opposite things. He said he wanted to marry me and live with me, and **in the same breath** he said he wanted to go off travelling on his own.

They asked me to make a speech, but I was so overwhelmed by the presents they gave me I couldn't think of anything to say. I was completely **lost for words**.

I have a feeling inside me that what she said was a lie. It just **didn't ring true**.

I couldn't understand what he was trying to tell me. I just didn't know what he **was on about**. (very informal)

B Commenting on the words you are using

You ask if I think we should help him. **In a word**, no. [said when you are about to give your opinion in a short, direct way]

I think he's behaved very stupidly. He's an idiot, **for want of a better word**. [not quite the exact or best word, but good enough for the situation]

I was, **to coin a phrase**, as sick as a parrot. [said when you use a phrase that sounds a bit silly]

C Joking and being serious

joking	meaning	serious	meaning
People are always **taking the mick/mickey out of** him.	laughing at him, by copying funny things he does or says	Hiccups are funny when other people have them, but they're **no laughing matter** when you get them yourself.	not something to laugh at, quite serious
We shouldn't **make light of** her troubles; she's very upset.	treat as a joke something that is serious	I have to do the work of three people. **It's no joke.**	used about serious or difficult situations

Exercises

27.1 Answer these questions.

1 If someone says 'Swedish' instead of 'Swiss' then quickly corrects themselves, what can we call this? *Slip of the tongue*
2 If someone makes people laugh by copying the way someone else talks, what are they doing to that person? *taking the mickey out of him!*
3 If someone can't find words to express their feelings, what are they? *He's lost 4 words!*
4 If two people talk about the weather, or about hair styles, just to pass the time, what kind of a conversation is it? *Small talk*
5 If someone tells stories or relates a series of events which are all deliberately untrue, what can we call it? *Pack of lies!*

27.2 Use the idioms from exercise 27.1 to rewrite these sentences.

1 I didn't know what to say. I'm *completely lost 4 words*.
2 Not one word of his story was true. It *just didn't ring true*.
3 I didn't mean to say it; it *was just an off-the-cuff*.
4 I didn't mean to offend her. I was just *slip off my tongue*.
5 It wasn't a very serious conversation, just *small talk really*.

27.3 Rewrite each sentence with an idiom that means the opposite of the underlined words. Make any other changes necessary.

1 She's had a big personal problem. We <u>should have a good laugh at</u> it.
2 He told me he had studied maths at Harvard, <u>and it sounded as if he was telling the truth.</u>
3 She said she was a princess who had lost all her money and position in a revolution. <u>That's a story anyone can believe!</u>
4 She has to get up at 5 a.m. and drive 50 miles to work every day. <u>It's great fun.</u>
5 I said I thought she should get herself a boyfriend. It was <u>a carefully prepared</u> remark.

27.4 Complete the crossword.

				¹B			
²M		³W	O	R	D		
i		A		E			
⁴C	O	i	N	⁵A	B	O	U T
K		T		T			
				H			

Across
3 Do I want to be a millionaire? In a _word_ , no.
4 You can do this to a phrase. *coin a phrase*
5 I don't know what you're on _about_ .

Down
1 She said it in the same _breath_ .
2 Stop taking the _mick_ !
3 For _want_ of a better word.

1. We shouldn't make light out of her problem.
2. It sounded like a pack of lies.
3. It was didn't ring true.
4.

28 Communication 2: getting the message across

A Ways of expressing yourself

example	meaning
The message from doctors and researchers has come through **loud and clear**: smoking harms your health.	clearly and very definitely
You mustn't be afraid to **speak your mind**; it's important that everyone hears your views.	state your opinion very clearly and openly
She told me the bad news in a very **matter-of-fact** way.	without any feeling or emotion

B Problems with communication

In these conversations, the second person repeats or sums up what the first person says using an idiom.

Brian: I told Henry a dozen times not to use that computer, but he still keeps asking if he can.

Liz: Yes, he just **won't take no for an answer**.

Anna: Jim just never stops! You try to tell him something and he goes on talking while you're talking.

Olivia: I know, it's impossible to **get a word in edgeways**.

Rita: I was trying to tell Liam that I know who stole the key, but he just kept talking about how expensive new locks are, which is a different question altogether.

Steve: I know. It's completely **beside the point**.

Gina: I think Carol completely misunderstood the main thing we were trying to say.

Gail: Yes, she completely **missed the point**.

C Other useful idioms connected with communication

Don't ask Ken to relax. He **doesn't know the meaning of the word**. [it is pointless to talk to him about relaxing; it's not in his character to do so]

She repeated what the doctor said **word for word**. [the exact words the doctor had used]

If I were you, I'd read **the small/fine print** before you use your new credit card. [the rules, restrictions and conditions, which are often written in very small letters]

To ask me to look after her three children for a week is rather **a tall order**, don't you think? [a task, request or favour which is not reasonable / too big to ask someone to do]

Whether she is cleverer than her brother is **a matter of opinion**. [something different people will have different opinions about – it usually means you don't agree with the idea]

There's **a question mark (hanging) over** the future of the tennis club. [nobody knows if it will continue to exist or not]

English is **a lingua franca** in a lot of countries nowadays. [/ˌlɪŋgwə ˈfraŋkə/ a language used for day-to-day public communication, which is not the speakers' own language]

Exercises

28.1 **Match each idiom on the left with the situation in which it could be used on the right.**

1 get a word in edgeways ⁴She keeps on asking, even though we said no.
2 miss the point ⁵She told me exactly what her friend said.
3 speak your mind ¹It's impossible to interrupt her, she talks non-stop.
4 won't take no for an answer ²She didn't really understand what I wanted to say.
5 (repeat) word for word ³He doesn't hide his personal opinions at all.

28.2 **Use the idioms from exercise 28.1 to rewrite these sentences.**

1 Hilary will never just accept a refusal. *She won't take NO for an answer.*
2 Joss always states his opinions quite openly. *He speaks his mind.*
3 Sally never seems to understand what we're trying to say to her. *She missed the point.*
4 She told us everything the teacher said to her in every detail. *She said word for word.*
5 I tried to tell her, but it was impossible to interrupt her. *It was impossible to get a word in edgeways.*

28.3 **Answer these questions.**

1 There's a question mark hanging over the whole wildlife area project.
   In your own words, what's the problem?
2 It's no good asking her to help. She doesn't know the meaning of the word.
   Does she usually help people? Explain. *No cos she's too selfish.*
3 If you read the small print, you'll see you can't get your money back. *Yes*
   Where do we usually find *small print*? What is another way of saying this idiom?
4 Tom: Miranda's a brilliant musician.
   Sue: That's a matter of opinion.
   Does Sue think Miranda's a brilliant musician? Explain. *No, he doesn't.*
5 English is a lingua franca in several Asian countries.
   Is English the official language in these countries? Explain. *No*

28.4 **Complete each of these idioms.**

1 The government's message to the voters is .... *loud* .... and clear: vote
   for us and we'll reduce taxes.
2 I think it's rather a ...... *tall order* .... to ask students to write a 500-word
   composition in one hour. It would take at least two hours.
3 That has nothing to do with what we are talking about; it's completely
   .... *beside* .... the point.
4 He has a very ...... *matter-of-fact* .... way of telling you things: no emotion or
   feelings whatsoever.

> **FOLLOW UP**
> Try to collect more idioms connected with speaking, writing and communicating in general. Look up
> keywords connected with these topics in a good general dictionary or in an idiom dictionary and see
> what idioms you find, for example, words like *talk*, *speak*, *hear*, *word*, etc.

29 Life and experience: proverbs

A Proverbs

A proverb is a short statement usually known by many people. It states something that is common experience or gives advice. Here are some examples.

you say	you mean
Absence makes the heart grow fonder.	Being apart from someone you love makes you love them more.
Actions speak louder than words.	What people do is more important than what they say.
There's no point / It's no good crying over spilt milk.	There's no point in getting upset over something bad that's happened when you can't change it.
Don't put all your eggs in one basket.	It is not a good idea to put all your efforts or all your money into one project as, if it fails, you may lose everything.
Many hands make light work.	A job is done quickly and easily if plenty of people help.
Blood is thicker than water.	Family relationships are stronger than any other relationships.

B Half proverbs

There are a number of proverbs, which we often use only half of. The endings are so familiar that it isn't necessary to say them. Here are some examples.

you say	ending of proverb	you mean
Too many cooks	spoil the broth.	If too many people work on something, they will spoil it.
People who live in glass houses	shouldn't throw stones.	People shouldn't criticise other people for faults that they have themselves.
It's the last straw	that breaks the camel's back.	Something is the last in a series of unpleasant events, and which finally makes you feel that the situation cannot continue.
While the cat's away,	the mice will play.	When the person in authority is not there, other people will not do what they should do.
Take care of the pennies/pence	and the pounds will take care of themselves.	If you don't waste small sums of money, you'll end up with plenty of money.
Birds of a feather	flock together.	People who have similar characters or interests will often choose to spend time together.
A bird in the hand	is worth two in the bush.	It's better to keep what you have rather than to risk losing it by trying to get more.
The grass is always greener	on the other side of the fence.	Other people always seem to be in a better situation than you.
All work and no play	makes Jack a dull boy.	Someone who spends all their time working becomes a boring person.

Exercises

29.1 Which proverbs do these pictures make you think of?

[handwritten: There's no point / It's no good crying over the spilt milk.]

[handwritten beside picture 1: It's the last straw which breaks the camel back.]

[handwritten: Too many cooks spoil the broth]

[handwritten beside picture 2: Birds of a feather flock together]

[handwritten: Don't put all ur eggs in one basket.]

[handwritten below picture 4: While the cat's away]

1 3 5
2 4 6

29.2 Can you find a proverb on the left-hand page that contradicts each of these proverbs?

1 Too many cooks spoil the broth.   3 Out of sight, out of mind.
2 Opposites attract.

29.3 Write the first bits of these proverbs – the bits that we usually use.

1 *Take care of the pennies* .... and the pounds will take care of themselves.
2 *The grass's always greener* .... on the other side of the fence.
3 *All work and no play* .... makes Jack a dull boy.
4 *People who live in glass houses* .... shouldn't throw stones.
5 *A bird in the hand* .... is worth two in the bush.
6 *Birds of a feather* .... flock together.
7 *While the cat's away* .... the mice will play.
8 *It's the last straw* .... that breaks the camel's back.

29.4 What proverbs could you use in these situations?

1 Your brother's girlfriend is going abroad for six months. He is afraid that she will lose interest in him while she's away. You could say: 'Don't worry. *Absence makes the heart grow fonder* .'

2 A friend thinks that he will not get a job because the boss's nephew is interested in the same position. You agree: '*Blood is thicker than water* .'

3 Three friends offer to help you build a new shed. You say: 'Thanks! *Too many cooks spoil the broth Many hands make light work.*

4 You are discussing two friends: Bob who is full of grand promises and Ben who says little, but is always very willing to help. You could say: 'I prefer Ben. *Birds of a feather flock together Actions* speak louder than words.'

5 A friend of yours is very upset that he has scratched his new car. You could say: 'Don't make such a fuss. *There's no point crying over spilt milk* .'

6 Your brother is thinking about resigning from a not very well-paid job in order to spend time looking for something better. You think he would be better to find a new job first. You say: '*Don't put all your eggs in one basket* .'

[handwritten: A bird in a hand is worth two in the bush.]

30 Memory

A   Idioms based on the word *memory*

idiom	meaning	example
commit something to memory	make yourself remember something	He never writes phone numbers down – he just commits them to memory.
take a stroll/trip down down memory lane	remember some of the happy things you did in the past	They went back to the place where they'd spent their honeymoon and took a stroll down memory lane.
jog someone's memory	make you remember something	The police are reconstructing the crime to try to jog the memory of possible witnesses.
in/within living memory	can be remembered by people still alive	Streets lit by gas lamps are still within living memory.

B   Idioms containing the word *mind*

idiom	meaning	example
come/spring to mind	immediately think of something	I'd like to get him a special birthday present, but nothing springs to mind.
slip your mind	forget about something	I was going to ring her to wish her happy birthday, but it slipped my mind.
bear/keep something in mind	remember information when making a decision or thinking about a matter	Bearing in mind that it was your first attempt, I think you did very well.
your mind goes blank	you can't think of anything to say	When I looked at the exam questions, my mind went blank.
cross your mind	think about something for a short time	Of course, I don't think you broke the window. The thought never even crossed my mind.
Out of sight, out of mind.	something you say which means that, if you do not see someone, you forget about them	Annie hasn't thought of her boyfriend since he went abroad. Out of sight, out of mind!

C   Other idioms relating to the topic of memory

idiom	meaning	example
something is on the tip of your tongue	you know it, but can't quite remember it	Her name is on the tip of my tongue – what is it?
ring a bell	think you've heard something before	Jill's face rings a bell, but I don't think we've ever met.
a train of thought	a series of consecutive thoughts	Oh no! I've lost my train of thought.
rack your brains	think very hard	I racked my brains, but couldn't think where I'd left the book.

Exercises

30.1 Complete each of these idioms with *memory* or *mind*.

1 Out of sight, out of ...... mind ....
2 The class reunion gave us a great opportunity for a trip down ...... memory ...... lane.
3 I'm sorry I forgot to post your letters. It just slipped my ...... mind ....
4 You can't remember what you did last night? Let me jog your ...... memory ....
5 Please bear me in ...... mind ...... if you need someone to work on this project.
6 I was so embarrassed that my ...... mind ...... just went blank.
7 It never crossed my ...... mind ...... to tell Nigel about our meeting.
8 Streets full of horse-drawn carriages are still within living ...... memory ...... – just!
9 I wanted to give her a surprise, but nothing suitable came to ...... mind ....
10 Try to commit your mobile phone number to ...... mind ....

30.2 Complete each of these idioms.

1 I don't think I know him, but his name rings ...... a bell ....
2 What is the word for it? I can't remember it. Oh dear, it's on ...... the tip of my tongue ....
3 If I try, I should be able to remember the recipe for you. Let me rack ...... my brains ....
4 Try not to interrupt his train ...... of thought ....
5 My son is much more adventurous than I was. At his age the thought of travelling abroad alone would never ...... cross my mind ....

30.3 Answer these questions.

1 Which idiom could also be included in the Proverbs unit (Unit 29) of this book?
2 Find two idioms that mention parts of the body other than *mind* or *memory*.
3 What is the literal meaning of *jog* in the idiom *jog someone's memory*?
4 *Rack* is the name of a medieval instrument of torture on which people lay and were stretched. How does it fit this idiom?
5 What is the literal meaning of *stroll* in the idiom *take a stroll down memory lane*?
6 What is the literal meaning of *spring* in the idiom *spring to mind*?
7 What is the literal meaning of the word *bear* in the idiom *bear in mind*?
8 Which of the idioms is based on a metaphor of hearing something?

30.4 Complete each of these idioms with the correct form of a verb.

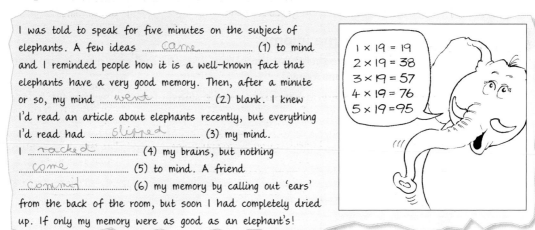

I was told to speak for five minutes on the subject of elephants. A few ideas ...... came ...... (1) to mind and I reminded people how it is a well-known fact that elephants have a very good memory. Then, after a minute or so, my mind ...... went ...... (2) blank. I knew I'd read an article about elephants recently, but everything I'd read had ...... slipped ...... (3) my mind. I ...... racked ...... (4) my brains, but nothing ...... came ...... (5) to mind. A friend ...... commit ...... (6) my memory by calling out 'ears' from the back of the room, but soon I had completely dried up. If only my memory were as good as an elephant's!

1 × 19 = 19
2 × 19 = 38
3 × 19 = 57
4 × 19 = 76
5 × 19 = 95

31 Time 1: the past and the future

A Looking back, looking forward

One of the major divisions in idioms involving time is between those that look back from now into the past and those that look forward into the future.

Looking back

example	meaning
This camera **has seen better days**.	is old and not working so well
My computer is **out of date**.	old and not useful or correct any more
She didn't study when she was young, but she's **making up for lost time** now.	doing now what she did not have the opportunity to do previously
People have fallen in love with one another **since/from the year dot**.	from the beginning of time

Looking forward

example	meaning
E-commerce seems to be **the shape of things to come**.	an indication of what is likely to become popular in the future
Use this room **for the time being** until your new office is ready.	temporarily; instead of
We are **on the threshold of** exciting new developments in medicine.	likely to happen very soon
The economy looks healthy **in the short/medium/long term**.	for a short/medium/long time in the future
It's **only a matter of time** before we start to colonise other planets.	it will definitely happen, even though we cannot say exactly when
I can't say if I like the job or not. **It's early days yet.**	it's too soon to say/decide
In the long run you'll see it was the right decision.	a long time from now

B Other related time idioms

He spends money **like there's no tomorrow**. [eagerly and very quickly (or, more formally, **as if there was/were no tomorrow**)]

At the end of the day, you have to be a little selfish. [something you say before stating a very important fact or idea]

The fact that he had been dead for a week in his apartment before anybody found him is **a sign of the times**. [something that shows that society now is worse than it was in the past]

> **TIP** Although the idioms on this page do not all contain the word *time*, their meanings are all related to time in some way. Grouping idioms by meaning is another way of learning them, in addition to grouping them by keywords.

Exercises

31.1 Match each idiom on the left with the situation in which it could be used on the right.

1 it's early days yet   4 · Someone shows you a car which is driven by solar energy.
2 within living memory   3 · You tell someone about a very ancient tradition.
3 since the year dot   5 · A scientist claims to be on the point of discovering a cure
                                                           for cancer.
4 the shape of things to come   1 · Someone asks you if you like an English course after only
                                                           one day.
5 on the threshold of   6 · Someone is spending all their savings carelessly.
6 like there's no tomorrow   2 · Never, for as long as anyone can remember, has there
                                                           been so much rain.

31.2 Write an appropriate comment for each of the situations in exercise 31.1 using the idiom you chose.

1 This car really is _the shape of things to come_ .
2 People have been doing this every spring ~~within living memory~~ since the year dot.
3 A scientist is _on the threshold of discovering a cure for cancer_
4 I've only been to a couple of lessons. _It's early days yet_
5 Jim's spending money _like there's no tomorrow_ .
6 There's never been rain like this _within living memory_ .

31.3 Rewrite the underlined part of each sentence with an idiom.

It's only the matter of time to
1 Some time soon we will inevitably discover life on other planets.
2 I think the main point is that you can never trust a politician. _At the end of the day_
3 I never learnt the piano as a child, so I'm solving that problem now by taking lessons. _I'm making up for the lost time_
4 Looking at just the next few years, the economic situation looks good, but looking at the next 30 to 40 years, the outlook is not so good. _In the short term / long term_
5 This bicycle is a bit old and broken down now. I should really get a new one. _'s seen better days_
6 Could you use this computer just temporarily till the new one arrives? _for the time being_
7 It's a typical thing about the time we live in that you can't speak to a real human being when you telephone the bank. All you get is an automatic voice. _sign of the times_
8 This milk has an old date on it. I'll throw it away and open a new carton. _out of date_
9 It costs a lot of money now, but over a longer period it will be a good investment, I'm sure. _In the long run_

31.4 These idioms involving *time* are not on the left-hand page. Using a dictionary if necessary, see if you can find the missing prepositions. Then choose the most suitable paraphrase.

1 I felt as if I was _in_ a time warp as I sat in the ancient cottage talking to the old man.
   a) time was passing very slowly   (b) I felt as if I had gone back in time to a different era
2 My dad can remember the first home computers, but that was ... my time.
   a) when I was too young to use one   b) before I was born _before_
3 I have a lot of time _for_ Gerry; he's a very interesting and intelligent person.
   (a) I like and respect him   b) I spend a lot of time with him
4 I turned off the water supply in the nick _of_ time. Five minutes later and the whole house would have been flooded!
   (a) just in time to prevent a disaster   b) very quickly indeed
5 Shakespeare's plays have stood the test _of_ time. They are as powerful today as they were hundreds of years ago.
   a) have never been changed   (b) have not been weakened by the passing of time

32 Time 2: clocks and frequency

A Clocks / time passing

If you ...	then you ...
work against the clock to get something done/finished	work fast because you only have limited time
do something **in no time at all**	do it very quickly
call it a day	decide to finish (usually finish working)
don't have a minute to call your own	are very busy indeed
do something **there and then** (or **then and there**)	do it immediately, right at that moment
get up / start **at the crack of dawn**	start very early in the morning

Jake **worked against the clock** to get the report finished before the meeting.

The homework is very easy. You'll be able to do it **in no time at all**.

I'm really tired. Let's **call it a day** now and come back to it next week.

Ever since the twins were born, I **haven't had a minute to call my own**.

If a new idea is suggested, Allan is always keen to try it out **there and then**.

As our plane was leaving at 8 a.m., we had to get up **at the crack of dawn** to be at the airport on time.

B Frequency

These idioms refer to how often (or how rarely) something happens.

idiom	meaning
once in a lifetime	never likely to happen again
once in a blue moon	very rarely
once and for all	finally and definitely
off and on / on and off	sometimes, but not regularly or continuously
from time to time	sometimes, but not regularly
nine times out of ten	almost always

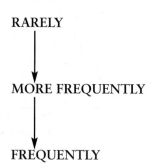

RARELY

MORE FREQUENTLY

FREQUENTLY

C Other time idioms

If something **goes/works/runs like clockwork**, it happens exactly as planned and without problems.

If you do something / start **from scratch**, you go right back to the beginning and start again.

> **TIP** Wherever possible, put groups of idioms onto a scale, like the frequency scale in B above. You could use scales for idioms connected with size, feelings, difficulties, etc.

Exercises

32.1 Complete each of these idioms.

1 It runs like _clockwork_ .
2 We set off at the crack _of dawn_ .
3 We were working against _the clock_ .
4 I've had enough. Let's call _it a day_ .
5 It happens this way nine _times out of ten_ .

32.2 Match each idiom on the left with the sentence on the right which best reflects its meaning.

1 there and then
2 once in a blue moon

3 in no time at all
4 off and on
5 doesn't have a minute to call her own

4 Bill plays golf occasionally, but not often.
5 Paula looks after three kids and has a full-time job.
1 The doctor examined me immediately.
2 I only see Patrick very rarely.
3 The new house was built very quickly.

32.3 Complete these idioms with prepositions.

1 _from_ scratch
2 once _in_ a lifetime
3 once and _for_ all
4 _from_ time _to_ time
5 work _against_ the clock
6 nine times _out of_ ten

32.4 Choose four of the idioms from exercise 32.3 and write a sentence for each one to illustrate its meaning.

32.5 Rewrite the underlined part of each dialogue with an idiom.

1 A: Do you go and see your mother and father very often?
   B: Well, occasionally, but not on a regular basis. _off and on_
2 A: Should we wait and do it as and when we need to?
   B: No, I think we should do it now, so that we never need to do it again. _once and for all_
3 A: Shall we try and speak to Mr Sanders about it?
   B: Well, we can try, but on almost every occasion he's too busy to meet anyone. _nine times out of ten_
4 A: The boss wants this report by Friday!
   B: Well, we'll just have to work very fast to get it finished by then. _against the clock_
5 A: Do you want to go on working a bit longer?
   B: No, I've had enough. Let's finish now. _call it a day_

'It must be the crack of dawn.'

33 The elements

A Earth

idiom	meaning
He's the **salt of the earth**.	a very good and honest person
She'd **go to the ends of the earth** to save her child.	do anything possible
The royal couple were **run to ground** in Wales.	discovered after a lot of searching
All my warnings **fell on stony ground**.	were ignored

B Air

If you **pluck a number out of the air,** you choose one at random.

If someone **blows hot and cold,** they sometimes seem to like someone or something and sometimes don't so that others are confused about how they really feel.

If you **get wind of something,** you hear information that others hoped to keep secret.

If you see **how / which way the wind is blowing,** you decide to see how a situation develops before making up your mind about it.

C Fire

Tanya is **playing with fire**[1], agreeing to go out with Rick. Rumours about his violent temper have been **spreading like wildfire**[2] ever since he moved to the area. Of course, most people sometimes say things **in the heat of the moment**[3] that they do not really mean and I don't know how much truth there is in the rumours. However, you can't help thinking that **there's no smoke without fire**[4]. Anyhow, don't **add fuel to the flames/fire**[5] by criticising Rick in front of Tanya as you'll only make her keener on him.

[1] doing something that could be dangerous (*play* in this idiom is normally used in continuous tenses)
[2] going round very quickly
[3] without thinking because they are angry or excited
[4] if people are saying something is true and you don't know whether it is true or not, it probably is true
[5] do something to make a bad situation worse

D Water

idiom	meaning
in deep water	in a difficult situation which is hard to deal with
out of your depth	in a situation that you do not have the knowledge or skills to deal with
jump / throw someone in at the deep end	do or make someone do something difficult without giving them any help
in hot water	in a situation where people are angry with you
be between the devil and the deep blue sea	have to choose between two equally difficult options
be a drop in the ocean	be a very small amount in comparison to what is needed

Exercises

33.1 **Match each idiom on the left with its definition on the right.**

1 get wind of something	move very fast
2 go to the ends of the earth	be an insignificant part of something
3 spread like wildfire	observe how a situation is developing
4 be in deep water	make a difficult situation worse
5 be a drop in the ocean	be in a difficult situation
6 blow hot and cold	hear about something secret
7 see how the wind is blowing	react in different, unpredictable ways
8 add fuel to the flames	do everything you can

33.2 **Rewrite each sentence with an idiom. Use the keyword in brackets.**

1 You'll be fine working for someone like that – he's a very decent man. (EARTH)
2 Unfortunately, no one paid any attention to my advice. (GROUND).
3 Unfortunately, her angry words have only made the situation worse. (FUEL)
4 I think Rosie must be in trouble – the boss has asked to see her at once. (WATER)
5 Lance doesn't really have the experience to cope with his new job. (DEPTH)
6 Spreading rumours like that is a risky thing to do. (FIRE)
7 Choose a number at random and multiply it by 3. (AIR)
8 The police were unable to find where the escaped convicts were hiding. (GROUND)

33.3 **Put the words in order and make sentences.**

1 like / The / of / news / wildfire / spread / their / divorce
2 the / the / sea / devil / blue / between / I'm / deep / and
3 no / fire / There / smoke / is / without
4 heat / the / of / Don't / anything / moment / in / say / the
5 and / I / the / cold / hot / he / way / blows / hate
6 the / thrown / when / I / I / university / end / was / in / deep / started / at

33.4 **Which idioms do these pictures make you think of?**

1   2   3

33.5 **Look at the different idioms relating to earth, air, fire and water both in this unit and in Unit 42. Which abstract concepts do each of these elements seem to represent in the English mind?**

FOLLOW UP

Here are some more idioms connected with the elements. Look them up in your dictionary. Write a definition and then write the idioms in sentences of your own.

not set the world on fire	go up in smoke
it's all water under the bridge	pour cold water on something
the tide is turning	make waves

34 Colour

A Red

idiom	meaning	example
red tape	official rules and bureaucracy that make it difficult to do something	There's a great deal of red tape involved in getting a work permit.
be in the red	have a negative amount in your bank balance	I can't afford a holiday this year. I'm 500 pounds in the red.
catch someone red-handed	catch someone at the moment they are doing something wrong	He was caught red-handed stealing money from the cash register.
a red herring	something unimportant that takes attention away from the main subject	Then he started talking about the cost of a new computer, which was a red herring, because we've got plenty of computers.

B Blue

I argued with Tim **till I was blue in the face,** but he wouldn't listen. [say the same thing many times, but someone refuses to listen]

I think there's **blue blood** in her family; her great-grandmother was a Russian princess. [belonging to the highest social class / aristocratic]

Blue-collar workers at the local car factory were on strike for six weeks. [workers who do physical work, especially in factories] (See *white-collar* in D below.)

C Green

example	meaning
I was **green with envy** when she got the job.	very envious
My mother's **got green fingers**. Everything she plants in the garden grows well.	is a very good gardener
The boss has **given** the project **the green light**.	given permission for something to start
Our house is in **the green belt**, so no other houses can be built near it.	countryside around a town or city which is protected from building development

D Black, white and grey

White-collar workers[1] at the Mirage car factory have gone on strike over pay and conditions. The union says management has broken an agreement, and it wants a new one in **black and white**[2]. The management says that the agreement is a **grey area**[3] that must be made clear in proper discussions. Meanwhile, the factory owners, the Merschott Company of Germany, consider that the plant is **a black hole**[4], into which more and more money is disappearing. They are threatening to close the factory altogether.

[1] workers who work in offices, not doing physical work
[2] written, not just a spoken agreement
[3] something that is a problem, and is not very clear because there are no rules
[4] something which has no bottom, and everything put into it just disappears

Exercises

34.1 Match each newspaper headline with its text.

1 **HEALTH SERVICE BUDGET JUST A BLACK HOLE, SAYS MINISTER**

2 **GOVERNMENT PROMISES TO DEAL WITH GREY AREA OF INTERNET LAW**

3 **GREEN BELT ROUND LIVERPOOL EXTENDED**

4 BLUE-BLOOD CHILDREN NO MORE INTELLIGENT THAN OTHERS, SAY SCIENTISTS

3/ A
There was a real need to protect the environment from further damage, the Director of Planning said.

4/ C
Any claim to the contrary simply could not be proved, said Doctor Wills, one of the team who investigated twenty upper-class families.

2/ B
It was not at all clear what the situation was, and it was now time for governments to co-operate to clarify things.

1/ D
Every year, more and more money simply disappears, without any real results in terms of improvements, she said.

34.2 Answer these questions.
1 Which colour workers work in offices and which ones do physical work?   *blue   white*   *white   blue*
2 What colour are you if you wish you had something someone else has?   *green*
3 What colour are you if you repeat something, but the other person pays no attention?   *blue in the face*
4 What colour is your bank balance when you have spent more money than there was in it?   *in the red*
5 What colour light do you see when someone gives you permission to do something?   *green*

34.3 Use the idioms from exercise 34.2 to complete these sentences.
1 I was absolutely ....*green*.... with ....*envy*.... when she won a trip to Los Angeles.
2 I'm 750 pounds ....*in*.... the ....*red*...., and the bank has asked me to pay it back immediately.
3 The ....*blue*.-....*collar*.... workers are on strike, but the office staff are still working.
4 You can talk to her till you're ....*blue*.... in the ....*face*....; she won't listen.
5 If the city authorities ....*give*.... the ....*green*.... light to the new conservation project, it will begin next year.

34.4 Rewrite the underlined part of each sentence with an idiom.
1 I want to see a contract <u>in written form</u>, not just an informal agreement.   *black & white*
2 I wanted to apply for a visa, but a friend told me there <u>are so many forms to fill in and complicated rules</u>, so I've decided to forget ~~it. is a red herring~~ it's too much   *red tape*
3 My new house has a big garden, but <u>I'm no good with plants</u>, so I'll probably never do any gardening.   *I don't have a green fingers*
4 She was <u>caught just as she was</u> stealing food from the school kitchen.   *red-handed*
5 He's always introducing <u>unimportant points</u> into the discussion <u>which distract everybody from the main argument</u>.

35 Games and sport

A Ball games

Right then, I've **started the ball rolling**[1] by telling you what I think our company should do now. I would like anyone who has any comments or questions to speak now. **The ball is in your court**[2]. Don't forget that our rival companies are **on the ball**[3] and if we don't act quickly and do something **off our own bat**[4], they will. I know my proposals will involve people doing overtime, but I hope that the workers may agree to **play ball**[5] given the circumstances we are all in. It's not our fault we are in this situation. Different rates of tax in different countries mean that we are not competing **on a level playing field**[6].

[1] started an activity and encouraged others to join in
[2] you have to do something now before any progress can be made
[3] quick to understand and react
[4] on our own initiative, without being asked to by anyone else
[5] co-operate in order to achieve something (usually used in a negative context)
[6] in a fair situation

B Cards

If you **play your cards right**, you behave in the right way to achieve what you want. It is informal and is often used in the expression *If (you) play (your) cards right, ...*

If you **put/lay your cards on the table**, you tell someone honestly what you think or what you plan to do.

If you **pass the buck**, you blame someone or make them responsible for something that must be done next (from an object used in the card game poker).

If you **follow suit**, you do the same as everyone else has just done. (This is a reference to playing the same suit, i.e. hearts, diamonds, spades or clubs, in cards.)

If you **call someone's bluff**, you make someone prove that what they are saying is true or prove that they will really do what they say they will do, because you don't believe them. To call someone's bluff in a card game is to force them to show you their cards.

C Miscellaneous sports and games

sport or game	idiom	meaning
swimming	**take the plunge**	do something important or difficult that you've been thinking of doing for a long time
board games	**go back to square one**	go back to the beginning of a project, because previous attempts have failed
archery	**be wide of the mark**	be wrong or miss what you were trying to hit
horse-riding	**do something on the spur of the moment** (spur = metal on boot which makes horse go faster)	do something suddenly, without planning
tarot cards (used for fortune-telling)	**be on the cards**	be likely to happen
gambling	**your best bet**	the best thing you can do to achieve the result you want
roulette	**when the chips are down** (chips = gambling pieces)	when you are in a difficult situation, especially one which tests whether you can trust people

Exercises

35.1 Which idioms do these pictures make you think of?

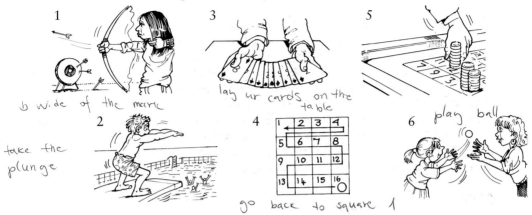

1   *wide of the mark*

2   *take the plunge*

3   *lay ur cards on the table*

4   *go back to square 1*

5

6   *play ball*

35.2 Match the beginning of each sentence on the left with its ending on the right.

1 If you play your cards right,   off their own bat.
2 When the chips are down,   would be your best bet.
3 The ball is in their court,   others will soon follow suit.
4 If you sign the contract,   we decided to go away for the weekend.
5 On the spur of the moment   so we'll have to wait and see what they do.
6 The children picked Mother some flowers you learn who your real friends are.
7 Going by train rather than bus or car   you should get an invitation to her party.

35.3 Complete each sentence with an idiom from the box.

> a level playing field   put his cards on the table   follow suit   call his bluff   off his own bat
> on the ball   on the cards   pass the buck   start the ball rolling

1 Let's ask Pete for advice – he's usually *put his cards on the table or the ball*
2 The government always tries to *pass the buck* when there are economic problems, saying the previous regime is to blame.
3 I'd like you each to tell us why you have decided to do a creative writing course; Marie, would you *start the ball rolling*, please?
4 Applicants all have to agree to the same conditions for the interview in order to ensure *a level playing field*.
5 No one asked him to help – he did it *off his own bat*.
6 If you keep your things tidy, the others may *follow suit*.
7 It is still *on the cards* that I'll get a contract for the job.
8 He's been very frank and has *put his cards on the table*; now we'll have to do the same.
9 He claims he can speak fluent Japanese; let's *call his bluff* and invite him to dinner with our Japanese guests.

> **FOLLOW UP** Can you find any idioms related to your favourite sport or game? You might be able to find some by looking up keywords relating to that sport or game in a good English–English dictionary or a dictionary of idioms. For example, if you are interested in horse-riding, you might look up *horse*, *saddle*, *reins*.

36 Animals 1: describing people

In this unit and in Unit 37 we look at idioms connected with animals. Here we look at ways of describing people and their actions. In Unit 37 we look at using animal idioms to describe situations.

A Animal names

These idioms are based on compound nouns related to animals.

A person who ...	is ...
is **a dark horse**	someone who is clever or skilful in a way that no one knew or expected
is **a lone wolf**	someone who does not mix socially with other people
is **a cold fish**	someone who is not very friendly and does not show their feelings
is/acts **as a guinea pig** /ˈgɪnɪ pɪg/	someone who acts as a subject in an experiment or trial of something
is **a party animal**	someone who loves parties and socialising
would love to be **a fly on the wall**	someone who would love to be present to see an important private or secret event

Note also:
There was a **fly-on-the-wall** documentary on TV last night about hospital waiting-rooms. [programme filmed in a real-life situation, sometimes with hidden cameras]

B People's characters and their actions

John's **bark is worse than his bite**. [he may seem fierce/tough, but he is not really]

You don't need to be afraid of him. He **wouldn't hurt a fly**. [is totally harmless and would never hurt anyone]

Larry's really got **the travel bug** ever since he won that holiday in the Caribbean. [a strong desire to travel (*bug* here means virus; the original meaning of *bug* is a small insect)]

She's working very hard for her exams. She's really **got/taken the bit between her teeth**. [has started to work/act in a very determined way (a *bit* is a piece of metal put between a horse's teeth to control it)]

They've **given me free rein** to do what I like in this new job. [complete freedom (*reins* are what you hold in your hands to control a horse when riding)]

Tim: How did you know I was getting married?
Linda: **A little bird told me**. [said when someone has told you a secret, but you do not want to say who]

As soon as the meeting was over, we all **made a beeline for** the food. We were so hungry! [went quickly and directly to]

I always **have butterflies in my stomach** just before an exam. [feel very nervous]

I **made a real pig of myself** last night, so I'm not going to eat any lunch today. [ate too much]

I have so much work to do these days. I'm just **chasing my tail** trying to catch up. [doing a lot, but it is all pointless / without effect]

Exercises

36.1 Which idiom from the left-hand page can be used to describe ...

dark horse 1 ... a person who has hidden or unexpected skills or talents that no one knows about?
2 ... a person who loves parties? *party animal*
3 ... a person who is the subject of an experiment or trial of something new? *guinea pig*
4 ... a person who is not very friendly? *cold fish*

36.2 Here are some facts about animals. Which idioms on the left-hand page are based on them?

1 When you ride a horse, it has a *bit* in its mouth, which is a metal bar that helps you control the horse. *taken the bit between its teeth*
2 A bee can fly in a straight line back to a place where it found food. *make a beeline for*
3 Wolves usually hunt together in a group or pack. *a lone wolf*
4 Dogs will often bark more out of fear than out of aggression. *it's bark is worse than its bite*
5 Cats and dogs often run round in circles thinking their tail is running away from them. *chasing the tail*
6 Pigs have a reputation for eating a lot of food very quickly. *make a real pig of urself*

36.3 Use the idioms from exercise 36.2 to repeat or sum up what the first speaker says.

1 Jack: Harry never seems to want to go out with other people.
  Pat: No, he's a bit of a *lone wolf* .
2 Liam: Are you busy these days?
  Chris: Busy! It's ridiculous! I try to keep up with things, but I'm just *chasing my tail* .
3 Keith: Dan is in the boss's office again today. That's the third time this week he's gone to complain about the computers.
  Mike: Yes, he won't give up. He's really got *a bit between his teeth* .
4 Orla: You seemed to be enjoying your lunch today!
  Fiona: Yes, I *made a real pig of myself* . I feel so full now!
5 Brian: Philip scared everyone yesterday. He looked really angry.
  Eve: Oh, don't worry about him. His *bark is worse than his bite* .
6 Alan: Look at Charles! He's already talking to a gorgeous girl over there!
  Joe: Oh yeah, he always *makes a beeline* for the prettiest girl in the room.

36.4 Complete each of these idioms.

1 Big Joe is quite harmless really, although he looks tough. He wouldn't *hurt* a *fly* .
2 I already know about Jill getting divorced. A *little bird* told me.
3 I hate making a speech to a big audience. I always get *butterflies* in my *stomach* .
4 It's a very unusual school. The pupils are .... free .... to do just what they like.
5 I really got the travel *bug* after I went on a trekking holiday to Nepal. I can't wait to go away again.
6 I'd love to be a *fly* on the *wall* when Nigel tells the boss he's resigning.

37 Animals 2: describing situations

A Cats and dogs

In the 'situation' box, note how the 'if-clause' tells you whether the idiom is normally used with things (something), people (you) or with an impersonal construction such as *there is*.

situation	idiom	meaning
If something	**goes to the dogs**	it goes from a good situation/condition to a bad one
If you	**let the cat out of the bag**	you accidentally tell people a secret / something you should not tell them
If you	**put the cat among the pigeons**	you create a crisis or a problematic situation
If there is	**not (enough) room to swing a cat**	there is very little room or space somewhere

The country **has gone to the dogs** since the new government took over.

We didn't tell anyone the news, but she **let the cat out of the bag** and now everyone knows.

Kim's report really **put the cat among the pigeons**. Now everyone's in a state of crisis.

There's not enough room to swing a cat in our flat, so I don't think a party is a good idea.

B Other animal-related expressions

In these dialogues, the second speaker uses an idiom to repeat and sum up the situation described by the first speaker.

Ron: Everyone is so selfish. They would sell their own mothers to get what they want, and they don't care how much other people suffer.

Tania: Yes, it really is **the law of the jungle**. It's very depressing.

Mary: We shouldn't even think of discussing the voting system for the committee. It's very complicated and unfair in many respects, and could raise huge problems.

Ricky: I agree. It's a real **can of worms**. I think we should avoid discussing it.

Iris: If you ask me, it's a waste of time complaining to Robert. He doesn't take any notice, no matter how often you do it or no matter how angry you get.

Pat: Yes, it's **like water off a duck's back**.

Roger: We're all overworked and in a panic. We're trying to solve too many problems, and ending up not achieving anything!

Nancy: Yes, I agree. We're all just **running round like headless chickens**.

Note also:

I don't use **snail mail** these days. E-mail's easier. [the post, often said humorously when contrasting with e-mail]

I don't know if anyone would really want a job like this one, but we could **put out feelers** and see if anyone is interested. [make informal enquiries; talk to people unofficially]

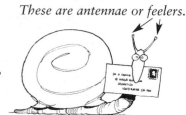

These are antennae or feelers.

> **TIP**
> When recording idioms in your Vocabulary notebook, make notes of typical situations in which they can be used. For example: *go to the dogs* – typical situation: a restaurant that was very good before is very bad now.

Exercises

37.1 Rewrite each sentence with an idiom that means the opposite of the underlined words.

1 There's <u>plenty of room</u> at my house. *not enough*
2 I'll let you know by <u>e-mail</u>. *snail mail*
3 Peter <u>has not told anybody the secret news</u>. *let the cat out of the bag*
4 The economy is <u>getting better and better</u>. *gone to the dogs*
5 The office staff were <u>working very calmly and efficiently</u>. *running round like headless chickens*

37.2 Which idioms do these pictures make you think of?

put the cat among the pigeons

 1

 2 *a can of worms*

 3 *like water off a duck's back*

37.3 Match each of the idioms from exercise 37.2 with one of these sentences.

1 a) What she said has raised some horrible problems which we'd all prefer to forget.
2 b) Oh dear! That is really going to cause huge problems and upset absolutely everybody!
3 c) You can insult him and be really awful to him, but he just never seems to care or even notice.

37.4 Answer these questions.

1 If you tell someone a secret, what do you let the cat out of? *a bag*
2 What can you put out in order to test whether people are interested in an idea? *feelers*
3 What kind of law do wild animals obey? *jungle*

37.5 Use a dictionary to find the missing words in these animal idioms if you do not know them. If you think you know the idioms, write your answers and then check them in a dictionary. Make a note of the meaning of the idioms in your Vocabulary notebook.

1 take the bull by the ___*horns*___ *being confident*
2 kill two birds with one ___*touch stone*___ *one action → two results*
3 at a snail's ___*pace*___ *slowly*
4 like a bear with a sore ___*head*___ *being bad tempered, irritable*
5 a ___*dog*___'s breakfast. *mess*

37.6 Use the five idioms from exercise 37.5 to rewrite the underlined parts of this paragraph.

at a snail's pace
take the bull by the horns
like a bear with a sore head

I was trying to finish my essay for my English class by the end of the week, but it all seemed to be going <u>very slowly</u> and I was not very motivated. So I decided to <u>face the situation and act positively</u>. I stayed up until after midnight every day for four days and worked on my essay. I was tired in the mornings, and went round <u>feeling very bad-tempered and irritable</u> all day, but, in the end I managed to <u>do two useful things in one go</u>: I finished the essay and I read a number of important books I should have read weeks ago. My last essay was a bit of <u>a mess</u>, but I'm hoping this one will get a better grade.

kill two birds with 1 stone / a dog's breakfast

FOLLOW UP Think of two animals which have idioms connected with them in your language. Then use a dictionary to see if there are any idioms connected with these animals in English.

38 Weapons and war

A Idioms based on guns and knives

If you ...	then you ...
bite the bullet	face a difficult situation and act decisively / do not avoid it
jump the gun	do something too soon, before you should do it
stick to your guns	don't let other people change your mind/ideas/principles
look daggers at someone	look at them in a very angry or hateful way
put the knife in	deliberately do or say something really hurtful to someone
twist the knife	do or say something which makes a bad/hurtful situation even worse

B Idioms connected with firing/shooting

In these dialogues, the second speaker uses an idiom to repeat part of the question.

Henry: Have you ever tried snowboarding?
Nigel: No, but I'd like to **have a shot at** it one day.

Carol: Now that you're the Head of Department, do you find people always blame you immediately for any problems that arise?
Liz: Oh yes, I'm **in the firing line** all the time.

Mick: So it's Peter Smith who makes all the important decisions and has all the power?
Rita: Oh yes, Peter Smith **calls the shots** these days.

Hilary: It must have been awful for you, being in the middle of such a terrible argument between Roz and Barbara?
Jane: Yes, I was really **caught in the crossfire**; I found it very difficult.

Aaron: So you think we should wait and not ask for the funds yet?
Beth: Yes, I think we should **hold fire** till the future is more certain.

C War and fighting in general

The village people are **up in arms** over the plan to build a motorway very near their homes. [angry and protesting loudly]

Jim's **his own worst enemy** when it comes to getting promotion at work. He's just so negative about everything. [his own attitude/behaviour will prevent him from reaching his goal]

I think you're **fighting a losing battle** trying to get a pay rise. The boss never listens to anyone. [trying to achieve something that you will probably fail to achieve]

I wouldn't give up this job till you're absolutely sure you've got the new one if I were you. You don't want to **burn your bridges**. [do something that makes it impossible to go back to a situation you were in before]

Joe can be very boring sometimes. He always seems to **have an axe to grind**. [has a strong view or opinion and wants to persuade everyone he is correct; normally used critically]

When it comes to the crunch, I won't let you down. [when a situation becomes serious or difficult]

I think we've found **a chink in his armour**. [a weak point that we can exploit / take advantage of]

Exercises

38.1 Complete each of these idioms.

1 She was looking ....*daggers*...... at me last night. I wonder what I've done to upset her?
2 Her last remark was so hurtful, especially as I was already upset. I think she was just trying to ...*twist*........ the ...*knife*........ even further.
3 I really think you should ....*bite*.......... the bullet, and go and speak to him.
4 She ...*stuck*........ to her ...*guns*...... and didn't sign the contract. So they've changed it.
5 You're ...*jumping*... the gun. Wait till we know whose fault it was before you complain.
6 Freddy really puts the ...*knife*........ in sometimes. He is capable of saying such cruel things.

38.2 What could you say? Using idioms from the left-hand page, tell someone ...

1 ... who is trying to persuade the teacher to tell you the exam questions before the exam takes place that they will not succeed. *You're fighting the losing bottle.*

in the firing line 2 ... that if a real crisis occurs, you will be there to support them. *when it comes to the crunch.*
call the 3 ... that you yourself are the main problem when it comes to trying to save money. *I'm my own worst enemy*
shots 4 ... that they will be the one to face all the criticisms and complaints in their new job.
5 ... that you'd like to try bungee-jumping one day if you ever get the chance. *Have a shot at*
6 ... that they should wait before they send a very angry letter they've written. *Hold fire.*

38.3 Horoscopes often use idioms. Read these horoscopes and then say or write exactly what you would tell a friend with that birth-sign about their future, without using the idioms.

| **TAURUS** Someone you thought was a good friend will say something very hurtful today, and later on will twist the knife even further. Stay calm and don't lose your temper. | **GEMINI** Two people you like and respect will quarrel today, and you'll be caught in the crossfire. Try to stay neutral, or you'll risk losing a good friend. | **CAPRICORN** Someone close to you will try to tell you what to do, but it's time you called the shots, so don't be afraid to make your own decisions. | **VIRGO** You've always thought of yourself as a strong, determined person, but someone discovers a chink in your armour and makes life difficult for you. |

38.4 Choose the correct answer.

1 If you were up in arms, you'd be ... .
   a) holding someone you love   (b) protesting strongly
   c) feeling much stronger than before

2 If someone puts the knife in, they ... .
   a) make an important point   b) test the situation before acting
   (c) do or say something very damaging

3 If you burn your bridges, you ... .
   (a) make it impossible to return to a former situation   b) get extremely angry and violent
   c) destroy a good friendship

4 If you have an axe to grind, you have ... .
   a) a serious quarrel with someone   b) a desire to hurt someone
   (c) a strong opinion and you want to persuade people you're right

 FOLLOW UP If you can, look at a popular English-language magazine or tabloid newspaper and see if the horoscopes contain idioms. Make a note of any idioms you find, especially for your own star sign.

39 Food

A Appetite

If something **makes your mouth water**, it makes you want to eat it:
One look at those cakes **makes my mouth water**.

If you say that someone **has a sweet tooth**, you mean that they particulary like sweet things.

The word *appetite* can be used to refer to a desire for food or for something other than food. In the same way, **whet your appetite** can be used to mean awaken a desire:
Cinemas use trailers to **whet viewers' appetites** and make them want to see the whole film.

B Sweet and sour

Sweet things are generally considered to be particularly pleasant and luxurious. **The icing on the cake**, for example, refers not only to the sugar coating on a cake but also to something that makes a good situation even better:
This trophy is **the icing on the cake** for Julie who has had a great year as a tennis player.

The expression **you can't have your cake and eat it** or **you want to have your cake and eat it** is used to refer to the fact that two good things are impossible to do or have at the same time:
He **wants to have his cake and eat it**: he wants a well-paid secure job, but he doesn't want to have to work evenings or weekends.

Sour and *bitter* generally have unpleasant associations in idioms. If an experience **leaves a sour taste in your mouth**, you have an unpleasant memory of it. If you do something **to the bitter end**, you see it through to the end even though it takes a long time and is difficult.

C Specific foods

idiom	meaning	example
have egg on your face	be left feeling stupid or embarrassed because of something you did	You'll have egg on your face if your plan doesn't work!
be the best/greatest thing since sliced bread	be fantastic (informal)	I love my walkman. For me, it's the best thing since sliced bread.
be your bread and butter	be an activity or job you do to get the money you need	Taxi-driving is his bread and butter though he also writes music.
bear fruit	produce a positive result	At last our work is bearing fruit.

D In the supermarket

If you say something or someone is **flavour of the month**, it means that that thing or person is very popular. This is a reference to supermarkets' practice of putting a particular flavour of something – strawberry ice cream, for example – on special offer for a month:
Flavour-of-the-month actress, Becci Carr, stars in tonight's TV drama.

The phrase **be past** or **pass one's sell-by date** is often used humorously to refer to a person or thing that is not wanted or used any more because they are too old. It refers to the way supermarket food is marked with a *sell-by date* after which the product must be removed from the shelves before it goes bad:
I certainly feel as if I've **passed my sell-by date** this morning!

Exercises

39.1 What might Jo say in each situation? Match the remarks in the box with the situations.

> *a*   You can't have your cake and eat it.   *d* He had egg on his face!
> *b*   I was left with a sour taste in my mouth!   *e* It's the best thing since sliced bread!
> *c*   It provides the bread and butter.

   e 1 Jo's husband asks her what she thinks of some new computer software she's using.
   c 2 Jo asks her brother how he likes his new, rather boring job.
   b 3 Jo's husband asks her how she felt after a meeting at work where people said some very unpleasant things to each other.
   d 4 Jo tells her husband about her boss – whom she doesn't like – who made a mistake in some basic figures at a meeting where all the main company managers were present.
   a 5 Jo's son tells her that he's going to spend his (not very large) savings on an expensive new guitar as well as going on a trip to Australia.

39.2 Circle the correct word to complete each sentence.

1 Although it was too slow-moving for my taste, I sat through the film to the ~~bitter~~ / sour / sweet end.
2 Watching that cookery programme on TV has really watered / wetted / ~~whetted~~ my appetite for trying some new recipes.
3 All the effort Mandy has put into training is beginning to bear food / ~~fruit~~ / vegetables.
4 Although the pop group DK1 is bargain / ~~flavour~~ / taste of the month at the moment, their popularity is unlikely to last.
5 Grandad was exhausted after his long walk and said he had passed his sell-by day / time / ~~date~~.
6 Staying in a hotel room that Elvis Presley had once used was really the icing on the biscuit / ~~cake~~ / sugar.
7 Having such a sweet mouth / tongue / ~~tooth~~ makes it very difficult for her to lose weight.
8 The wonderful smells from the kitchen are really making my eyes / ~~mouth~~ / nose water.

39.3 Match an idiom from the left-hand page with each of these definitions.

have sweet tooth
1 love chocolates and cakes   4 be in an embarrassing position *have egg on ur face*
b the best thing since sliced bread 2 be absolutely fantastic   5 bring about good results *bear fruit*
3 be too old to be useful   6 make you want something (Give two answers.)
passed my sell by date   *makes my mouth water / whet my appetite*

39.4 Complete these sentences in any way you like.

1 .... is her bread and butter though she still hopes to succeed as an actress.
2 .... *it piece of chocolate cake* .... always makes my mouth water.
3 .... *Nelly & Usher* .... seems to be flavour of the month in the pop music world at the moment.
4 Kate had egg on her face when ....
5 For me .... *mobile phone* .... is the best thing since sliced bread.
6 I hope that .... will bear fruit.

> **FOLLOW UP**
> Look up these food words in a good dictionary: *apple, cheese, jam, tea*. Find an idiom for each of them and write it in a sentence.

40 Roods

A People: character, emotions and relationships

example	meaning
Goodbye. I hope **our paths cross** again soon.	I hope we meet again soon.
I'm really **stuck in a rut** in this job. I think I'll look for something new. (rut = deep track or mark made by a vehicle on the surface of a road)	In a boring situation, with no hope of excitement, or future prospects.
This computer's **driving me round the bend**! It keeps crashing each time I try to save my work.	The computer is making me angry and frustrated.
This book is **right up your street/alley**. It's called 'How to make a million in a year'. (alley = narrow street or lane with buildings on either side)	It's perfect for you; exactly what interests you.
Josh is very **middle-of-the-road** politically.	Neither left-wing nor right-wing, has no radical views.

B Road idioms that comment on situations

I think the government is **on the right/wrong track** these days. [thinking or acting rightly/wrongly]

It's **an uphill battle/fight/struggle** trying to persuade Joe to get a job. [a very difficult task]

That restaurant's really **gone downhill** lately. [it was good, but is not any longer]

She lives right **off the beaten track**, but she loves the peace and quiet. [in a very isolated place]

The Conservative Party is **at a crossroads**. [at a decisive moment in its history]

This job I have now is **a complete dead end**. [it has no future / no prospects]

be on the right/wrong track

go downhill

at a crossroads

an uphill battle/fight/struggle

off the beaten track

a dead end

I use a bicycle these days **to go/get from A to B**. [to make simple/typical journeys]

The new hotel has really **put the village on the map**. [now everybody has heard of the village]

Well, it's almost midnight. We should **hit the road**. [start our journey (home)]

Road rage is increasing in many countries. [violent incidents resulting from traffic disputes]

Exercises

40.1 Complete each of these idioms from A on the left-hand page.

1 Airlines _are driving_ me round the _bend_ ! You can never get simple information from them when you phone them up.
2 I don't have any extreme views about anything. I'm quite _middle- of_ -the- _road_ .
3 I didn't like her at all, and I hope our _paths_ never _cross_ again, to be honest.
4 It's a good idea to change your job every few years. It's very easy to get stuck _in_ a _rut_ if you're not careful.
5 This video's _right_ up your _street / alley_ . It's all about how violins are made.

40.2 Use the idioms from exercise 40.1 to rewrite the underlined parts of these sentences.

1 Well, it's been nice talking to you. Maybe <u>we'll see each other again somewhere</u>. _our paths cross again_
2 That TV programme about birds is <u>just right for you</u>. You should watch it. _right up your alley_
3 Jim is fairly <u>neutral</u> when it comes to environmental issues. _middle of the road_
4 The photocopier <u>makes me absolutely crazy</u>. It always breaks down just when you need it most. _drives me round the bend._
5 I gave up my job and went round the world. I felt I had <u>got into a boring routine with no prospects for the future</u>. _stuck in a rut_

40.3 True or false? Tick (✓) the correct box.

	True	False
1 If someone lives off the beaten track, they live in the middle of a city.	☐	☒
2 If a street is a dead end, you can't drive down it and out the other end.	☐	☒
3 Road rage is when people get angry and violent because of problems and arguments while driving.	☐	☒
4 If something is an uphill struggle, it's like the pleasant feeling of travelling up a beautiful hill.	☐	☒
5 If someone is on the wrong track, they are dialling a wrong number on a telephone.	☐	☒

40.4 Use idioms from the left-hand page to ...

1 ... tell someone it's time to start a journey. _hit the road_
2 ... tell someone that the bus is the easiest way to travel round in your area. _to get from A to B_   _To use a bus_
3 ... tell someone not to go to the Imperial Hotel as it's not as good as it used to be. _it's gone downhill_
4 ... tell someone that you think what they are going to do is the right course of action. _you're on the right track_
5 ... tell someone that a new rock music festival has really made your town famous. _put the town on the map_
6 ... tell someone that you think your country is at an important and decisive point in its history. _at a crossroads_

FOLLOW UP Think of idioms connected with roads, paths and tracks in your language. Do any of them match the idioms in this unit? If they don't, try to find out the equivalent expression in English. Use a dictionary of idioms or another good dictionary, or go online to dictionary.cambridge.org/idioms

41 Houses and household objects

A Home

Home is the place where people feel comfortable and safe. If you **are/feel at home** somewhere, you are/feel comfortable there. If you **make yourself at home,** you relax and make yourself comfortable. Similarly, if something is **as safe as houses,** it is extremely safe.

The implications of what she had said didn't **come home to me** until some days later. [I didn't understand it fully]

Her news reports have really **brought home** to me the horrors of war. [made me understand, usually something unpleasant]

B Doors and fences

Doors give you access to somewhere new.

They don't pay me very well for the work I do there at the moment, but at least I've **got my foot in the door.** [started working at a low level in an organisation because you want to get a better job in the same organisation later on]

Doors have keys and handles.

Female voters **hold the key to** the party's success in the election. [provide the explanation for something you could not previously understand]

Her father **flew off the handle** when she said she wasn't going to return to university. [reacted in a very angry way (informal)]

A fence marks the boundary between two areas of land.

If you **sit on the fence,** you delay making a decision or fail to choose between two alternatives. Usually in the end, though, you have to **come down on one side or the other.** [make a choice]

C Household objects

Alf **hit the ceiling/roof**[1] this morning for no reason at all. I thought he'd just **got out of bed on the wrong side**[2], but then his girlfriend explained that he's been **burning the candle at both ends**[3] because of his exams. I'm glad she **put me in the picture**[4] because now I can understand why he reacted so crossly. However, I wish he'd **take a leaf out of his girlfriend's book**[5] and go to bed at a reasonable time.

[1] reacted angrily
[2] got up in a bad mood and has stayed in a bad mood all day
[3] staying up late and getting up early
[4] explained the situation to me – *picture* also means *situation* in **get the picture** [understand the situation (informal)] and **keep someone in the picture** [keep someone informed]
[5] copy something someone else does, often in order to gain an advantage that they have

Exercises

41.1 Match the beginning of each idiom on the left with its ending on the right.

1 sitting on the — home
2 getting your foot in the — handle
3 getting out of bed on the wrong — fence
4 flying off the — picture
5 putting someone in the — ends
6 feeling at — door
7 burning the candle at both — side

41.2 Answer these questions.

1 Is a decisive person likely to sit on the fence or come down on one side or the other?
2 If a student takes a holiday job in a big company in order to get a foot in the door, what does that suggest about the student's plans?
3 In what circumstances do people often burn the candle at both ends?
4 Are you more likely to say that something important or something trivial is brought home to you?
5 Do you think someone would be pleased or displeased if you took a leaf out of their book?
6 If you keep someone in the picture, are you being honest to them or not?
7 How do you feel if you get out of bed on the wrong side?
8 If someone hits the roof, what sort of mood are they in?

41.3 Which idioms do these pictures make you think of?

put sy in the picture   fly off the handle
feel at home   as safe as houses

41.4 Rewrite the underlined part of each sentence with an idiom.

1 It will take some time before the impact of the new legislation <u>is fully felt by</u> the person in the street.
2 Sophie will make herself ill if she goes on <u>allowing herself so little sleep</u>.
3 Before you take over the project, I'll <u>let you know exactly what the situation with it is</u>.
4 The police think that DNA testing <u>will provide the evidence necessary for</u> proving who the murderer must have been.
5 Jim<u>'s been in a really bad mood all day</u>.
6 The government can't <u>postpone making a decision</u> for ever.
7 Rob <u>gets really angry</u> at the slightest provocation these days. (Give two answers.)
8 If you want to get fit, why don't you <u>do as Katie has done</u> and join a gym?

41.5 Write sentences using six of the idioms from the left-hand page about your own life or experiences.

42 Nature

In this unit we look at idioms connected with the earth, the planets and the air, and other basic elements.

A The air

The air (or sky) is often seen as something associated with feelings and emotions, or is in some way connected with unknown or future events. Look at these newspaper clips.

There was a sense of relief **in the air**[1] when the 'not guilty' verdict was announced.

Whether the government will change the law on football hooliganism is **up in the air**[3] at the moment.

The discussions have not solved the problem, but they have helped to **clear the air**[5] to a certain

The news has come as **a breath of fresh air**[2] for students worried about the high level of fees.

Mr Watson said the news had come **out of the blue**[4] and it had shocked everyone. He

[1] everyone could feel it
[2] something new / more exciting
[3] undecided
[4] completely unexpectedly (*the blue* = the sky)
[5] make bad feelings between people disappear

B The earth, planets, ground

Idioms about the earth often refer to the ground beneath our feet and to being practical/realistic.

If ...	this means ...
someone is a **down-to-earth** person	they are very practical
you **come (back) down to earth with a bang**	something brings you suddenly back to reality
an idea or plan/project **bites the dust**	it fails/dies
someone is **(living) on another planet**	they have no awareness of the real world
you are **over the moon** about something	you are extremely happy
something **is/hits rock bottom**	it is as low as it can possibly be/go
you **find out how the land lies**	you see how the situation is before you get involved
a person is **upper-crust***	they belong to a very high social class

* The *crust* is the top surface of the earth; under it are other layers of very hot rocks.

Note also:

If you are **in the dark** or someone **keeps you in the dark**, you are not told important things that other people know.

If you are **in your element**, you are happy/relaxed in the situation because you are good at the things it involves.

If you are **out of your element**, you feel unhappy/uncomfortable because you are not good at the tasks involved. (*element* here refers to the four basic natural elements: earth, water, fire and air)

Exercises

42.1 Complete each of these idioms.

1 The news .... out of the blue. No one was expecting it.
2 What a crazy idea! I think she's living .... another planet.
3 The price of computers has .... rock bottom this year.
4 I think we should .... out how the land lies before we decide.
5 They've .... me in the dark about their future plans. I wish they'd tell me.

42.2 Match each question on the left with the most likely response on the right.

1 Is Anna Conda really a princess?	Yes, it bit the dust.
2 I guess he was delighted with the news?	Yes, he was in his element.
3 So your new project failed after all?	No, he's very down-to-earth.
4 Did your long talk with David help at all?	I don't know, but she's very upper-crust.
5 Did your dad enjoy his golfing holiday?	Yes, he was over the moon.
6 Is Alfie a very romantic type of person?	Well, it did help to clear the air a bit.

42.3 Rewrite the underlined part of each sentence with an idiom.

1 You could feel a sense of fear <u>in everyone</u> when the planes came overhead.
2 It really is <u>something new and exciting</u> for us that the company has decided to move to London. We are all bored with working in a small town.
3 Sally <u>was brought suddenly back to reality</u> when the bank manager told her she had spent all her money.
4 Things are <u>very undecided</u> at the moment. I'll let you know when a decision is made.

42.4 Answer these questions.

1 Think of one person you know who is down-to-earth and another person you know who is just living on another planet. In what ways are they so?
2 When was the last time you felt over the moon, and why?
3 Think of an occasion when someone you hadn't seen for a very long time suddenly appeared out of the blue.
4 Think of one situation where you could personally say 'I'm in my element here!'

42.5 The underlined idioms below are not on the left-hand page. Try to work out the meaning of the idioms from context. If you can't, then check their meaning in a good general dictionary or in a dictionary of idioms.

1 I was <u>shaking like a leaf</u> as I waited to hear if I had passed the exam.
2 I <u>slept like a log</u> last night. It was so quiet and the bed was very comfortable.
3 I hate making big decisions. I usually prefer to just <u>go with the flow</u>.
4 It <u>goes against the grain</u> for him ever to say he was wrong. It is not in his character to admit that he has made a mistake.

FOLLOW UP Look up *sun*, *star(s)*, *moon*, *rock(s)*, *sea* and *mountains* in a good dictionary or a dictionary of idioms. What idioms do you find? Write the idioms in sentences which illustrate their meaning.

43 Boats and sailing

A Boats

idiom	meaning	example
push the boat out	spend a lot of money, usually because you are celebrating	Bill was happy to push the boat out for his daughter's wedding.
rock the boat	do or say something that causes problems, usually when you try to change a situation that other people do not want to change	Party members were told firmly not to rock the boat by publicly criticising the government just before the election.
miss the boat	be too late to get something you want	Can I still get tickets for the concert or have I already missed the boat?
burn one's boats/bridges	do something that makes it impossible for you to go back to the situation you were in before	Don't sell your house to finance your business – that would be burning your boats.
be in the same boat	be in the same, usually difficult, situation	It's a pity you can't use a dictionary in your exam, but at least everyone's in the same boat.

B Sailing

idiom	meaning	example
steer clear of	avoid someone or something because it is dangerous for you	I'd try to steer clear of Maggie if I were you – she's trouble!
sail close to the wind	take risks that could cause problems or danger (usually used in the continuous)	You're sailing a bit close to the wind by speaking to the boss like that!
be plain sailing	be very easy	I was a bit apprehensive about doing so much in just one day, but it was all plain sailing.
be in the doldrums (doldrums = area of sea with no wind)	(of a business) be not very successful; (of a person) feel sad and without energy	His business has been in the doldrums for several years now.
put/stick your oar in (oar = long piece of wood used for rowing a boat)	join a discussion when the other participants do not want you to (informal)	I hope John has the sense not to stick his oar in at tomorrow's meeting.
show someone the ropes	show someone how to do a job or activity	As it's your first day at work, Sue will show you the ropes.
be a nervous wreck (wreck = boat that's been destroyed, e.g. by hitting rocks)	be mentally and physically exhausted	I'm a nervous wreck after a day with those terrible children.
clear the decks (deck = flat open area on boat)	get ready for action	We'd better clear the decks before we paint the room.
be (all) at sea	be confused	I'm all at sea with this computer.

Exercises

43.1 **Answer these questions.**

1 If you miss the boat, have you lost a means of transport or an opportunity?
2 If you say that a project was plain sailing, are you happy with how it went or not?
3 If you burn your boats, are you taking a risk or not?
4 If a friend is in the doldrums, would you try to calm them down or cheer them up?
5 Are you more likely to be a nervous wreck if you're bored or if you're overworked?
6 If you are all at sea in a new job, do you need someone to show you the ropes or to stick their oar in?
7 If you rock the boat, will people be pleased with you or annoyed with you?
8 If you show someone the ropes, are you helping them or threatening them?

43.2 **Complete each of these idioms with one word.**

1 Things here are very difficult, but at least we're all in the .... boat.
2 It'll be hard climbing the mountain, but should be .... sailing on the way down.
3 Everyone would like to dance, so let's clear the .... and make as much space as we can in the middle of the floor.
4 Speaking to the press about what's going on is .... a bit close to the wind.
5 I know the party is costing a lot, but you have to .... the boat out occasionally.
6 Joe's been in the .... ever since he lost his job.
7 Trust Simon to stick his .... in – he never knows when it's better to say nothing.
8 I don't trust Paul – I'd steer .... of him if I were you.

43.3 **Here are some more idioms based on sailing concepts. Match each idiom on the left with its explanation on the right. (Note that *tack* = direction taken in sailing in order to catch the wind.)**

1 change tack   be familiar with how things are done
2 know the ropes   be in a weak mental or physical condition
3 try a different tack   act in a way that is not extreme
4 learn the ropes   take a different course of action
5 be a quivering wreck   get to know how to do things
6 steer a middle course   attempt to do something in a different way

43.4 **Complete each sentence with an idiom from the left-hand page or from exercise 43.3.**

1 Leave things as they are – it's better not to .... (Give two answers.)
2 Everything must seem strange at first, but you'll soon ....
3 Finish your course before you go travelling – there's no point in ....
....
4 Parents usually try to .... between leniency and strictness.
5 Sally's very miserable – do you know why she's .... ?
6 The new boy is bound to be feeling .... on his first day at school – perhaps you can help.
7 Things are not working out – let's .... (Give two answers.)
8 I hate job interviews – I'm always .... before them.

44 Science, technology and machines

A Engines and cars

Look at these conversations. The second speaker uses an idiom to agree with what the first speaker says.

Eva: We'll have to get ready to start work on the new system.
Lars: Yes, we'll have to **get into gear,** I suppose.
(like putting a car into gear before driving)

Ron: I hate having Lisa in my car. She always tells you what you're doing wrong, or when the lights have gone red, and so on.
Peter: Yes, she's a real **back-seat driver,** isn't she?

Olga: I think we've spent over the budget these last three months. We'll have to be more careful.
Mick: Yes, we'll have to **put the brakes on** our spending; we've paid out some large sums.

Hugh: Things are going well these days, aren't they? Everything's working quietly and smoothly.
Ben: Yes, things are **ticking over** nicely.
(A car engine *ticks over* when it is running quietly, but the car is not moving.)

Will: Well, it was quite an angry meeting, but I think it was good that people could just say exactly what they were thinking and get angry if they wanted to.
Mia: Yes, I think it was good that they were able to **let off steam.**
(like a steam engine which lets off steam to reduce the high pressure that has built up)

Jim: I'm glad we organised our own travel instead of going with a group, aren't you?
Russ: Yes, I'm glad we decided to **go under our own steam.**

B Electricity, phones and radio

If you ...	this means ...
get your lines/wires crossed	there is a misunderstanding between you and someone
are on the same wavelength as someone (wavelength = fixed position on a radio band, e.g. FM/AM)	you view the world or think in the same way as them
blow a fuse/gasket (gasket = kind of seal in an engine)	you lose your temper and react very angrily to an event
give someone a buzz	you phone them (informal)

C Other idioms from the world of technology and machines

The government is **back-pedalling** over its plans to lower taxes. [is beginning to say the opposite of what it said before, like pushing the pedals of a bicycle backwards]

His comments really **put/threw a spanner in the works.** [spoilt something, e.g. a plan, or prevented it from succeeding]

She always buys the latest, **state-of-the-art** computer. [one which has all the newest features]

Plans for a new bridge across the river are **in the pipeline.** [are being discussed/prepared but are not public yet]

Exercises

44.1 Advertisements often use idioms to sell products. Match each slogan with its text.

1 **Want to let off steam tonight?**   3 **State-of-the-art digital technology in your home**

2 **We're on your wavelength**   4 **Give us a buzz for lower bills**

A   **Local Radio is changing, and here at Homestyle FM we believe you'll want to listen to us with our new programmes for the autumn.**

C   **By 2005, most TV channels will no longer broadcast in the traditional way. Buy a new TV set now and you will be ready for the changes.**

B   **Are you paying too much for your mobile phone? Call us on 07965 34352 and find out how you can pay less.**

D   **At Broadnet.com we offer more chatrooms where you can say what you think about everything than any other Internet Service Provider.**

44.2 Agree with what A says. Complete each response with an idiom from the left-hand page.

1 A: Her e-mail caused real problems for our plans, didn't it?
  B: Yes, it really ....

2 A: I think George is beginning to change his mind about joining our committee.
  B: Yes, he seems to be ....

3 A: Wow! Eric really lost his temper last night, didn't he?
  B: Yes, he absolutely ....

4 A: Good. Things seem to be nice and quiet and working smoothly.
  B: Yes, everything seems to be just quietly ....

5 A: It seems there was a misunderstanding between us.
  B: Yes, I think we ....

6 A: I think we should give her a call this evening.
  B: Yes, it's probably a good idea to ....

44.3 Which idioms do these pictures make you think of?

44.4 Rewrite each sentence with an idiom from exercise 44.3.

1 It took us a long time to really start to do our work properly and efficiently.
2 Brad is one of those people who always knows the road better than the person driving.
3 There are plans for a new railway, but it will be some years before the project starts.

44.5 Complete each sentence with a preposition or particle.

1 We're .... the same wavelength.
2 I'd prefer to go .... my own steam.
3 Everyone needs to let .... steam occasionally.
4 You've really put a spanner .... the works.
5 Business is ticking .... nicely these days.
6 We'll have to put the brakes .... with regard to how much we spend.

45 Finger, thumb, hand

Idioms connected with the hand can refer to ownership, control, acting and exercising skills.

A Idioms based on the fingers

In these conversations, the second speaker repeats the meaning of the idiom in bold.

Alison: Rosa had all the statistics **at her fingertips.**
Geoff: Yes, I was amazed she was able to quote them immediately.

Ron: I'm getting my exam results tomorrow. **Keep your fingers crossed** for me!
Pat: Yes, I will. I'll be wishing you good luck all day and hoping you do well.

Ben: I think he's **put his finger on** the problem.
Liz: Yes, I think he's identified exactly what's wrong.

Mick: Jane never **lifts a finger** at home.
Nancy: I know. She never helps out. She's so lazy.

Larry: He **got his fingers burnt** in a financial deal in 1998.
Lily: Yes, I know. He suffered badly and lost a lot of money at the time.

Oscar: Paula **has** really **got green fingers,** hasn't she?
Ruth: Yes, everything she plants in her garden seems to grow beautifully.

B Idioms based on the thumb and the whole hand

example	meaning
The plan has been **given the thumbs up/down**.	has been approved (up) or rejected (down)
That office block **sticks/stands out like a sore thumb** next to such a beautiful park.	looks different from everything else in its environment (in a negative sense)
As **a rule of thumb**, always write down the code.	as a general, useful rule
The boss has **given me a free hand** at work.	allows me to take whatever action I want to
Ed can **turn his hand to** any job round the house.	has the skill/ability to do unfamiliar jobs without any previous experience
Things **got out of hand** and the police arrived.	got out of control
I don't really have any **first-hand** knowledge of nature conservation.	direct / from experience
That restaurant has **changed hands** twice.	been sold to a new owner
I **have my hands full** with three children.	am very busy / have a lot of things to do
I'd like to **try my hand at** scuba-diving one day.	try it for the first time
I play golf occasionally just **to keep my hand in**.	in order not to lose my skill/knowledge
I always like to have a dictionary **to hand** when I'm reading English newspapers.	available; nearby
Give me a hand with this big box, will you?	help me, e.g. to carry/lift it
I've **washed my hands of** the whole project as it caused so many problems.	stopped being involved in

Exercises

45.1 Complete these idioms with *hand(s)*, *finger(s)* or *thumb(s)*.

1 I have my .... full at the office these days. I'm doing two people's jobs.
2 I'm sorry, but the plan's been given the .... down by the committee.
3 She's been given a free .... to change the entire computer system for the whole company.
4 Yes, he's just lazy. You're right. You've put your .... on it.
5 Things are getting out of .... ; we need someone to organise things properly.
6 As a rule of .... you should never use the present perfect in English with words like *yesterday* or *last year*, but journalists do it sometimes.
7 If you need help with your garden, ask Liz – she's got green ....
8 I get my exam results tomorrow. Keep your .... crossed for me!
9 Their teenage kids never lift a .... at home; they just leave everything to the parents.
10 That shop has changed .... again. It's owned by someone from Hong Kong now.

45.2 Rewrite the underlined part of each sentence with an idiom from the left-hand page.

1 I think it would be good if you got some <u>direct</u> experience of working in a poor country before working for an aid organisation at home.
2 Jerry has <u>withdrawn completely from</u> the club committee. He was so disgusted that he just quit, and never wants to see any of them again.
3 That new power station on the coast <u>is such an ugly sight</u>! You'd think they would have built it to blend in with the landscape.
4 Have you ever <u>had a go at</u> water-skiing? My sister's got a boat if you would like to try.
5 I always have to have the cookbook <u>right next to me</u> when I'm trying out a new recipe.
6 I'm too busy to play football every week now, but I really should play occasionally, just to <u>keep my skills alive</u>.
7 She <u>lost out badly</u> on the stock exchange. She bought shares in an Internet company that went bankrupt.

45.3 Correct the mistakes in these idioms.

1 Do you think you could bring me a hand this weekend? I have to move some furniture to our summer cottage.
2 If you're the sort of person who is prepared to make your hand to anything, you'll be able to earn a lot of money; people are always looking for willing workers.
3 I was very pleased when they told me my project had been given the up-thumb.
4 I decided to wash my hands with the whole idea and to have no involvement whatsoever in it.
5 If you want to make a good impression at a business meeting, it is a good idea to have all the facts and figures in your fingertip.
6 To build a horrible concrete bridge over such a beautiful river is terrible. It stands out like a sick thumb!

FOLLOW UP Look again at the idioms on the left-hand page and see if you can see any further pattern of meanings for the different sets of idioms connected with hands, fingers and thumbs. What do fingers do? Are the thumb idioms different? Make a few notes in your Vocabulary notebook and see if your ideas are still valid as and when you add new idioms connected with the keywords.

46 Foot, heel, toe

A Foot

Several idioms involving the word *foot* refer to someone's personal situation.

example	meaning
You're an adult now; you have to learn to **stand on your own two feet**.	be independent; look after yourself
I'm **rushed off my feet** at work.	extremely busy/hectic
He's famous, but he's always **kept both feet on the ground.**	always remained normal and realistic
I accepted the job, but then **got cold feet**.	became afraid to do it
Don't worry. It will take you a while to **find your feet**. It's always like this in a new job.	get used to things; feel you can cope
Nancy and I **got off on the wrong foot**.	our relationship started badly
The children are always **under my feet** when I'm trying to do the housework.	in my way, disturbing my activities
He really seems to have **landed/fallen on his feet.** He got a new job and found a flat within a week of arriving in the city.	been very lucky or successful in a difficult situation (The idiom is based on the notion that cats always land on their feet when they fall.)
She lived at home for a while, but **got itchy feet** again and went off travelling for a year.	got a desire to travel

Other idioms with *foot* refer more to actions.

I really **put my foot in it** when I told Mario I hated Italian food; he's Italian! [accidentally said/did something very embarrassing]

I think you should **put your foot down** and say no. [assert your authority or independence]

He **followed in** his father's **footsteps** and became a doctor. [take the same course of action as somebody else]

B Heel and toe

These two idioms with *heel* refer to preventing or slowing down movement.

I don't think Sara wants to join us; she's **dragging her heels** a bit. [deliberately being slow]

They're **digging their heels in** and refusing to compromise. [refusing to change their position]

The boss always **keeps us on our toes**. [keeps us busy; makes us give our full energy to our work]

TIP Whenever you find idioms that seem to have something in common in their meaning (as with the two *heel* idioms or the *foot* idioms referring to situations), group them together on one page in your Vocabulary notebook. Add any new idioms that have similar meanings as you meet them.

Exercises

46.1 Match each idiom on the left with its definition on the right.

1 have itchy feet	be very busy
2 find your feet	start off in a bad way
3 be under someone's feet	feel familiar with something
4 land/fall on your feet	be restless / want to travel
5 get off on the wrong foot	regret a decision
6 be rushed off your feet	remain connected to the real world
7 get cold feet	be constantly in the way
8 stand on your own two feet	be lucky/successful
9 keep both feet on the ground	be independent

46.2 Write sentences which relate to *your* life with any five of the idioms in the list in exercise 46.1.

EXAMPLE *I applied for a place at an American university and was accepted, but then I got cold feet.*

46.3 Rewrite these sentences with five of the idioms from exercise 46.1.
1 I said I would join Jim on the protest march, but then regretted it and didn't go at all.
2 She was very busy in the shop last month, but she's pleased that the business is doing well.
3 He'll have to learn to make his own decisions now that he's at college and not living at home any more.
4 Mavis and I started off rather badly when she first joined the company, but now we're working very well together.
5 I'm feeling restless these days. I'd love to go off on a backpacking holiday somewhere.

46.4 Which idioms do these pictures make you think of?

46.5 True or false? Tick (✓) the correct box.

	True	False
1 If you drag your heels, you deliberately act slowly or delay something.	☐	☐
2 If you put your foot down, you tell someone very firmly to act in a particular way.	☐	☐
3 If someone keeps you on your toes, they keep you very excited.	☐	☐
4 If you follow in someone's footsteps, they are your boss and you are below them.	☐	☐
5 If you dig your heels in, you are very determined not to be persuaded to do something you don't want to do.	☐	☐

FOLLOW UP Use a good dictionary to find the meanings of these idioms if you do not already know them.
foot the bill
toe the line
hard/hot on the heels of

47 Bones, shoulder, arm, leg

A Idioms and meaning associations

Sometimes groups of idioms have some aspect of meaning in common. For example, our *bones* are inside our body, they have flesh/meat on them and they form our skeleton. Note how some basic associations of the word *bone(s)* play a part in this meaning of these idioms.

example	meaning	association
I **have a bone to pick with** you.	You have done something that has annoyed me, and we must discuss it.	Animals pick the flesh off bones when they eat their prey.
She's going to get that job; **I can feel it in my bones**.	I have a feeling deep inside me / an instinct.	Bones are deep inside us.
How best to use the money we raised has become **a bone of contention**.	People are arguing and disagreeing over it.	Animals fight over bones/food.
Let's try and get to **the bare bones** of the problem.	Get to the heart / the most basic aspects of the problem.	The bones are our skeleton, our basic form.

B Shoulder and arm

Main association: Shoulders support or carry things.

She **has a chip on her shoulder** about the fact that she was not promoted in her job years ago. [blames other people for something negative that has happened to her and goes on carrying these feelings for ever]

Fiona, can I talk to you? I'm having a horrible time and I need **a shoulder to cry on**. [sympathy or support in time of trouble]

You are not alone in your fight against the authorities. We will **stand shoulder to shoulder with you**. [support you in a difficult time]

I didn't have much success trying to get to know that good-looking guy at the party. He **gave me the cold shoulder**. [reacted to me in an unfriendly or cold way for no obvious reason]

Main association: Arms hold and/or control things.

I didn't really want to do the job, but he **twisted my arm** and I said yes. [persuaded me to do something I didn't really want to do]

I don't really want to talk to her. I've been trying to **keep/hold her at arm's length**. [keep a distance between myself and her]

C Leg

I haven't really won the lottery. I was only **pulling your leg**. [only joking / trying to fool you]

He'll find it difficult to convince the police that he's innocent. He **hasn't (got) a leg to stand on** really. [has nothing to support his claim or position]

> **TIP**
>
> There are ten units in this book that deal with idioms connected with the body. Try to build a picture in your mind of a human body as you work through the units and remember which parts of the body are most strongly associated with idioms, e.g the hand.

Exercises

47.1 Use idioms to complete the network.

A bone of ....

The .... bones

BONE

I have a bone ....

I can feel ....

47.2 Use the idioms from exercise 47.1 to rewrite these sentences in as brief a way as possible.
1 I want to talk to you about something very annoying that you have done.
2 This book will give you the most basic information, but it doesn't go into great detail.
3 I don't think we should allow the cost to become a matter that we argue about.
4 There's going to be trouble at work. I can really sense it in a subconscious way.

47.3 Choose the correct answer.
1 Janet has a chip on her shoulder because she never got a chance to go to university.
   a) She is disadvantaged in trying to find a job.
   b) She has an ambition she has not yet fulfilled.
   c) She carries a negative feeling about it throughout her life.
2 Brian is pulling Helen's leg.
   a) He is annoying her.   b) He is trying to fool her about something.
   c) He is attacking her.
3 Louise needs a shoulder to cry on.
   a) She needs to cry publicly.   b) She needs a friend to listen to her troubles.
   c) She needs something to cry about.
4 Rita is trying to twist Sally's arm because she wants to borrow Sally's car.
   a) Rita is trying to persuade Sally even though Sally doesn't want to do it.
   b) Rita is trying to blackmail Sally to do it.
   c) Rita is trying to pay Sally to lend her car.
5 Lorna gave Mark the cold shoulder when he asked her to go with him to the school party.
   a) She put her head on Mark's shoulder in a romantic way.
   b) She rubbed her shoulder against Mark's as a way of saying 'yes'.
   c) She behaved in a rather distant way and said 'no'.
6 Clare said she would stand shoulder to shoulder with Irene.
   a) She promised to fight Irene with all her strength.
   b) She promised to stand next to Irene in a queue for something.
   c) She promised to support Irene in a difficult situation.

47.4 Write a sentence or a couple of sentences for each of these idioms to show their meaning.

hold/keep someone at arm's length   not have a leg to stand on

47.5 Here are two more idioms using *arm* which are not on the left-hand page. Using a dictionary if necessary, complete each idiom.
1 The tickets for the Michael Jackson concert <u>cost us an arm and a</u> .... ;
   they were the most expensive I have ever bought.
2 I think I'll .... <u>my arm</u> and apply for that job. I know I'm not at all
   qualified, but I've got nothing to lose by applying.

48 Head

A Emotions

Head is used in a number of idioms that relate to emotions and staying calm and in control.

keep your head
[keep calm, especially in a difficult or dangerous situation]

lose your head
[panic or lose control]

laugh/scream/shout your head off
[laugh/scream/shout very much and very loudly (informal)]

be banging or hitting your head against a brick wall
[ask someone to do something which they won't do]

bring something to a head / something comes to a head
[an unpleasant situation is so bad that it has to be dealt with]

If you can **keep your head** when all around are losing theirs, you'll be a man, my son. (written by 19th century poet Kipling)

They were **shouting their heads off** until late at night and I just couldn't fall asleep.

Trying to get the boys to tidy their bedroom is just **banging your head against a brick wall**.

Andy and Jill had been upset with each other for some time, but things eventually **came to a head** last night when they had a terrible row.

B Thought

Sometimes *head* is used in idioms to mean the place where ideas or thoughts are produced.

idiom	meaning	example
put ideas into someone's head	make someone want to do something they had not wanted to do before (usually something stupid)	Louisa was always quite happy in the village until Rex started putting ideas into her head.
get your head (a)round (usually – **can't get (my) head (a)round**)	come to fully accept or understand something (informal)	I just can't get my head around what's happened. It's been such a shock!
off the top of your head	without thinking about it for very long or looking at something that has been written about it	Off the top of my head, I couldn't tell you where they live, but I could soon find out.

C Other head idioms

Rebecca is so beautiful; she always **turns heads**[1] whenever she walks into a room. My brother Barney is beginning to fall in love with her, but our parents would like to **knock that on the head**[2]. This is a very busy year for Barney and he is going to have to work very hard to **keep his head above water**[3]. However, he **bites/snaps their heads off**[4] if they tell him to ignore her. I'm taking care not to get involved – it's safer to **keep my head down**[5].

[1] people notice that person because they look interesting or attractive
[2] put a stop to it (informal)
[3] have just enough money in order to live or keep a business going (an image from swimming)
[4] speaks to them angrily
[5] say as little as possible in order to avoid arguments

Exercises

48.1 **What do these underlined idioms mean?**

1 I <u>can't get my head around</u> how much she's changed since she met Joel.
2 Mary will never <u>turn heads</u> in the way that her older sister does.
3 You'll <u>laugh your head off</u> when you see Bill wearing a dinner jacket.
4 Dick hadn't had time to prepare a speech, but he spoke very well <u>off the top of his head</u>.
5 If I were you, I'd <u>keep my head down</u> until the situation improves.
6 Sam wants to use your saw to build a treehouse – you'd better <u>knock that idea on the head</u>.
7 My boss <u>snapped my head off</u> just because I asked for an extra day off.
8 It was the first time that Joanna had talked about wanting to work abroad and her father blamed her new boyfriend for <u>putting ideas into her head</u>.

48.2 **Complete each sentence with an idiom from the box. Make any other necessary changes.**

bang your head against a brick wall	bring things to a head	come to a head	keep your head
lose your head	scream your head off	snap someone's head off	

1 Mel .... when she saw a rat under the table.
2 When the pilot announced that the plane was having engine problems, all the passengers behaved calmly and no one ....
3 I'm trying to get him to give up smoking, but I ....
4 You'll easily pass your driving test as long as you ....
5 I wish he wouldn't .... when I ask him about his work.
6 Jack and Sue have not been getting on well for some time now, but Jack's rudeness to her last night .... and they had a blazing row.
7 The disagreement over pay .... at a meeting yesterday.

48.3 **Which idioms do these pictures make you think of?**

48.4 **Answer these questions.**

1 Has anyone ever bitten your head off? Why did they do this?
2 Under what circumstances would you find it hard to keep your head?
3 When was the last time you laughed your head off?
4 What kind of person would turn your head in the street?
5 Can you think of someone who has been criticised for putting ideas into people's heads?
6 Would a business be pleased if it were keeping its head above water? Why (not)?

 This unit includes just some of the idioms based on the word *head*. Look in a good dictionary, find three more idioms and write them down in example sentences.

49 Face, hair, neck, chest

A Face

Our face presents the image we show people and that is reflected in most of the idioms with *face*.

idiom	meaning	example
make/pull a face	show that you do not like something by making an unpleasant expression	Emma pulled a face when she heard that Jim was coming to the party.
keep a straight face	not to laugh or change your expression even though you want to laugh	It was all I could do to keep a straight face when I saw Jim in his new suit.
put a brave face on something	pretend you are happy about something when you are not happy	Chris was disappointed about not getting the job, but he's put a brave face on it.
take something at face value	accept something as it looks without thinking about whether it might, in fact, not be quite what it appears	I decided to take his words at face value although my brother told me I was being naive.
on the face of it	according to the appearance of something	On the face of it, it's a generous offer. But I feel there might be a trick in it.
face to face	with another person in their presence rather than, say, by phone or letter	You should really discuss this with her face to face.

B Hair

Hair in idioms often has associations with being calm and in control.
If you say to someone **Keep your hair on!** (informal) you mean Calm down!

Her boyfriend has disappeared again. She's **tearing/pulling her hair out!**
[getting very anxious (usually used with continuous verb forms)]

My boss **didn't turn a hair** when I handed in my notice. [showed no reaction at all]

C Neck and chest

> It's uncomfortable at home at the moment because my two flatmates, Tom and Dick, **are at each other's throats**[1] all the time. It started when Tom used Dick's computer and managed to destroy some files. Tom decided to **make a clean breast of it**[2]. Now Dick won't let him use the computer without **breathing down his neck**[3] all the time and he's always going on about how stupid Tom was. Tom finds this **a real pain in the neck**[4] and he wishes he had never **got it off his chest**[5], but had just let Dick think it was a computer virus that had destroyed his files. Tom knows he is in the wrong, but he wishes Dick wouldn't keep **ramming it down his throat**[6] all the time and would just show his annoyance by **giving him the cold shoulder**[7].

[1] arguing in a very angry way
[2] tell the truth about what he had done so that he did not feel guilty any more
[3] paying close attention to what he is doing in an annoying or threatening way
[4] really annoying
[5] told him what he was feeling guilty about
[6] forcing him to listen to his opinions
[7] ignoring him in a deliberate way

Note how idioms with *throat* or *neck* often describe someone behaving in a way that the speaker finds aggressive or intrusive. Note also how the idea of a guilty secret being a weight on your chest is reflected in two idioms – **make a clean breast of** and **get it off your chest**.

Exercises

49.1 Complete each idiom with a word from the box. Use some of the words more than once.

> chest   face   hair   neck   shoulder   throat(s)

I haven't been enjoying my job recently. On the ....[1] of it, it's a good job, but my colleagues don't get on with each other. They are either at each other's ....[2] or giving each other the cold ....[3] and I don't know which is worse. My boss is always breathing down my ....[4] and ramming his reactionary views down my ....[5]. I find him a terrible pain in the ....[6]. I had to get my feelings off my ....[7] and, today, I decided to unburden myself to his secretary. Suddenly, I realised that my boss was standing behind me. 'You should have told me this ....[8] to ....[9],' he said and, without turning a ....[10], he added 'You're fired!' I was so angry that I pulled a ....[11] at him and stormed out of the office.

49.2 Match the beginning of each sentence on the left with its ending on the right.

1 You try to keep a straight face	when you get very upset about something.
2 You put a brave face on something	when you admit to doing something wrong.
3 You can be said to be pulling your hair out	when you accept it in a straightforward way.
4 You make a clean breast of something	when you are showing your anger.
5 You may make a face	when you want to control your laughter.
6 You take something at face value	when you deliberately ignore them.
7 You may be told to keep your hair on	when you are not pleased about something.
8 You give someone the cold shoulder	when you try to hide your disappointment.

49.3 Correct the mistakes in these idioms.

1 Rose's father didn't pull a hair when she told him she was going to get married.
2 I wish my boss would let me get on with my work instead of breathing down the neck.
3 You should tell him directly how you feel rather than just giving him the cold shoulders.
4 Nina is very worried about her husband's illness, but she's putting her brave face on it.
5 Keep your hair up!
6 If you take what they say with face value, you'll soon get disappointed.
7 Having to do homework is such an ache in the neck!
8 I have to tell you a terrible secret. I'll go mad if I don't get it on my chest soon.

49.4 Which idioms do these pictures make you think of?

1 GUILT WORRY   3   5

2   4   6

50 Eyes

The eyes are the basis of a large number of idioms. Note the idioms and their meanings in these paragraphs.

eyebrow   *eyelid*

> I couldn't believe my eyes[1] when I first saw her. She was so beautiful, I just couldn't keep my eyes off[2] her. I tried to catch her eye[3] to say hello.

> As a teacher myself, I know that teaching is not easy. You always have to keep an eye on[4] the students, but sometimes you just have to turn a blind eye[5] if they behave badly. If you want to be a teacher, you have to go into the profession with your eyes open[6].

> Jenny and I were good friends at first, but now we don't see eye to eye[7]. I know the fact that we stopped being friends raised a few eyebrows[8] at the time.

> Could you run/cast your eye over[9] this report and see if there are any spelling mistakes? My computer's on the blink[10] and the spell-checker refuses to work. These reports are important, and I always have to have/keep one eye on[11] how the boss will react to them if they look untidy.

> It all happened in the blink of an eye[12] and no one could do anything to prevent it. It was horrible. But the police officer standing nearby didn't bat an eyelid[13]. Then something caught my eye[14] which shocked me even more.

> Working in such a poor country opened my eyes to[15] how unjust the world is. It was indeed a real eye-opener[16].

[1] couldn't believe what I was seeing
[2] couldn't stop looking at her
[3] get her attention; make her look at me
[4] keep your attention on
[5] ignore behaviour which you know is wrong
[6] aware of all the problems there could be
[7] agree with each other
[8] surprised/shocked people
[9] have a quick look at
[10] is beginning to break down and go wrong, probably because it is old (*to blink* means to close and open your eyes very quickly)
[11] observe carefully
[12] extremely short time
[13] didn't react at all
[14] made me look
[15] made me understand for the first time
[16] an event or situation that I unexpectedly learnt something from

Exercises

50.1 Write a suitable response to each of these remarks with an idiom. Use the keyword in brackets.

1 A: Oh! We're doing 58 and the speed limit is 50. There's a police car there!
   B: Don't worry, if it's just over the limit, they usually _turn blind eye_ . (BLIND)
2 A: There's Petra over there. I wonder if she's seen us?
   B: I don't know. Let's wave and see if we can _catch her eyes._ . (CATCH)
3 A: Are you and Sally not friends any more?
   B: No, not really, we just don't _see eye to eye_ . (SEE)
4 A: Is there something wrong with this photocopier?
   B: Yes, it's been _on the blink_ for a while now. (BLINK)
5 A: Was it an interesting experience working for Social Services?
   B: Yes, I learnt a lot of things. It was a real _____ . (OPEN)
6 A: Did she react in any way when you told her the awful news?
   B: No, she didn't _bat an eyelid_ . (BAT)

50.2 Circle the correct word to complete each sentence.

1 If you want to be a professional athlete, you have to go into it with your eye / **eyes** open.
2 Will you cast your **eye** / eyes over this report? I have to hand it in tomorrow.
3 Erik is so crazy about Margaret. Look at him! He can't keep his eye / **eyes** off her!
4 The events of last night really opened my eye / **eyes** to just how arrogant he really is.
5 I couldn't believe my eye / **eyes** when I saw what a mess they had made of the room.

50.3 Rewrite the underlined part of each sentence with an eye idiom.

1 An accident can happen so quickly you can't stop it. _in the blink of an eye_
2 His behaviour at the meeting surprised a few people. _raised a few eyebrows._
3 You should take into consideration your chances of promotion when taking up a new job.
4 A very strange sight forced me to look as I was driving along the motorway yesterday.
   caught my eye

50.4 Here are some random examples from a computer database containing lines from real conversations. The figures in diamond brackets, e.g. <s1>, <s2>, mean 'first speaker', 'second speaker', etc. How many of the examples use *eye* as an idiom, and how many use the word *eye* in its literal sense as 'the organ we see with'? Use a dictionary if necessary.

1	go into town and get erm an **eye** test. <s1> Mm. <s2 > In town.
2	you er keep an **eye** out for tramps, do you then?
3	In your mind's **eye** how are you going to do that?
4	<s1> So I'll keep a general **eye** on it. And er <s3> Yeah
5	<s1> There's something in my **eye**. There's that thing floating
6	difficult to put that to your **eye**. You also have to have one eye
7	good offer? <s2> Yeah it caught my **eye** <s1> Yeah it's
8	I'm casting my **eye** over this form and I think
9	this year. <s4> Just keep an **eye** out for it. <s4> Yeah.
10	<s2> You'll have to keep an **eye** on her. <s1> Yeah. <s2> Oh my
11	so you're about **eye** level with the monitor.
12	saw her out of the corner of my **eye**. <s3> Her lipstick is all over

51 Ear, lips, mouth, nose, teeth, tongue

A Ear

The association of *ear* with hearing/listening is prominent in most of these idioms.

example	meaning
In my opinion, you should just **play it by ear**.	respond to the situation as it occurs, don't decide what to do beforehand
Do you **play** the guitar from music or **by ear**?	play without music; just by sensing the right notes
I **couldn't believe my ears** when she told me.	couldn't believe what I was hearing
Bill never listens when you tell him important things. It just **goes in one ear and out the other**.	doesn't listen or pay attention; forgets things immediately
Go on! Tell me the gossip. **I'm all ears!**	I'm very keen to hear what you have to tell me.

B Other face idioms: lips, mouth, nose, teeth, tongue

Some literal associations remain strong in these idioms. But remember, these are only guidelines, and some idioms may be less transparent in their meanings.

Main association: Lips are associated with saying/talking.
The company **pays lip service to** the principle of equal rights for women. [says it believes in, but does not carry out]
I promise I won't tell anyone. **My lips are sealed**. [I shall keep the secret / tell no one]

Main association: Mouths are associated with speaking or eating.
I heard about the school **by word of mouth**. Everyone said it was good. [by being told directly]
Those cream cakes are really **mouth-watering / making my mouth water**. Take them away before I eat them all! [making me want to eat them]

Main association: Noses are associated with feelings/reactions and involvement.
Stop **poking/sticking your nose into** other people's business! [interfering in]
You shouldn't **turn your nose up at** 200 pounds a week. It's better than nothing. [refuse]
That new secretary **gets right up everybody's nose**. Someone will have to talk to the boss about it before it's too late. [annoys/irritates everyone]

Main association: Teeth are associated with hard work / determination / struggles.
He achieved it **in the teeth of** serious opposition. [despite]
I escaped disaster **by the skin of my teeth**. [I only just escaped a disaster]
We can't change what's happened. We'll just have to **grit our teeth** and do our best to carry on as before. [accept the situation and handle it with determination]
Joe is **lying through his teeth**. I never said any such thing! [telling a deliberate lie]

Main association: Tongues are associated with speaking.
I was upset by her remarks, but I **bit my tongue**. [remained silent; didn't react]
Her name's **on the tip of my tongue**, but I just can't remember it. [I know it and will be able to remember it very soon]

TIP Where idioms do carry indirect associations with their literal meanings, try to group them in some way, e.g. 'lips and tongue are associated with speaking', as this may help you to remember them.

Exercises

51.1 True or false? Tick (✓) the correct box for these statements.

<table>
<tr><td></td><td>True</td><td>False</td></tr>
<tr><td>1 If someone plays a musical instrument by ear, they can read the notes directly from a sheet of music.</td><td>☐</td><td>☐</td></tr>
<tr><td>2 If your lips are sealed, you refuse to tell other people a secret you know.</td><td>☐</td><td>☐</td></tr>
<tr><td>3 If you escaped by the skin of your teeth, you only just escaped and came close to disaster.</td><td>☐</td><td>☐</td></tr>
<tr><td>4 If a person gets up your nose, you are crazy about them and can't stop thinking of them.</td><td>☐</td><td>☐</td></tr>
<tr><td>5 If you achieve something in the teeth of opposition, you do it in spite of that opposition.</td><td>☐</td><td>☐</td></tr>
<tr><td>6 If information spreads by word of mouth, it is kept as a secret known only to a small number of people.</td><td>☐</td><td>☐</td></tr>
</table>

51.2 Rewrite each underlined idiom with a literal expression that has the same meaning.

1 She said some very hurtful things to me, but I just bit my tongue, because I didn't want to show her I was upset.
2 I can't really advise you on how to behave at the interview. Just play it by ear, and I'm sure you'll be great.
3 The government pays lip service to low taxes, but then puts up indirect taxes without people realising it.
4 We offered him a holiday at our house near the beach, but he turned his nose up at it.
5 He said, 'Do you want to hear some gossip about Tom and Lily?' I said, 'Oh yes! Tell me. I'm all ears.'
6 I wish you wouldn't poke your nose into other people's affairs.
7 The table was piled high with mouth-watering desserts.

51.3 Correct the mistakes in these idioms.

1 There's no point talking to her. Everything just enters one ear and leaves the other.
2 I just didn't believe in my ear when they told me I had won first prize.
3 When I knew how bad the situation was, I just ground my teeth and continued fighting.
4 The name of the village where he lives is on the top of my tongue. Give me a few minutes and I'll remember it.
5 What she said is simply not true. She's lying with her tooth.
6 The sight of all those delicious pizzas is watering my mouth, but I'm on a diet, so I shouldn't really have any.

51.4 Here are four more idioms which are not on the left-hand page. Using a dictionary if necessary, choose the correct answer.

1 My heart was in my mouth.
   a) I was feeling ill.   b) I was feeling anxious/nervous.   c) I was falling in love.
2 Could I have a word in your ear?
   a) Could you tell me the facts?   b) Could I tell you a secret?
   c) Could I speak to you privately?
3 These people just live from hand to mouth.
   a) They steal food.   b) They just earn enough money to survive.
   c) They eat with their hands.
4 The boss was foaming at the mouth when it emerged how much money had been lost.
   a) He was feeling sick.   b) He was spitting at people.   c) He was very angry.

52 Heart

A Feelings

idiom	meaning	example
open your heart	share your deepest feelings	Tony opened his heart to me.
bare your heart/soul	share secret (often dramatic) feelings with someone else	I find it rather painful to bare my heart to anyone else.
pour your heart out	share secret worries with someone else	Imelda poured her heart out to me – I wished I could help her.
your heart misses/skips a beat	you suddenly feel so excited or frightened that your heart beats faster	When I first saw Pat, my heart missed a beat. I knew he would be important to me.
someone's heart is in the right place	someone is good even if they sometimes behave the wrong way	He is a bit rude sometimes, but his heart is in the right place.
have a change of heart	change your opinion or the way you feel	Ben wants to buy the boat before his wife has a change of heart.
break someone's heart	make someone very sad (often someone who loves you)	It breaks my heart to see the refugees on the news.
your heart sinks	start to feel sad or worried	My heart sank as Bob approached.
a man/woman after my own heart	you admire them because they do or believe the same as you	He loves dogs – he's a man after my own heart!
talk to someone heart-to-heart / have a heart-to-heart	you have a serious conversation and express your feelings openly	They had a heart-to-heart and sorted out their differences.
take something to heart	take something (usually criticism) seriously	Don't take it to heart. He really didn't mean to upset you.

B Determination

lose heart
[stop believing that you can succeed]

to your heart's content
[you do it as much as you want to because you enjoy it]

put your heart and soul into something
[put a great deal of effort and determination into something]

set your heart on something / have your heart set on something
[you are determined to achieve something]

know something by heart / learn something off by heart
[memorise it so that you can recite it perfectly]

Paul **didn't lose heart** even though he had failed his driving test six times.

Rowena **put her heart and soul into** a project aimed at helping blind children.

Tom **set his heart on / had his heart set on** emigrating to Australia.

When you've done your homework, you can play computer games **to your heart's content**.

Actors get very good at **learning things by heart**.

Exercises

52.1 Match each remark on the left with the person who the remark might be addressed to on the right.

1 Don't lose heart!	Someone who has a rather unrealistic ambition.
2 Don't take it to heart!	A loved one who is causing you grief.
3 You're a man after my own heart!	Someone who has to give a speech.
4 Don't set your heart on it!	Someone with the same tastes.
5 Learn it by heart!	Someone who is feeling discouraged.
6 You're breaking my heart!	Someone with a secret to share.
7 Your heart is in the right place!	Someone who is upset after being criticised.
8 You can open your heart to me!	A kind person who tries to do the right thing (but doesn't always succeed).

52.2 Complete each sentence with an idiom from the left-hand page.

1 My .... when the handsome man smiled at me.
2 When we are on holiday, the children can build sandcastles
   .... while we lie on the beach and read.
3 Jim used to support the Green Party, but he's ....
4 If you ask Roy to help you, I'm sure he'll .... and the
   job will be finished in no time.
5 It's not a good idea to .... to a journalist unless you
   want your secrets to become public knowledge. (Give three answers.)
6 Your dissertation is nearly finished, so don't .... now.
7 It .... to see my brother making such a fool of himself.
   (Give two answers.)
8 My .... when I realised pay day was still a week away.

52.3 Rewrite each underlined idiom with a literal expression that means the same.

Emily (1) had set her heart on getting a promotion. She had been (2) putting her heart and soul into her work, but had not yet been offered a better position. So she decided to (3) have a heart-to-heart with her boss. Over several cups of coffee she (4) poured her heart out to him, telling him all about her achievements and her ambitions. Her boss listened (5) with a sinking heart. When she had finished (6) baring her heart, he said: 'You're a great worker, Emily, and (7) your heart is certainly in the right place. In many ways, (8) you're a woman after my own heart. But you do need to improve on your people skills before we can consider promoting you. (9) Don't lose heart, though. I'm sure you will make it one day.' Emily (10) took his words to heart and was at first very upset. But then she bought a book called *People Skills and How to Get Them* and decided she'd (11) learn it by heart.

52.4 Answer these questions.

1 What might a boy who is very good at playing the guitar set his heart on doing?
2 If you do something to your heart's content, do you do it very well or do it a lot?
3 If you say that someone is a woman after your own heart, do you mean that she likes you or that she is like you?
4 If you say that someone's heart is in the right place, are you praising them?
5 If your heart misses a beat, which of these might you be: sick, excited, afraid, in love?
6 Who does a teenage girl often open her heart to?
7 Why might a woman have a change of heart about getting married and what would she then do?
8 What sort of thing might break a young lover's heart?

53 Brain, mind, blood and guts

A Brain

If you **have something on the brain** (informal), you can't stop thinking or talking about one particular thing.

If you **pick someone's brains,** you ask for information or advice from a person who knows more about something than you do.

The phrase **the brain drain** is used to refer to the movement of highly skilled and educated people from their own country to another one where they are paid more.

B Mind

idiom	meaning	example
be a load/weight off your mind	feel relieved because a worry is removed	Knowing he was safe was a load off my mind.
have/keep an open mind	wait until you have all the facts before forming an opinion	The PM is keeping an open mind until the report is ready.
have a mind of its own	(of a machine) it doesn't work the way you want it to	My word processor seems to have a mind of its own.
make up your mind	decide	I made up my mind to leave. My mind's made up! I'm leaving.
put/set someone's mind at rest	help someone to stop worrying	If it'll put your mind at rest, I'll phone home every day.
at the back of your mind	always in your mind although you don't spend too much time thinking about it	The thought of having to make a decision soon is always at the back of my mind.
in your mind's eye	in your imagination or memory	In my mind's eye I can still see the house I grew up in.

C Blood and guts

If a film is said to be full of **blood and guts*** (informal), it means that it is very violent.

If something is done **in cold blood,** or in a **cold-blooded** way, it is done in a cruelly planned and unemotional way. It is strongly associated with the verbs *kill* and *murder*.

If making someone tell or give you something is **like getting blood out of a stone,** it is very difficult to do.

If you say you have a **gut feeling/reaction,** you mean that feeling or reaction is instinctive.

If you **slog/sweat/work your guts out** (informal), you work extremely hard.

* *Guts* is an informal word for intestines.

Exercises

53.1 Match the beginning of each sentence with its ending.

1 Getting him to agree to spend money is like   his mind at rest.
2 He's exhausted because he's been slogging   at the back of his mind.
3 I'm sure the doctor will set   pick his brains.
4 I've got that computer game   in his mind's eye.
5 He can still see her quite clearly   getting blood out of a stone.
6 He tries not to think about it, but it's always   cold-blooded.
7 If you can't do it alone, you could try to   his guts out.
8 Crimes of passions are less horrific than murders which are   on the brain.

53.2 Complete each of these idioms with *brain(s)*, *mind*, *blood* or *gut(s)*.

1 There was a large .... drain from the UK to the US in the second half of the 20th century.

2 Knowing that you're going to take responsibility for the job is a major weight off my
....

3 My .... reaction is to trust him.
4 This horrible car has a .... of its own.
5 There is too much blood and .... on TV these days.
6 I can't finish this crossword. Can I pick your .... ?
7 The man was murdered in cold ....
8 I can see my grandmother's face now in my ....'s eye.

53.3 Complete each sentence with an idiom from the left-hand page.

1 The government are rather worried about ....
2 I like both the shirts. I can't .... which one to buy.
3 Don't think too long about the question. Just tell me your ....
....
4 Why do people enjoy films that are full of .... ?
5 Don't decide until you know all the facts. It's best to ....
.... until then.
6 I know you must be worried, but I'm sure we can ....
7 I've had that awful song .... ever since hearing it on the radio this morning.
8 Getting him to tell me anything about his work is like ....

53.4 What do you think is the main metaphorical or non-literal meaning of these words as shown by the idioms in this unit?

1 mind   2 blood   3 brain   4 guts

FOLLOW UP Look up *brain(s)*, *mind*, *blood* and *gut(s)* in a good dictionary. Can you find any other examples of idioms using these words? If so, do they have the same metaphorical meanings as those you suggested in exercise 53.4?

A The body

idiom	meaning	example
be on someone's back (informal)	constantly ask someone to do something or criticise them in an annoying way	My parents are always on my back about doing my homework on time.
you wouldn't be sorry / you'd be pleased/glad/happy to see the back of someone/ something	you'd be glad when someone leaves or something ends because you don't like that person or thing	I'll be glad to see the back of this government. They've been a bit of a disappointment.
could do something with one arm/hand tied behind your back	could do something very easily	The test was easy. I could've done it with one hand tied behind my back!
get/put someone's back up	offend someone	I put her back up when I criticised Americans – I didn't know she came from New York.
stab someone in the back	do something harmful to a person who trusted you	Although she's friendly to my face, I suspect she'd happily stab me in the back.
do something when/while someone's back is turned	do something while someone can't see what you are doing (usually something that person would not approve of)	As soon as the teacher's back was turned, the children started passing notes to each other.
you scratch my back and I'll scratch yours	if you help me, I'll help you	We can help each other – you scratch my back and I'll scratch yours.
know a place/person/thing like the back of your hand	know a place/person/thing extremely well	He's a great guide as he knows the town like the back of his hand.

B Position

In these idioms *back* has the sense either of being distant or not taking the main route.

If a plan **is on the back burner**, it isn't being dealt with now but hasn't been totally forgotten.

If somewhere is **at/in the back of beyond**, it means that it is far from any town.

If you **take** or an activity **takes a back seat**, something else becomes more important.

If you say that something **came/fell off the back of a lorry**, you think it has been stolen.

If something comes **by/through the back door**, it comes in a way that is not honest or official.

C Backward(s)

I had **leant/bent over backwards** to please her [tried very hard]. However, she **left without a backward glance** [left with no regrets or sad feelings].

Exercises

54.1 **Answer these questions.**

1 If your boss is always on your back about tidying your desk, is your desk usually tidy and how does your boss feel about this?
2 If you put someone's back up, has your relationship with that person improved?
3 What sort of thing might children do when the teacher's back is turned?
4 If someone says *You scratch my back and I'll scratch yours*, what do they want you to do?
5 If someone leaves home without a backward glance, are they happy to leave?
6 If doing housework takes a back seat while you are revising for your exams, which is more important – housework or revision?

54.2 **Complete each of these idioms with one word.**

1 My aunt loves living miles from anywhere, but I'd hate to live in the back of
   ....
2 You must have known that a new TV for that price could only have come off the back of
   a ....
3 You won't get lost if you keep with Tom. He knows the mountains like the back of his
   ....
4 Although my hosts .... over backwards to give us a good time, we didn't really enjoy our holiday.
5 I wouldn't trust Mr Girton. He's charming to your face, but he'll .... you in the back as soon as he gets the chance.
6 We'd better put our discussion of plans for the new building on the back
   .... and get on with trying to deal with the current crisis.
7 Smiths must have got the contract through the back .... – I'm sure at least one other company put in a cheaper offer.
8 Amelia is retiring this week and I certainly shan't be sorry to .... the back of her. She's always stirring up trouble.

54.3 **Match each question on the left with the most likely response on the right.**

1 Do you know the area well?	Somewhere in the back of beyond.
2 Was the test difficult?	By the back door, I'm sure.
3 Where is the castle?	She's always on my back about it.
4 Where did they get the computer?	I'll be glad to see the back of it.
5 How on earth did she get that position?	Like the back of my hand.
6 Do you like this hot weather?	It's taking a back seat at the moment.
7 Does your girlfriend like your motorbike?	It fell off the back of a lorry.
8 How's your Japanese project going?	I could have done it with my hands tied behind my back.

54.4 **Rewrite the underlined part of each sentence with an idiom from the left-hand page.**

1 Jim <u>offended May</u> by telling her she was too young to go out with the others.
2 <u>If you do me a favour now, I'll do one for you too.</u>
3 Sue <u>tried hard</u> to give her grandmother an enjoyable holiday.
4 The teacher <u>is always complaining</u> about my handwriting.
5 Let's <u>postpone any discussion of the merger</u> until after next week's meeting.
6 My dream is to go off to a cottage <u>in the middle of nowhere</u> and work on a novel.
7 Joe went off to join the navy <u>without any regrets</u>.
8 Quick! We can leave now <u>while Sasha isn't looking</u>.

55 Long

A Idioms with *long* used frequently in conversation

Ben: Hi Jill! I haven't seen you for ages.
Jill: Yeah, **long time no see!** [I haven't seen you for a long time]

Nancy: Hey, what happened to your plan to go on holiday with Ken?
Rita: Oh, **it's a long story**. I'll tell you next time I see you. [it's all very complicated and difficult to tell]

Bernard: How long do we normally have to wait till they give us an answer?
Malcolm: (laughing) **How long is a piece of string?** It could be three days or three months! [That's an impossible question to answer. Used in answer to questions beginning 'How long … ?']

Karen: But how did it happen? I don't understand.
Laura: Well, **to cut a long story short**, Peter fell in love with the restaurant owner, married her and now he's the manager. [tell the main points, but not all the fine details]

Sandy: Did you write down the names of everyone who complained?
Elsa: Yes, I've got **a list as long as your arm!** [very long list indeed]

A: *What are you doing?*
B: *I think it's time to cut a long story short.*

B Compound idioms

If ...	then ...
a story/lecture/speech is **long-winded** /ˈwɪndɪd/	it's too long and boring
a task or a process is going to be **a long haul** /hɔːl/	it's not going to be easy and it will take a long time
someone has **a long face**	they look sad and depressed/gloomy

C Idioms with *go/come* and *long/length*

She always **goes to great lengths** to make us feel welcome. [makes a very big effort]

He would **go to any lengths** to avoid meeting Christine; he hates her. [do anything he could]

I think Jane will **go a long way**; she's very clever and she studies hard. [will be very successful; rise to the top of her profession]

Helen and I **go back a long way**. [have known each other for many years]

Kyoko has really **come a long way** since she first started learning English; she's quite fluent now. [made great progress]

Note also: I think we should **take a long, hard look** at the cost of all this. [consider carefully]

Exercises

55.1   Complete each of these idioms.

1   My parents always go .... to make any new friend of
mine feel welcome if I bring them home.

2   You've come .... since the last time we played tennis.
You must have been practising hard.

3   Georgina and I go .... I've known her since 1984.

4   My teacher at school always told me I would go .... ,
but she was wrong; I'm stuck in a very boring job and don't earn much.

5   I'd be prepared to go .... to get that job. I've never
wanted anything so much in all my life.

6   It's time to take .... at our personal finances. I think
we're spending too much.

55.2   Use the idioms from exercise 55.1 to make sentences of your own, based on these outlines.

1   Tell a young person just leaving high school who has done well in their exams that you
think they have an excellent career ahead of them.

2   Tell someone that you and your best friend have known each other for years and years.

3   Tell someone that the family you stayed with when you were learning a new language did
everything possible to make you feel at home.

4   Tell someone who plays the violin for you that you think they've made great progress
since the last time you heard them play.

5   Tell someone that you think you should reconsider very seriously a plan you have made
with them to start a business together.

6   Tell someone you would be prepared to do absolutely anything to persuade the owner of a
beautiful flat to sell it to you.

55.3   Which idioms with *long* could you use to answer someone who said to you ... ?

1   Hi! Wow, it's been ages, hasn't it?

2   How long does it take to get a computer repaired?

3   Hey, what happened to you and Hilary? I thought you were going to get married.

4   What happened at the meeting last night? Don't tell me all the details, just the main
points.

55.4   What is the opposite of ... ? Use an idiom from the left-hand page in each answer.

1   a short, interesting lecture

2   a happy-looking face

3   a quick, easy process

4   a short list

 During the next week, each time the word *long* comes up in your reading or when you are speaking
English, note whether it is being used with its ordinary meanings or in an idiom. If any of the idioms
you hear/read are not in this unit, make a note of them in your Vocabulary notebook.

56 Line

A Line as track

Imran knew he **was in line for**[1] promotion last year. However, foolishly, he said something **out of line**[2] at a meeting and that was the end of his hopes for a while. I'm not sure what he said exactly, but it was something **along the lines of**[3] the problems of the company being down to inefficient management. Anyhow, he's learnt that it is not a good idea to **step out of line**[4] – at least not in his **line of work**[5] – and he seems to be **going along/on the right lines**[6] now. As long as he doesn't say anything **along/on the same lines**[7] again – at least not until he's got his promotion, when he can be one of the inefficient managers himself.

[1] likely to get (used about something good)
[2] not suitable, that should not have been said (or sometimes done)
[3] similar to
[4] behave in a way that is not what is expected of you
[5] profession
[6] be doing something in a way that will bring good results
[7] of a similar kind (sometimes in a similar way)

B Lines as limits

idiom	meaning	example
draw the line	think of or treat one thing as different from another	At what point does a child stop being a minor? You have to draw the line somewhere.
draw the line at something	not do something because you think it is wrong or too extreme	I quite like modern fashions, but I draw the line at body-piercing!
draw a line under something	decide that something is finished and you are not going to think about it again	Let's draw a line under this episode and try to make a fresh start.
there is a fine/thin line between one thing and another	two things are very similar, although the second thing is bad while the first is not	There is a fine line between determination and pig-headedness.

C Lines of writing

Drop me a line when you have a spare moment. [send me a short letter, postcard or e-mail]

Reading between the lines, I think he's feeling a little lonely. [I am trying to understand his real feelings from what he says]

It is foolish to **sign on the dotted line** until you have checked all the details. [formally agree to something by signing a legal document]

The bottom line is that children must be protected. [the most important fact]

Exercises

56.1 Complete these idioms with prepositions.

1 I hope I'm .... line .... a pay rise this year.
2 You must read .... the lines of her letter to understand what she's saying.
3 I'd like to design a house .... the lines of a place I read about.
4 I'll help with the play, but I draw the line .... taking a speaking role.
5 There's a fine line .... generosity and extravagance.
6 It's uncanny how we always seem to be thinking .... the same lines.
7 You were quite .... line. Don't do it again!
8 When our house purchase is agreed, we'll sign .... the dotted line.
9 It's time to draw a line .... this sad occurrence and to make a fresh start.
10 Would you mind having a look at my essay plan and telling me whether you think I'm going .... the right lines or not?

56.2 Explain the difference in meaning between the sentences in each pair.

1 A: Jane drew a line under her relationship with Tim.
  B: Jane drew the line at a relationship with Tim.
2 A: David's actions were quite out of line.
  B: David's actions were along the right lines.
3 A: Rebecca said she'd try to drop me a line.
  B: Rebecca said she'd try to read between the lines.
4 A: Accountancy is Jim's line of work.
  B: Jim's in line for the accountancy job at our company.

56.3 Match each statement on the left with the most likely response on the right.

1 Drop me a line soon.   Why ever not?
2 You're absolutely out of line.   It was great.
3 I'm in line for promotion.   So do I.
4 What's Tony's line of work?   I'm sorry.
5 Shall we draw a line under our past problems? Of course, I will.
6 Nick doesn't dare step out of line.   He's in computer programming.
7 I draw the line at going on strike.   That's fine by me.
8 Was my talk along the right lines?   Congratulations.

56.4 Rewrite the underlined part(s) of each sentence with an idiom from the left-hand page.

1 Please <u>write to me</u> as often as you can.
2 What's Natasha's <u>job</u>?
3 What Paul did was totally <u>inappropriate</u>.
4 My dream is to open a school <u>similar to</u> the one I attended myself as a child.
5 Genius <u>is in some ways very close to</u> insanity.
6 <u>Doing enough exercise is of course essential, but too much might be harmful</u>. Where <u>does enough become too much?</u>
7 Let's now try to <u>forget</u> our previous disagreements.
8 Marcus <u>should be getting</u> a new company car this year.
9 We'd like to visit you in Australia, but the <u>key problem</u> is that we just can't afford it.

56.5 Write sentences using six of the idioms from the left-hand page about yourself or people that you know.

57 Act, action, activity

Idioms with *act* have two main meanings, one connected simply with doing things, the other with acting as in a theatre or drama. Idioms with *action* can refer to what is happening or to whether something/someone is working/functioning normally.

A Act

Here, the second speaker uses an idiom to repeat or sum up what the first speaker says.

Josh: The boss saw Jim and Margaret kissing in the office yesterday. He was furious.
Simon: Yes, I heard about it. They were **caught in the act**. Amazing!

Kim: Lisa should fill out her application for university or she'll be too late.
Erica: Yes, it's time she **got her act together**.

Paul: Keith wants to join us now that we're doing well.
Bill: Yes, now that we're successful he wants to **get in on the act**!

Edith: Brian is crying and saying he's ill. I don't believe him.
Yvonne: I don't either. I think he's just **putting on an act** because he doesn't want to work.

Note these other idioms with *act*:

It's always **a difficult balancing act** to please the younger people and the older ones at the same time. [trying to treat the two groups of people equally]

A lot of people think the tabloid newspapers should **clean up their act** and stop destroying famous people's lives. [stop doing something a lot of people don't like or agree with]

Stop behaving like a child! You're over 18 now. **Act your age!** [don't behave in a childish way]

Stop **acting the fool/goat**! This is a serious matter. [playing around / not taking things seriously]

B Action and activity

Note that it would normally be very unusual to find all these similar idioms together in one text.

Normally, the office is a **hive of activity**[1], but the boss has been **out of action**[2] for a week, so everyone's taking it easy. He'll probably be **back in action**[3] next week. He says there are opportunities for huge sales on the Internet and that we should **get a slice/piece of the action**[4]. But usually he's **all talk and no action**[5], so unless he **follows/takes a different course of action**[6] from his usual way of doing things, then nothing will happen.

[1] a very busy place (like a beehive) with people working hard all the time
[2] not been working in the normal way, perhaps because he's ill
[3] be back at work again
[4] take part in something exciting, profit from it
[5] someone who promises/says they will do a lot of exciting things, but doesn't do them
[6] acts in a particular way (rather formal)

Exercises

57.1 Use an idiom from the left-hand page to repeat or sum up what the other person says.

1 A: Ken has been off work for a couple of weeks, hasn't he?
   B: Yes, he's been _____ for a while now.

2 A: Doreen is so silly. She's 31, but she acts like a teenager sometimes.
   B: Yes, I agree. She should learn to _____ .

3 A: Eva is always saying what fantastic plans she has to travel round the world, but she never actually does it.
   B: Yes, she's _____ .

4 A: Bob should go and get a job. He finished university over a year ago and has never had a job.
   B: Yes, it's time _____ .

5 A: I think we always have to try to give the kids a lot of fun, but at the same time show their parents we're giving them a serious education.
   B: Yes, it's a very delicate _____ .

57.2 Complete the crossword.

1		2		3	
4			5		

Across
1 Time to get your act _____ .
4 Don't _____ on an act!
5 I want to _____ in on the act.

Down
2 Don't act like this animal.
3 Bees are busy there.

57.3 Rewrite the underlined part of each sentence with an idiom from the left-hand page.

1 He was stealing a car, and the police caught him <u>just at the moment when he was getting into it</u>.
2 I was out of the team for three weeks with a knee problem, but now <u>I'm playing again</u>.
3 I think it's time we <u>acted in a different way</u>.
4 The film industry should <u>change its present wrong way of doing things</u> and stop making violent films.
5 Everyone wants <u>to be part of the exciting situation</u> now that we are making a lot of money. (Give two answers.)
6 Our office is <u>a very busy place</u> these days as we prepare for the launch of our new products.

Try to follow a particular theme and learn as many idioms as you can connected with it. For instance, *act* gives us idioms connected with the theatre. Look up other theatre words (*stage*, *curtain*, *scene*) and see if you can find any new idioms.

58 Good and bad

A Good and better

Our daughter, Sharon, wanted to be an actress. I used to be involved in amateur theatre and I think Sharon wanted to go one better[1]. Against our better judgement[2], we agreed that she could go to drama school. However, we managed to persuade her to do a secretarial course first – she agreed that this would always stand her in good stead[3]. After completing the course and rather to our relief, she thought better of[4] a life on the stage and decided to go for a job in theatre management instead.

[1] do more or do something better than it has been done before
[2] although we did not think it was a sensible thing to do
[3] be useful in the future
[4] decided not to do what she had intended to do

B Best

idiom	meaning	example
second best	not as good as the thing you really want	If you know what kind of job you want, you really shouldn't settle for second best.
get the best of both worlds	have the advantages of two different things at the same time	Living in France and working in Switzerland gives them the best of both worlds – Swiss salaries and a French lifestyle.
for the best	unpleasant now but will turn out well in the future	It may well be that the break-up of their relationship is for the best.
make the best of a bad job	be positive about a situation that you do not like but cannot change	It was difficult for her to move to such an isolated place, but she made the most of a bad job and slowly began to enjoy it.
be on your best behaviour	make an effort to behave as well as possible	Jack hates formal parties, but he has promised to be on his best behaviour at the reception tonight.

C Bad, worse and worst

The company has been **in a bad way** ever since it lost a major order last July. [in a poor condition]

The situation at school was dreadful last Christmas when a number of teachers were fired and it has **gone from bad to worse** since then. [got even worse than it was before]

I was learning the piano, but I've **given it up as a bad job.** I couldn't find time to practise. [stopped because I felt it was not worth continuing]

If the worst comes to the worst, we'll sell the house and move back to my parents. [if the situation becomes very difficult or serious]

 TIP Use the example sentences on this page as models, but alter them a little if possible so that they describe something in your own life.

Exercises

58.1 Complete each of these idioms with *good, bad, better, best, worse* or *worst*.

1 Learning a little Japanese should stand you in .... stead when you visit Japan.
2 Chris has been in quite a .... way ever since he had flu in January.
3 I didn't want to have a karaoke machine at our party, but, against my .... judgement, I agreed.
4 People who live here enjoy the .... of both worlds: the peace of the countryside, and fast and frequent rail connections with the city.
5 If the .... comes to the .... , we can always walk home.
6 The headmaster warned the children to be on their .... behaviour while the inspectors were in the school.
7 When Terry was made redundant, he decided to make the .... of a .... job and use his extra time by taking a computer course.
8 The situation at the scene of the disaster seems to be going from .... to ....

58.2 Put the words in order and make sentences.

1 else / to / better / Sarah / has / one / go / everyone / always / than
2 to / to / worse / going / be / bad / Conditions / seem / from
3 the / tried / to / best / we / was / make / bad / a / job / weather / The / of / bad / but
4 it / I / I / the / of / her / better / nearly / thought / told / but / truth
5 very / As / he / never / ambitious / second / Mark / settle / is / for / will / best
6 gave / Rose / as / job / up / tried / ski / a / it / learn / soon / but / bad / to / to
7 worst / ask / If / a / we / worst / always / Dad / comes / the / to / can / loan / for / the
8 the / happens / Whatever / for / best / happens

58.3 Look at the pictures and answer the questions.

1 Is the boy on his best behaviour?
2 What might happen if things go from bad to worse?

3 How are the people at number 10 trying to go one better than their neighbours?

4 In what sense is Mike in a bad way?
5 How might he make the best of a bad job?

58.4 Choose two idioms from each of the three sections on the left-hand page. Then write sentences about your own personal experiences.

EXAMPLE: I'm studying English because I'm sure it will stand me in good stead in the future.

59 Ground

The ground, meaning the earth under our feet, is associated with a number of idioms which refer to positions people occupy in giving arguments and opinions. The ground is also seen as a starting point from which plans, actions, etc. can take off, like a plane.

A Attitudes, arguments, positions

Agreeing / accepting ideas

We share a lot of **common ground**, so I think we'll work well together. [things we agree on; similar opinions and experience]

The idea that organic food is better for people as well as the environment is **gaining ground**. [becoming more popular/accepted]

Disagreeing/opposing

The Prime Minister's speech has **cut the ground from under the feet of** the Opposition. [made their position weaker by saying something better]

She was determined to **hold/stand her ground** and not to be persuaded by the others. [refuse to change her opinion/behaviour]

I think you**'re on dangerous ground** if you try to insist that they change the financial system. [hold a view/opinion that will probably offend/upset people]

Changing your opinion/argument

For a long time, neither side would **give ground**, but now it seems they are ready to consider each other's position. [change their opinion or accept the other side's position]

It's very difficult to argue with Rosa; she keeps **shifting her ground**. [changing her opinion/argument]

B The ground as starting point

If someone ...	this means they ...
gets a project/idea **off the ground** (or if a project/idea **gets off the ground**)	help it start off well/successfully (or it starts well/successfully)
gets in on the ground floor	become involved in something right at the beginning (and which is often successful later)
prepares the ground (for some activity)	create a good/suitable situation for something to take place

C Other useful *ground* idioms

I felt so embarrassed I just **wished the ground would swallow me up**. [wished I could just disappear]

Good restaurants **are thick/thin on the ground** in this town. [there are a lot / very few]

Living near the airport **suits me down to the ground** since I travel a lot. [suits me perfectly]

As a result of the media attention, she has **gone to ground**. [hidden, not appeared in public]

This part of town was my old **stamping/stomping ground** when I was a student here ten years ago. [place where I spent a lot of time]

Exercises

59.1 Complete these idioms with prepositions.

1 The Minister cleverly cut the ground .... her opponents' feet by announcing new tax cuts.
2 He got .... the ground floor with e-commerce and became a millionaire when it took off.
3 Good hotels are thin .... the ground in the smaller cities; you have to go to the capital to get hotels of international standard.
4 The project has got .... the ground quicker and more smoothly than we expected.
5 Part-time work suits me .... the ground at the moment as I'm trying to study at the same time.

'Well I think it suits you down to the ground.'

59.2 Use the idioms from exercise 59.1 to rewrite these sentences. Make any other necessary changes.

1 I'm afraid there aren't many good cafés in the town centre.
2 Working from home is perfect for me as I can look after our small child at the same time.
3 If you join our company now, I promise you are coming into it at the beginning of some really exciting developments.
4 Reducing the price now will enable us to get a big advantage over our competitors, because they will not be able to do the same.
5 It's a good idea, but I don't know if it will ever become popular.

59.3 Rewrite each sentence with an idiom from the left-hand page which means the opposite of the underlined words.

1 She let them persuade her and had a meeting with the boss to tell her everything.
2 We have no ideas or experiences we can share, so we need to discuss how we can work together.
3 I think you can quite safely raise the subject of longer holidays at the staff meeting.
4 There are very few English Language schools in the capital city.
5 The idea that public transport is better for the environment is becoming less popular.

59.4 Answer these questions.

1 If a famous person goes to ground, what do they do?
2 How do you feel if you wish the ground would swallow you up?
3 If someone refuses to give ground, what do they refuse to do?
4 Which idiom on the left-hand page means changing your position in an argument?
5 One idiom on the left-hand page gives you a choice between *stamping* and *stomping*. What is it and what does it mean?
6 If you want to sell a new product in a new country and someone has prepared the ground for you, what does that mean?

60 Similes and idioms with *like*

In this unit we look at idioms with *as ... as ...* and *like*. *As ... as ...* idioms make an adjective stronger / more intense, so as *blind as a bat* means very blind / with very poor sight indeed.

A As ... as ... and *like* idioms involving animals/birds

Try to memorise the keywords. They may help you to remember the whole idiom more easily. They also tell you something about what the animals are associated with in British culture.

animal	keyword	example	meaning
bat	blind	I'm **as blind as a bat** without my glasses!	can't see
bat	hell	It must be urgent. She left **like a bat out of hell**.	moving very fast indeed
bear	head	He's **like a bear with a sore head**.	very bad-tempered/irritable
bee	busy	I've been **as busy as a bee** all morning.	very busy
bird	free	When I set off round the world, I felt **as free as a bird**.	very free
bull	the colour red	Telling him not to smoke in here is **like a red rag to a bull**.	will make him extremely angry
cat	bring/drag things into the house	He arrived looking **like something the cat brought/dragged in**.	very scruffy/untidy/messy
eel	slippery	Be careful. He's **as slippery as an eel**.	changes his attitude/position; constantly escapes control
fish	water	As the only football enthusiast in the group, I felt **like a fish out of water**.	uncomfortable because you are different from other people
fox	sly/cunning	I wouldn't trust her. She's **as sly/cunning as a fox**.	very sly/cunning
hawk	eyes	Janet will see you if you use the computer without permission. She **has eyes like a hawk**.	sees everything; never misses anything
ox	strong	My father was a big man, and **as strong as an ox**.	very strong

B Other common similes

There were tents **as far as the eye could see** at the rock festival. [covering the landscape]
It's **as plain as the nose on your face** that she's in love with him. [very easy to see]
Looks are not everything. It doesn't matter if you marry someone who is **as ugly as sin** as long as you love each other. [very ugly indeed]
Your suitcase is **as light as a feather** [very light]. Mine's **as heavy as lead** [/led/ very heavy].

C Other common *like* idioms

I've always tried to **avoid** exams **like the plague**. [/pleɪg/ avoid / have no contact with something unpleasant (*the plague* is a serious disease which kills many people)]
I'm sorry, I forgot to get your newspaper. **I have a memory like a sieve!** [/sɪv/ very bad memory (a *sieve* is a kitchen tool with a plastic net which separates liquids from solids)]
He'll be here **like greased lightning** if he hears there are free tickets. [very quickly indeed]

Exercises

60.1 This list of animals and the adjectives traditionally associated with them in British culture have got mixed up. Put the adjectives into the correct boxes and write sentences using the idioms.

	animal	wrong adjective	right adjective	example sentence
I	bat	free	blind	
2	ox	slippery	strong	
3	bee	sly	busy	
4	eel	busy	slippery	
5	bird	blind	free	
6	fox	strong	sly / cunning	

60.2 Rewrite these sentences with idioms from the left-hand page.

1 I don't mind carrying this box. It's extremely light. The other one was very very heavy.
2 If I were you, I would avoid that restaurant in every possible way. The food is awful.
3 Millie never misses anything you do in the office. She sees absolutely everything.
4 I felt completely out of place with my electric guitar among all those classical musicians.
5 There are hotels completely covering the landscape all along the coast.
6 She got up late and came down to breakfast looking scruffy and messy.

60.3 Answer these questions.

1 Which animal has a sore head? bear
2 Which animal doesn't like red things? bull
3 Which animal lives in hell? bat

60.4 Use an idiom from exercise 60.3 to complete each sentence.

1 He was very bad-tempered, like a bear with a sore head .
2 Her comments were like .
3 He ran off like a bat out off hell .

60.5 Complete each of these idioms.

1 She drove home like greased lightning the moment she heard Patrick had arrived.
2 Don't ask Robert to post a letter. He has a memory like a sieve .
3 Everyone could see what was happening. It was as plain as the nose on your face.
4 Even if a person is as ugly as sin, that doesn't mean that they are not good human beings. We should not judge people by their external appearance.

60.6 Use a dictionary of idioms or another good dictionary to find out which *as ... as ...* similes are associated with these things.

1 a pancake be as flat as a pancake
2 a brush be as daft as a brush
3 gold as good as gold
4 brass as bold as brass
5 a bone be as dry as a bone

Key

Unit i

i.1   1 **by hook or by crook**

	YES	NO	DON'T KNOW/ CAN'T TELL
means using illegal methods if necessary	☐	☐	✔
means nothing will stop me	✔	☐	☐
means I was very determined	✔	☐	☐

2 **at loggerheads**

	YES	NO	DON'T KNOW/ CAN'T TELL
means have a good relationship	☐	✔	☐
means hate each other	☐	☐	✔
means disagree very strongly	✔	☐	☐

3 **pay through the nose**

	YES	NO	DON'T KNOW/ CAN'T TELL
means suffer in some way	☐	✔	☐
means pay a small sum of money	☐	✔	☐
means pay a large sum of money	✔	☐	☐

i.2   1 E   2 A   3 D   4 F   5 C   6 B

i.3   1 My father **put his foot down** when I said I wanted a car for my seventeenth birthday. He said I was too young.
2 Her words put the cat among the **pigeons**; Jim is furious.
3 You'll be pleased to hear we arrived **safe and sound** in Peru.
4 He was lying **through** his teeth when he said he had got a first-class grade in his exam; the truth is he failed.

Unit ii

ii.1   In CIDI and CIDE these idioms are to be found under the following head words:
1 pick (both)
2 earth (both)
3 ground (CIDI); stand (CIDE)
4 knife (both)
5 head (CIDI); bang (CIDE)
6 daylights (CIDI); this idiom is not in CIDE

ii.2   1 *back* and *with a bump* can be omitted
2 either *all* or *the* could be omitted
3 *most* can be omitted
4 *living* could be omitted

ii.3   1 *bill* could be replaced by *tab*
2 *bump* could be replaced by *bang* or *jolt*
3 *stand* could be replaced by *hold*
4 *sticking* could be replaced by *putting*
5 *banging* could be replaced by *hitting*
6 *scared* could be replaced by *frightened*

ii.4 *Possible answers:*

1 **look a gift horse in the mouth** – always used in a negative sentence
You shouldn't look a gift horse in the mouth!
2 **be pushing up the daisies** – always used in a continuous form
We'll all be pushing up the daisies by then!
3 **be on the brink of** – always followed by a noun or an *-ing* form
Newspaper reports say that the company is on the brink of financial disaster.
4 **tie yourself up in knots** – always used reflexively
She tied herself up in knots trying to explain why she had written to him like that.
5 **be man enough** – always followed by an infinitive with *to*
Are you man enough to accept the challenge?

ii.5 1 informal   2 humorous   3 literary   4 old-fashioned   5 very informal
6 formal

Unit 1

1.1 **These two idioms both mean** *feel poorly / not very well:*
feel off-colour
feel under the weather

These two idioms both mean *be getting better after an illness:*
be on the road to recovery
be on the mend

These four idioms all mean *be crazy:*
be as nutty as a fruitcake
be not all there
be off your trolley
be a basket case

These four idioms all mean *die:*
give up the ghost
bite the dust
pop your clogs
fall off your perch

1.2 1 sore   2 bitter   3 itchy   4 warmed   5 pill   6 screw   7 recharge
8 fiddle   9 right   10 sandwich

1.3 1 fall off your perch
2 kick the bucket
3 bite the dust
4 pop your clogs
5 give up the ghost

1.4 1 I've got itchy feet. – Where would you like to go?
2 He's as right as rain now. – That is a relief!
3 He's not right in the head. – I know, Jane told me he was off his rocker.
4 I'm going to tell him what I think of him. – Good. Give him a dose of his own medicine.
5 Dad's a bit off-colour today. – Oh dear, I hope he's OK tomorrow.
6 Failing the exam was a bitter pill to swallow. – Yes, but she'll soon get over it.

Follow up

There are probably a lot of idioms relating to madness and death in English because these are difficult subjects and people feel more comfortable talking about them in an indirect way. As many of the idioms used are very informal, it would be easy to offend someone if you used them in an inappropriate situation.

Unit 2

2.1 in seventh heaven   on cloud nine   on top of the world   over the moon
thrilled to bits

2.2 1 jump for joy
      2 grin and bear it
      3 be floating on air
      4 do something for kicks / get a kick out of something
      5 sour grapes
      6 be on top of the world

2.3 1 The child was thrilled **to** bits to have her photo in the paper.
      2 I felt as if I was floating **on** air as I ran down the hill into his arms.
      3 Why does Marti look so out of **sorts** today?
      4 Don't make such a fuss. It's not the **end** of the world!
      5 Your telephone call has really **made** my day!
      6 Jill said she was on cloud **nine** and Jack agreed that he was in **seventh** heaven.
      7 Why does Mark always have to be such a **misery** guts?
      8 Stereotypically, happy footballers say that they are over the **moon**.

2.4 1 Good news – if something makes your day, it makes you feel happy.
      2 No – down in the dumps means miserable.
      3 Hot-air ballooning – boot cleaning is not something that many people find exciting.
      4 Unhappy – when you grin and bear it, you try to make the best of a situation that you are not happy with.
      5 News of the illness of a close friend. A heavy shower of rain might make you damp (wet), but it wouldn't put a damper on the event.
      6 No one enjoys the company of a misery guts – being with a miserable person can make you feel miserable too.
      7 'Of course, that model is very unreliable!' is the sort of unpleasant remark that someone might make out of sour grapes.
      8 Just as a damper makes a piano quieter, so something that puts a damper on an event quietens it down, makes it less fun.
      9 Quite a lot of the images are based on the concept of happiness making you feel as if you are not on the ground but up in the air.

Unit 3

3.1 These pairs of idioms mean more or less the same thing:
went off the deep end / did his nut
gave him an earful / gave him a piece of her mind
drove him up the wall / sent him round the bend
put his back up / rubbed him up the wrong way

3.2 1 here   2 terms   3 cat   4 went   5 after   6 out   7 screw
      8 wits'

3.3 Yesterday I had terrible toothache. It hurt a lot and I guess that's why I was in a bad temper all day. Everything anyone said seemed to put **my** back up and, in the end, I **blew** a fuse with the person I share my office with. Even when I'm in a good mood, she sends me **round** the twist with her constant chatter and yesterday I had had it **up** to here with her after only ten minutes. I really gave her an **earful** and the result is that we are no longer **on** speaking terms. I know I'll have to apologise for doing my **nut** like that, but perhaps I'll wait a while. It's much easier to work when she isn't talking to me! Perhaps I should give her a **piece** of my mind more often.

3.4 *Possible answers:*

The answers to the questions with even numbers here are fairly fixed, but those with odd numbers are more open. (The answers given below to the odd-numbered questions are those of one of the authors.) Check your answers with your teacher or another good speaker of English if you are not sure whether they are correct or not.

1 People sniffing drives me up the wall.
2 put/set the cat among the pigeons; ruffle someone's feathers
3 Yes, a teacher once went off the deep end when someone flew a paper aeroplane in the classroom.
4 fed up to the back teeth; your blood is up; after your blood; out for blood; get/put someone's back up; give someone an earful; give someone a piece of your mind
5 A friend recently rubbed me up the wrong way when he told me something I didn't want to hear.
6 *I've had it up to here* is usually accompanied by the speaker's hand indicating the top of his/her head.
7 I sometimes give people who make unsolicited phone calls selling things a piece of my mind – yes, I know they're only doing their job, but it can be extremely annoying.
8 blow a fuse

Unit 4

4.1
1 I don't have **the faintest** idea where he is today; you'll have to ask somebody else.
2 The title of the CD has **a familiar ring** to it, but I don't think I've ever heard it.
3 My cousin knows the tax laws **inside out**, so if you want advice on your tax, he'll help you.
4 I can't for **the life of me** think what it was I came into the kitchen for.
5 I saw Tom and Lily together in a restaurant looking adoringly into each other's eyes. **I put two and two together,** and decided they must be madly in love.

4.2 I always thought I knew my computer **inside out**, but the other day it started to crash every time I opened a certain program. I could not **for the life of me** understand why it was doing this, and I didn't have **the faintest idea / the foggiest (idea) / a clue** about what to do to fix it.
I rang the helpline which I had used in the past, and after about 20 minutes I spoke to someone who said his name was Patrick, and that he was there to help me. He gave me some advice which **had a familiar ring to it** from previous calls I had made to the same helpline. **I put two and two together,** and concluded that they give the same advice to everybody, and that it's just a way of getting rid of you. The computer still crashes every time I open the program.

4.3
1 No, that name doesn't ring any bells with me. I don't think I've met her.
2 I'm (really) out of touch with TV soap operas these days. I never watch them.

3 She knows her stuff when it comes to the history of this area. / She knows the history of the area inside out.

4 I got (hold of) the wrong end of the stick and it caused (a lot of) problems.

5 Her name rings a bell. I may have met her.

4.4 1 I **haven't (got) / don't have a clue** how to use the photocopier. Do you think you could help me?

2 I **haven't (got) / don't have the faintest idea** where I left that letter I brought for you. I'm really sorry.

3 I **haven't (got) / don't have the foggiest (idea)** what she's talking about. She's crazy!

Unit 5

5.1 1 Philip: Yes, I think he's **got the message.**

2 Gerry: Yes, that should definitely **teach her a lesson.**

3 Brad: Yes, they've certainly given us **food for thought.**

4 Nick: Yes, I'm sure the whole thing is a **figment of his imagination.**

5 Steve: Yes, it was important to **set/put the record straight.**

5.2

5.3 1 I want to know **where** I **stand.** One day you say you love me, the next day you say I'm just a friend. It's driving me crazy.

2 He spent £500 of my money. I'll never lend him my credit card again. I've **learnt** my **lesson.**

3 I don't know all the **ins** and **outs** of the situation, but I think one of the directors is going to resign. There must be a big problem.

4 I can understand that she needed help, but **what beats** me is that she should ask someone as stupid as Simon to help her!

5.4 *Possible answers:*

Check your answers with your teacher or another good speaker of English if you are not sure whether they are correct or not.

1 I bought a cheap brush to wash the dishes from someone who came to the door selling things. I learnt my lesson – it fell to pieces after a week!

2 I flew with a very bad airline once, just because the ticket was cheap. The flight was delayed and very uncomfortable. I decided not to complain and just put it down to experience.

3 I wanted to be a diplomat when I was about 18. I got some information about the job, then had second thoughts when I realised what it involved.

4 I heard on the grapevine that someone I know has decided to take early retirement from his job.

5 Many years ago I wasn't sure if someone loved me or just wanted me to be a friend, so I asked that person directly to tell me where I stood.

Unit 6

6.1 1 His Internet company has gone **from** strength **to** strength in the last six months. He's making a lot of money now.
2 The flood ruined our old kitchen, but it was a blessing **in** disguise, because the insurance company paid for a completely new one.
3 This new model is not the be-all-and-end-all **of** digital cameras, but it certainly has many technical features that others do not have.
4 Your offer to drive us to the airport makes all the difference **to** our travel plans.
5 Your plan to persuade Lela to join the committee worked **like** magic.

6.2 1 At first we thought the new road would spoil our village, but in fact it **was a blessing in disguise** and the village shops are doing more business.
2 I sprayed the stain remover onto my jacket and it **worked like magic / did the trick**.
3 This is not **the be-all-and-end-all of** cookery **books**, but it does have recipes from 100 different countries.
4 The school **has gone from strength to strength** since the new head teacher took over.
5 Getting new curtains has **made all the difference to** my flat. It feels like a new one.

6.3 1 b)   2 c)   3 a)   4 b)

6.4 1 The photocopier has completely **given up** the ghost. We need a new one.
2 I didn't think I **had the** ghost of a **chance** of passing the exam, but I did.
3 My new motorbike **works/goes/runs like** a dream; it's fast, but so smooth and quiet.

6.5 1 You succeed.
2 We don't use it with the simple tense forms. So we can say 'She's going places', 'I knew she would go places' or 'She'll go places, I'm sure', but not 'She goes places' or 'She went places'.
3 That it most often occurs in the negative, with *not*.

Unit 7

7.1 1 left holding the baby
2 brick wall
3 stumbling block
4 dire straits
5 draw a blank
6 have you over a barrel
7 face the music

7.2 1 Easier said than done.
2 Try not to spread yourself too thin.
3 I wish I hadn't put my foot in it.
4 Getting older is a fact of life.
5 Sarah's mother decided it was time to tell her about the birds and the bees.
6 Children are taught the facts of life in primary school.

7.3 1 dig yourself into a hole
2 be left holding the baby
3 a stumbling block
4 clutch at straws
5 come up against a brick wall
6 face the music

7.4 1 hole   2 blank   3 thin   4 straits   5 wall   6 block   7 barrel

Unit 8

8.1 1 tie up loose ends – finish off final little tasks
     2 come to light – be discovered
     3 give something a shot – try something
     4 get to grips with something – understand and deal with something
     5 make do – manage with something of worse quality
     6 to be on the safe side – just in case
     7 wave a magic wand – find an easy solution
     8 get to the bottom of something – uncover the truth

8.2 1 tunnel   2 wave   3 loose   4 prayers   5 it   6 bag   7 light
     8 fall

8.3 1 I'd like to try that new bowling alley. Let's **give it a whirl** this evening.
     2 I'm finding it quite hard **to get to grips with** my new role at work.
     3 When the business failed, Paul vanished, leaving his partner **to pick up the pieces**.
     4 Some important new evidence **has come / has been brought to light** in the last few days.
     5 I hope that we'll be able **to get to the bottom of** what's been going on.
     6 New medical research **has shed / is shedding light on** the causes of heart attacks.
     7 As soon as I met Joshua's family, everything **fell into place**.
     8 In the investigation into their accounts, a number of errors **have been brought / have come to light.**

8.4 1 I'll wash your car for you! – You're the answer to my prayers!
     2 Let's go home now. – Soon. I've still got some loose ends to tie up.
     3 The job's in the bag! – I hope you're right!
     4 We'd better take umbrellas. – OK, just to be on the safe side.
     5 Can you make do with a pencil? – Sure, that'll do fine.
     6 We just don't know what to do! – If only I could wave a magic wand!

8.5 1 light at the end of the tunnel
     2 pick up the pieces
     3 wave a magic wand
     4 get to the bottom of it

Unit 9

9.1 1 Tim: good situation. He has been freed from some unpleasant task or responsibility.
     2 Sally: bad situation. She has had to take the blame instead of other people.
     3 Carmen: bad situation. She has to do what everyone else tells her to do, whenever they want it.
     4 Fiona: good situation. She has persuaded someone to let her do what she wants.

9.2 1 into   2 down   3 at/on   4 unto   5 to

9.3 1 I think there is **a hidden agenda in** that letter she sent to the boss.
     2 I thought I was going to have to represent my class at the staff–student meeting, but **I've got off the hook / they've let me off the hook.**
     3 She's an awful boss to work for; the secretaries **are at her beck and call**, eight hours a day, seven days a week.
     4 He has **been at/on the receiving end of** a lot of criticism from the press in recent weeks.
     5 They cause all the trouble, and I always have to **carry the can.**
     6 I don't want someone telling me what to do all the time. I'd rather be **left to my own devices.**

Possible answers:

Check your answers with your teacher or another good speaker of English if you are not sure whether they are correct or not.

1 I think there is a hidden agenda in the proposal to reduce the staff in order to make the company more efficient. I think they want us to do more work for the same pay.
2 The Prime Minister's spin doctors immediately tried to make the bad situation sound positive when they spoke to reporters.
3 The school bent the rules and let him join the course even though he was under 18.
4 In my country we are due to go to the polls next year. I hope we get a new government.

Unit 10

10.1
1 a can of worms
2 the acid test
3 a vicious circle
4 in a nutshell
5 on the other hand
6 the other side of the coin
7 tie yourself up in knots
8 go round in circles
9 be called to account
10 won't give an inch

10.2
1 the acid test
2 tying yourself up in knots
3 the pros and cons of a situation
4 putting it in a nutshell
5 going round in circles
6 a vicious circle

10.3
1 In some ways it's glamorous being a pop star. But **the other side of the coin** is that you no longer have any privacy.
2 It's time these petty criminals were **called to account** for their irresponsible actions.
3 I know Bill's a nice friendly person, but, **be that as it may**, he still has to pull his weight in the office.
4 **On the one hand**, I think Janna might have the best personality for the job, but, on the other, Mina has more experience.
5 If he's apologised, I think you should **give him the benefit of the doubt**.
6 It would be opening **a can of worms** to inquire about his finances.

10.4
1 I **tied myself up in knots** trying to explain to Karl how I felt about him.
2 I'd like you to write an essay on **the pros and cons** of working abroad.
3 To put it **in a nutshell**, James needs to produce better homework.
4 Natasha was prepared to compromise, but Alex wouldn't **budge/give an inch**.
5 You need more money so you work more. You earn more so you spend more. So you need to work more. **It's a vicious circle.**

Unit 11

11.1
1 It's a small world.
2 The more, the merrier.
3 It's six of one and half a dozen of the other.
4 How time flies!

5 No such luck!
6 I can take it or leave it.
7 Don't make me laugh!
8 No way!

11.2   1 Get a life!
2 You haven't lived!
3 It's/That's the story of my life!
4 Such is / That's life!
5 This is the life!

11.3   1 It's a lovely present. Thanks a **million.**
2 You won't find it difficult to learn to ski. There's really nothing to **it.**
3 It's **neither** here **nor** there which hotel you decide to stay in – they're both excellent.
4 Let's have a really big wedding. The more, the **merrier.**
5 You **can** say that again! I couldn't agree with you more!
6 He's travelled a lot. You **name** it, he's been there.

11.4   1 It's six of one and half a dozen of the other.
2 It's a small world.
3 How time flies!

Unit 12

12.1   1 B: Yes, I know. One minute she was angry, the next minute she was **all sweetness and light.**
2 B: Yes, apparently they're **like gold dust.**
3 B: Yes, I think he's just **asking for trouble / asking for it** (*asking for it* is more informal).
4 B: Yes, it's **second to none.**
5 B: Yes, she's certainly **a hard act to follow.**

12.2   1 She really gets **on** my **nerves** sometimes.
2 The last President was an **out**-and-out cruel monster, and the new one is not much better.
3 I don't think you should cast **aspersions** on him. He's not here to defend himself.
4 The scientists did some ground-**breaking** research on human genes.
5 She had already upset me, but to add **insult** to **injury** she told me I was ugly.

12.3   1 poke fun at
2 grate

12.4   1 They criticised her very strongly, but she **gave** as good as she **got** and made them shut up.
2 This dining table is just **made** for this room. The wood matches the doors perfectly.
3 Why are you **giving** me such a **hard** time? I know I was wrong, but I said I'm sorry. I can't do any more.
4 We stayed at a luxurious five-star hotel. It was out of **this world.**

Unit 13

13.1   1 never do anything by halves
2 throw the baby out with the bathwater
3 leave a lot to be desired
4 get/jump/leap on the bandwagon
5 a laughing stock

13.2
1 The new documentary channel on TV **leaves a lot to be desired.**
2 My brother **never does anything by halves;** he designed and built his own house, and designed most of the furniture too!
3 He thinks everyone is afraid of him, but in fact **he is a laughing stock.**
4 Yes, I think we should change the system, but I think we should **not throw the baby out with the bathwater.**
5 Five years ago, there were not many companies selling on the Internet, but now everyone **has got/jumped/leapt on the bandwagon.**

13.3
1 She pretended to disagree with everyone else in order to make them discuss / think about things more deeply.
2 No, not nice to ride in. *Rough and ready* does not refer to time, but means of low or poor quality.
3 He claimed he was a trained electrician, but he was lying.
4 Probably not, since it is not as good as people say it is.
5 No. You'd be rather unhappy, since you would be very irritated or exasperated with your friend.

13.4
1 That new motorway project has **all** the **makings** of a disaster for the environment. It will go through the middle of a wildlife area.
2 Zara **made** a real **exhibition** of **herself** in class the other day. It was so embarrassing!
3 The Krona Hotel is a bit **on the** expensive **side.** Couldn't we stay somewhere cheaper?
4 This new digital camera is a **dead loss.** The batteries run out after about ten photos.
5 I think Paris **has** the **edge** over other European cities as a place for a holiday.
6 The government has got a **lot** to **answer** for with regard to unemployment.

Unit 14

14.1 Sentences 1, 2, 3 and 6 are basically negative whereas the others are positive. Notice that the context of sentence 3 suggests the *take less care of your appearance* meaning of *let yourself go* whereas the context of sentence 7 suggests the meaning of *relax completely*.

14.2 1 lid   2 hard/rough/tough   3 insignificance   4 of   5 blow   6 lump
7 balance   8 dream

14.3 *Possible answers:*

Check your answers with your teacher or another good English speaker if you are not sure whether they are correct or not.

1 Yes, I was once left in the lurch when I was preparing food for a big party and all my flatmates went out and left me on my own preparing food for fifty people.
2 A boss once gave me a bit of a rough time when he wanted a lot of work done very quickly.
3 I think nothing of giving a talk in front of a lot of people.
4 I think it is important to make the most of every day you live.
5 Writing a thesis was a big problem at the time, but has now paled into insignificance.
6 Beautiful music or poetry or children's innocence can bring a lump to my throat.
7 I've had to come to terms with the death of family members.
8 I would never dream of betraying a friend.

14.4 1 is/hangs in the balance
2 keep a lid on
3 blow out of (all) proportion

Unit 15

15.1
1 not on – inappropriate
2 one way or another – somehow
3 at the top of your agenda – important
4 over the top – exaggerated
5 if all else fails – as a last resort
6 strike while the iron is hot – now

15.2
1 There's no accounting for taste(s)!
2 You could've fooled me!
3 (Yes,) strike while the iron is hot.
4 (I suppose Smith's) the lesser of two evils.
5 If all else fails.

15.3
1 If I were in your **shoes**, I'd take the job in New York.
2 Asking the Managing Director for his ID was a really stupid mistake to make. I'm sure my colleagues will never let me live it **down**.
3 Improving office morale is said to be high on the new boss's **agenda**.
4 We hadn't intended to stay there so long, but one thing **led** to another.
5 Take your chance now. Strike while the **iron** is hot.
6 I can't understand what people see in the exhibition. There's no accounting for **tastes**.
7 If all else **fails**, I suppose I'll have to go and live somewhere else.
8 Given the choice between watching football or golf, I suppose football is the **lesser** of two evils.

15.4 Check your answers with your teacher or another good speaker of English if you are not sure whether they are correct or not.
1 If I were in **the Prime Minister's** shoes, I'd **listen to what the people are saying**.
2 **Sorting out my study** is at the top of my agenda at the moment.
3 **Speaking to his mother like that** is just not on, as far as I'm concerned.
4 I'm determined to **visit my nephew in Australia**, one way or another.
5 I think that **Sue's furious reaction to my saying she'd put on a bit of weight** was over the top.
6 In my opinion, if you compare **smoking a pipe** and **smoking cigarettes**, then **smoking a pipe** is the lesser of two evils.

Unit 16

16.1
1 be caught napping
2 have a narrow escape
3 safe and sound
4 be led astray
5 by the skin of your teeth
6 be panic stations
7 leave well alone
8 go out on a limb

16.2
1 When David suggested they should come and stay for a weekend, it set alarm **bells** ringing in my mind.
2 The patient's life is hanging by a **thread**.
3 Having to go to work is **a necessary evil**.
4 Why do some people always cut **things** fine?

5 They are on a knife-**edge** waiting for the results of Brian's medical tests.

6 As the building was on fire, he had no choice but to put his life in the firemen's **hands** and climb out of the window and onto their ladder.

7 You'll be taking **your** life in your hands if you make a speech like that to such an audience.

8 I think it would be more sensible to leave **well** alone.

16.3 1 be/go out on a limb
2 be caught napping
3 lead someone astray
4 have a narrow escape
5 set alarm bells ringing
6 on a knife-edge

16.4 1 I suppose that exams are **a necessary evil.**
2 It was such a relief when Ralph arrived back from his Arctic expedition **safe and sound.**
3 You took **your life in your hands** by agreeing to go up in a helicopter with such an inexperienced pilot.
4 The hurricane seems to be getting a bit too **close** to our town **for comfort.**
5 If I were you, **I would leave well alone.**
6 **It was panic stations** before the important visitors arrived, but we managed to get everything under control in time for their visit.
7 The Smiths **caught** the train **by the skin of their teeth.**
8 I hope the other students won't **lead** our son **astray.**

Unit 17

17.1 1 go all out – make a lot of effort
2 be a doddle – be very easy to do
3 go through the motions – do something without enthusiasm or effort
4 be heavy-going – be difficult or tiresome to do
5 pull your weight – do your fair share
6 have a bash – make an attempt

17.2 1 I wish you'd pull your **finger** out and help me move the furniture.
2 Sam didn't like the exam, but I thought it was a **piece** of cake.
3 I'm going to get the job somehow, by hook **or** by crook.
4 Sally could, **at** a push, take over the project for you.
5 The test was as easy as falling off a **log.**
6 Don't worry if you don't win the game – just as long as you give **it** your all.
7 Why don't you have **a** go at repairing the washing machine yourself?
8 Persuading him to do what I wanted was like taking candy from a **baby.**
9 Max will always go out of his **way** to help others.
10 I had no problems using the public transport system there – it was child's play. (i.e. no article used in this idiom)

17.3 1 out   2 through   3 out   4 out   5 of   6 by   7 by   8 from
9 at

17.4 1 Course, you will. It's **as easy as falling off a log.**
2 Let me **have a go.**
3 He is going **out of his way** to make a good impression on her.
4 It was **a piece of cake.**

17.5 Matt, Sam and Sonya are speaking in a more informal way.

Unit 18

18.1 1 I wouldn't be **seen dead** working in a hamburger restaurant. All my friends would laugh at me. I just couldn't do it.
2 I feel duty **bound** to go home and see my parents at least once a month.
3 I've had enough coffee, thanks, but another one of those lovely cakes wouldn't go **amiss**.
4 I think that CD player he's trying to sell is stolen. If I were you, I wouldn't **touch** it with a **barge pole**.
5 It's not **worth** my **while** trying the exam again. I failed the first time, and I'll probably fail again.

18.2

			¹T	²H	I	N	G
				O			
			³L	U	C	K	
⁴S	H	O	V	E			

18.3 1 You're **in luck**. We have just one room left for tonight.
2 **If push comes to shove**, we'll just have to sell the apartment.
3 I don't want to go with a big group of people. I want to **do my own thing**.
4 I got a bill today for £700 for repairs to my car. I'm telling you, **I need a bill for £700 like I need a hole in the head** right at this moment.

18.4 1 if need be
2 take your pick
3 *be dying to* is always in the continuous form (so we don't say 'I always die to meet him.')
4 in keeping with

18.5 *Possible answers:*

Check your answers with your teacher or another good speaker of English if you are not sure whether they are correct or not.

1 I'd possibly give anything to meet the singer Bob Dylan.
2 I'm dying to see a visitor from Spain who is coming to stay at my house.

Unit 19

19.1 1 It's unlikely he'll manage to climb the mountain without oxygen.
2 It's neither likely nor unlikely – all that is clear is that Molly herself now has no control over what might happen.
3 It's extremely likely you'll guess his role correctly.
4 It's unlikely that she'll be able to complete her course.
5 It's extremely likely, it even seems certain, that Beth will come top.
6 It's neither likely nor unlikely that Rob will pass – either result seems to be equally possible.
7 It sounds unlikely that the library will have the required book.
8 It is extremely likely, the speaker is in fact certain, that Green will lose his job.

19.2 1 No such luck!
2 Just my luck!
3 It's the luck of the draw.
4 Don't push your luck!

5 I'll take pot luck.

6 You should be so lucky!

19.3
1 They've been married for so long that they take each other **for** granted.

2 We've done all we can. Now the results of the election are in the lap of **the** gods.

3 Alex is chancing **his** arm a bit only applying to one university.

4 No prizes for **guessing** who got the job in the end!

5 The cards were stacked **against** Bart being able to persuade him.

6 It was touch-**and**-go who would win the match.

7 We could all see Jan's collapse **coming**.

8 Let's go down to the theatre **on** the **off**-chance that we can get some tickets that have been returned.

19.4 *Possible answers:*

Check your answers with your teacher or another good speaker of English if you are not sure whether they are correct or not.

I went to the theatre on the off-chance and managed to get a ticket.

I knew who would win the prize – it was a foregone conclusion.

I did as much work as I could for the exam. Now it's in the lap of the gods.

I ran all the way to the station, but still missed the train. Just my luck!

I went to the newsagent's to ask if they still had yesterday's newspapers. No such luck!

I haven't seen the cinema programme this week, so I'll take pot luck when I go this evening.

Unit 20

20.1
1 He is always the odd **one out**. If all his friends do one sport, he does a different one.

2 When he lost all his money, he still tried to keep **up** appearances even though he could not afford his lifestyle.

3 Sometimes it's better to **keep** a low profile at work. In that way, nobody asks you to do difficult jobs.

4 She **made** a name for herself by being the first woman to climb Mount Everest.

5 He's always putting on **airs** and **graces**, but everyone knows he's just an ordinary person with a very ordinary background.

20.2
1 **Anybody who is anybody** will be at the concert on Friday, so don't miss it.

2 It's not **politically correct** to refer to 'underdeveloped' countries any more. If you don't want to offend people, you should say 'developing nations'.

3 He was voted 'Best **up-and-coming** actor' of 2001.

4 They employed a lot of young people as they felt they needed **new blood.**

5 A lot of the people who live in those huge houses near the beach **are (rather /a bit / very) toffee-nosed.**

6 My boss **is a rough diamond,** but he's a very nice guy in fact.

7 She was **a pillar of society,** but then it turned out she was involved in the illegal drug trade.

20.3
1 You are rising to better positions; you are becoming very successful.

2 They have no home, no money and no job.

3 They are rising very rapidly in the industry and probably making a lot of money.

4 They think they are better than other people, especially people of a lower social class.

20.4
1 a pillar of society

2 a rough diamond

3 a high-flyer

Unit 21

21.1   1 of   2 for   3 down in   4 to   5 at   6 on

21.2   *Possible answers:*

Check your answers with your teacher or another good speaker of English if you are not sure whether they are correct or not.

1 I'm sick and tired of traffic jams.
2 I felt on top of the world when I finished writing this book!
3 The Victoria Falls in Africa took my breath away.
4 I feel on edge if a train or plane I am on is late in departing or arriving.
5 I gave a lecture once about words that are very frequent and words that are not frequent in English. I said that the word 'Belgium' was not frequent (compared with 'France', 'Italy', etc.), perhaps because British people don't talk about Belgium. There were two Belgian people in the audience! I was very embarrassed.

21.3   *Possible answers:*

1 When she told me, I **was so shocked I just stood there.**
2 I need help, I **don't know what to do / how I should react/act/behave.**
3 I had always been **very relaxed and in control in my job, but suddenly ...**
4 I'm writing because **I am desperate / I have no idea how I can solve my problem.**

21.4   1 Meeting her there when I wasn't expecting to see her **made my day.**
2 I'm not sure whether I want the job or not. I **have mixed feelings (about/towards it).**
3 The good news made me **jump for joy.**
4 I got a chance to go to Canada for a week. I was **thrilled to bits.**
5 He doesn't like people using his computer, so he won't **take kindly to** the idea of sharing one.
6 If you're feeling **down in the dumps**, why don't you come out with us tonight?
7 I've **had my fill of** job interviews – six in just two weeks! I never want another one.

Unit 22

22.1   The speaker has a good relationship with Anna, Pat, the Browns and Jimmy, but has a bad relationship with Rob, Jane, the dog and Jack.

22.2   1 I would immediately drop any boyfriend that tried to two-**time** me.
2 Susie has taken **a** shine to her new teacher.
3 Please stay **in** touch with me once you go home.
4 Nita's boyfriend promised to make **it up** to her for forgetting her birthday.
5 There's something about him that always rubs me **up** the wrong way.
6 We try to be friendly, but the Smith family prefer to keep **themselves** to themselves.
7 If you want to leave early, you'd better try and stay in the boss's good **books.**
8 Rana really seems to have it **in** for me today – I don't know how I've upset him.

22.3   1 b)   2 a)   3 b)   4 a)   5 b)

22.4   *Possible answers:*

Check your answers with your teacher or another good speaker of English if you are not sure whether they are correct or not.

1 Traditionally the child will bring an apple for the teacher, but they might try all sorts of other things like helping to tidy up, behaving well in the classroom, and so on.
2 You are confused – although you may not yet realise it.

3 You might pay for the repair and/or buy them flowers or chocolates, or do something nice for them.

4 You can keep in touch by phone, letter or e-mail. I like e-mail best because it is so quick and easy.

5 It rubs me up the wrong way when people say *Have a nice day* when you know they don't particularly mean it.

6 They should be dropped by both of the people that they were going out with.

7 You may be alone, but you are not necessarily lonely (i.e. unhappy) – you just prefer to be on your own.

8 Not necessarily – not in the way that it is if you get on like a house on fire, for example.

Unit 23

23.1   1 a small fortune
2 Big deal!
3 larger than life
4 make it big

23.2   1 Maria is **miles away**.
2 Chairs are sold in **all shapes and sizes**.
3 The new school is a **far cry from the old one**.
4 You can see he's in love. It **sticks/stands out a mile**.
Or: He's in love. You can see/spot it **a mile off**.

23.3   1 She's 40 next week, but she doesn't want to **make a big thing of it**. She'd prefer just to go out for a meal with her husband rather than have a big party with lots of people.

2 For any person in a temporary job, the possibility of unemployment **looms large**, especially in a time of economic recession.

3 The unions are prepared to discuss the problem, but the employers will not **budge an inch**. They say they have made their final offer, and that's that.

4 We have a new boss starting next week. He's a bit of **an unknown quantity** – nobody has met him or knows much about him.

5 I like having friends to stay in my flat, but only for a couple of days. In general, friends are nice **in small doses**; if they stay too long, they always irritate me.

6 We should think **big** when we come to plan the new website. There's no point in having one single, dull page; we should have lots of links and video clips, and as many colour pictures as possible, and sound.

23.4   *Meanings and possible sentences:*

the middle ground: something which two people who are arguing or who disagree can agree on
He is very good at finding the middle ground in meetings when people are disagreeing.

the middle of nowhere: a place which is remote and isolated, and very far away from cities or big towns
He owns a lovely summer cottage in the middle of nowhere, a perfect escape from the stresses of city life.

be caught in the middle: find yourself trapped between two people who are arguing or disagreeing
Jim and Mary were having a terrible argument and I was caught in the middle. I felt very embarrassed and uncomfortable.

Unit 24

24.1   on the breadline   well-to-do / well-heeled   living in the lap of luxury

24.2 1 Bob (So far Anne's business venture has been costly rather than profitable.)
      2 Colin (Both cars cost a lot, but Daisy clearly feels that it was not money well spent.)
      3 Fred (Ed's daughter is extravagant even though she may have plenty of money.)
      4 Harry (Gill has lost hope of success.)

24.3 1 making   2 pick   3 lap   4 fortune   5 money   6 tighten   7 nose
      8 pay   9 water   10 making

24.4 1 live in the lap of luxury
      2 tighten your belt
      3 pay through the nose
      4 spend money like water
      5 a money-spinner
      6 a rip-off

Unit 25

25.1 1 paper   2 mill   3 her   4 step   5 coming   6 rut   7 go   8 sack
      9 shop   10 head

25.2 1 snowed under with work
      2 be headhunted
      3 pull out all the stops
      4 be given the sack
      5 in a rut / get out of a rut
      6 (at the bottom/top of) the career ladder

25.3 1 behind the scenes – hidden
      2 dead-end – without prospects
      3 get the sack – be dismissed
      4 off the record – unofficially
      5 on hold – delayed
      6 pull out all the stops – make an effort
      7 rushed off your feet – very busy
      8 up-and-coming – promising

25.4 1 snowed   2 stops   3 cut   4 hold   5 get   6 climb   7 hands
      8 behind

25.5 *Possible answers:*

Check your answers with your teacher or another good speaker of English if you are not sure whether they are correct or not.

There isn't much of a career ladder in my profession.
Several people got the sack from my workplace last year.
The staff that are left are now up to their ears in work.
They certainly have their work cut out for them.
The shake-up has offered management opportunities for some up-and-coming workers.
My working day is very rarely run-of-the-mill.

Unit 26

26.1

Time	Place
by leaps and bounds	all over the place
drag your feet	left, right and centre
fast and furious	on the spot (when it means *in the same place*)
get a move on	the word spread
step by step	
on the spot (when it means *immediately*)	

26.2
1 Juan is making progress by leaps and bounds.
2 Excitement is at fever pitch.
3 Within minutes the fire brigade was on the spot.
4 The situation has gone beyond a joke.
5 The holiday got off to a flying start.
6 I looked for you all over the place.
7 The film is about two men on the run.
8 I'll take you through it step by step.

26.3
1 b)   2 c)   3 a)   4 a)   5 a)

26.4
1 Yes, because she would be complimenting you on your rapid progress.
2 No, because the speaker finds your behaviour seriously worrying.
3 To hurry.
4 No, it is criminals.
5 You may drag your feet when you are tired (in the literal meaning of the phrase) but, as an idiom, you drag your feet when you are reluctant to do something.
6 Thrillers tend to be fast and furious whereas love stories tend to be much more slow-moving.
7 Yes, because it suggests that it is successful from the very beginning.
8 You can keep a diary.
9 Very untidy.
10 Very excited or angry.

Unit 27

27.1
1 a slip of the tongue
2 taking the mick/mickey
3 lost for words
4 small talk
5 a pack of lies

27.2
1 I didn't know what to say. I **was (completely) lost for words**.
2 Not one word of his story was true. It **was (all) a pack of lies**.
3 I didn't mean to say it; it **was a slip of the tongue**.
4 I didn't men to offend her. I was just **taking the mick/mickey**.
5 It wasn't a very serious conversation, just **small talk**.

27.3
1 She's had a big personal problem. We **should not make light of** it.
2 He told me he had studied maths at Harvard, **but it (just) didn't ring true**.
3 She said she was a princess who had lost all her money and position in a revolution. **That's a likely story!**
4 She has to get up at 5 a.m. and drive 50 miles to work every day. **It's no joke / laughing matter.**

5 I said I thought she should get herself a boyfriend. It was **an off-the-cuff** remark.

27.4

				¹B			
²M		³W	O	R	D		
I		A		E			
⁴C	O	I	N	⁵A	B	O	U	T
K		T		T			
				H			

Unit 28

28.1
1 get a word in edgeways – It's impossible to interrupt her, she talks non-stop.
2 miss the point – She didn't really understand what I wanted to say.
3 speak your mind – He doesn't hide his personal opinions at all.
4 won't take no for an answer – She keeps on asking, even though we said no.
5 (repeat) word for word – She told me exactly what her friend said.

28.2
1 Hilary will never **take no for an answer.**
2 Joss always **speaks his mind.**
3 Sally **always seems to miss the point** (**of** what we're trying to say to her).
4 She **repeated word for word** everything the teacher said to her.
5 I tried to tell her, but it was impossible to **get a word in edgeways.**

28.3
1 The future of the project is very uncertain. No one knows if it will continue.
2 Probably not. The sentence means it is not in her character / not typical of her to help.
3 Small print is usually found at the bottom of contracts, insurance policies, advertisements, etc. We can also say *fine print*.
4 Probably not. If you reply 'That's a matter of opinion', you usually do not agree with the other person.
5 Not necessarily an official language, but a language that people use in everyday business and for communication between groups who have different first languages.

28.4 1 loud   2 tall order   3 beside   4 matter-of-fact

Unit 29

29.1
1 It's the last straw (that breaks the camel's back).
2 Birds of a feather (flock together).
3 Too many cooks (spoil the broth).
4 While the cat's away, (the mice will play).
5 There's no point / It's no good crying over spilt milk.
6 Don't put all your eggs in one basket.

29.2
1 Many hands make light work.
2 Birds of a feather (flock together).
3 Absence makes the heart grow fonder.

29.3
1 **Take care of the pennies/pence** and the pounds will take care of themselves.
2 **The grass is always greener** on the other side of the fence.
3 **All work and no play** makes Jack a dull boy.
4 **People who live in glass houses** shouldn't throw stones.

5 **A bird in the hand** is worth two in the bush.
6 **Birds of a feather** flock together.
7 **While the cat's away,** the mice will play.
8 **It's the last straw** that breaks the camel's back.

29.4 1 Absence makes the heart grow fonder.
2 Blood is thicker than water.
3 Many hands make light work.
4 Actions speak louder than words.
5 There's no point / It's no good crying over spilt milk.
6 A bird in the hand (is worth two in the bush).

Unit 30

30.1 1 mind   2 memory   3 mind   4 memory   5 mind   6 mind
7 mind   8 memory   9 mind   10 memory

30.2 1 I don't think I know him, but his name rings **a bell**.
2 What is the word for it? I can't remember it. Oh dear, it's on **the tip of my tongue**.
3 If I try, I should be able to remember the recipe for you. Let me rack **my brains**.
4 Try not to interrupt his train **of thought**.
5 My son is much more adventurous than I was. At his age the thought of travelling abroad alone would never **have crossed my mind**.

30.3 1 Out of sight, out of mind.
2 rack your brains, on the tip of your tongue
3 push
4 Thinking hard feels like stretching your brain, making it do something that is difficult for it to do.
5 leisurely walk
6 jump
7 carry
8 ring a bell

30.4 1 came/sprang
2 went
3 slipped
4 racked
5 came/sprang
6 jogged

Unit 31

31.1 1 it's early days yet – Someone asks you if you like an English course after only one day.
2 within living memory – Never, for as long as anyone can remember, has there been so much rain.
3 since the year dot – You tell someone about a very ancient tradition.
4 the shape of things to come – Someone shows you a car which is driven by solar energy.
5 on the threshold of – A scientist claims to be on the point of discovering a cure for cancer.
6 like there's no tomorrow – Someone is spending all their savings carelessly.

31.2 1 This car really is **the shape of things to come**.
2 People have been doing this every spring **since the year dot**.

3 A scientist is **on the threshold of** discovering a cure for cancer.
4 I've only been to a couple of lessons. **It's early days yet.**
5 Jim's spending money **like there's no tomorrow.**
6 There's never been rain like this **within living memory.**

31.3 1 **It's only a matter of time before we** discover life on other planets.
2 **At the end of the day,** you can never trust a politician.
3 I never learnt the piano as a child, so I'm **making up for lost time** by taking lessons.
4 **In the short term,** the economic situation looks good, but **in the long term,** the outlook is not so good.
5 This bicycle **has seen better days.** I should really get a new one.
6 Could you use this computer **for the time being** till the new one arrives?
7 It's **a sign of the times** that you can't speak to a real human being when you telephone the bank. All you get is an automatic voice.
8 This milk **is out of date.** I'll throw it away and open a new carton.
9 It costs a lot of money now, but **in the long run** it will be a good investment, I'm sure.

31.4 1 in, b) 2 before, b) 3 for, a) 4 of, a) 5 of, b)

Unit 32

32.1 1 It runs like **clockwork.**
2 We set off at the crack **of dawn.**
3 We were working against **the clock.**
4 I've had enough. Let's call **it a day.**
5 It happens this way nine **times out of ten.**

32.2 1 there and then – The doctor examined me immediately.
2 once in a blue moon – I only see Patrick very rarely.
3 in no time at all – The new house was built very quickly.
4 off and on – Bill plays golf occasionally, but not often.
5 doesn't have a minute to call her own – Paula looks after three kids and has a full-time job.

32.3 1 **from** scratch
2 once **in** a lifetime
3 once and **for** all
4 **from** time **to** time
5 work **against** the clock
6 nine times **out of** ten

32.4 *Possible answers:*

Check your answers with your teacher or another good speaker of English if you are not sure whether they are correct or not.

1 I'd lost the notes for my essay, so I had to start **from scratch.**
2 When I was offered the chance to study in the USA, I knew such an opportunity would come along only **once in a lifetime.**
3 The government should do something to solve the problem of illegal drugs **once and for all.**
4 I see my cousins **from time to time,** but not regularly.
5 Rescue teams are working **against the clock** to search for survivors of the earthquake.
6 **Nine times out of ten** if I buy something one day, I'll see the same thing cheaper in another shop the very next day.

32.5 1 B: Well, **off and on**. (Or, slightly more formally, **from time to time**.)
2 B: No, I think we should do it now, **once and for all**.
3 B: Well, we can try, but **nine times out of ten** he's too busy to meet anyone.
4 B: Well, we'll just have to work **against the clock** to get it finished by then.
5 B: No, I've had enough. Let's **call it a day**.

Unit 33

33.1 1 get wind of something – hear about something secret
2 go to the ends of the earth – do everything you can
3 spread like wildfire – move very fast
4 be in deep water – be in a difficult situation
5 be a drop in the ocean – be an insignificant part of something
6 blow hot and cold – react in different, unpredictable ways
7 see how the wind is blowing – observe how a situation is developing
8 add fuel to the flames – make a difficult situation worse

33.2 1 You'll be fine working for someone like that – he's **the salt of the earth**.
2 Unfortunately, **my advice fell on stony ground**.
3 Unfortunately, her angry words have only **added fuel to the fire/flames**.
4 I think Rosie must be in **hot water** – the boss has asked to see her at once.
5 Lance **is** really **out of his depth in** his new job.
6 Spreading rumours like that is **playing with fire**.
7 **Pluck a number out of the air** and multiply it by 3.
8 The police were unable to **run the escaped convicts to ground**.

33.3 1 The news of their divorce spread like wildfire.
2 I'm between the devil and the deep blue sea.
3 There is no smoke without fire.
4 Don't say anything in the heat of the moment.
5 I hate the way he blows hot and cold.
6 I was thrown in at the deep end when I started university.

33.4 1 play with fire
2 pluck a number out of the air
3 a drop in the ocean

33.5 You may give slightly different answers here, but basically earth seems to represent being practical and natural, air seems to represent vagueness and uncertainty, water seems to represent difficulty and fire seems to represent anger or passion.

Unit 34

34.1 1 D　　2 B　　3 A　　4 C

34.2 1 *White*-collar workers work in offices and *blue*-collar workers do physical work, usually in factories.
2 You are *green* with envy.
3 You are *blue* in the face.
4 It is / You are in the *red*.
5 You are given the *green* light.

34.3 1 I was absolutely **green** with **envy** when she won a trip to Los Angeles.
2 I'm 750 pounds **in** the **red**, and the bank has asked me to pay it back immediately.
3 The **blue-collar** workers are on strike, but the office staff are still working.

4 You can talk to her till you're **blue** in the **face**; she won't listen.
5 If the city authorities **give** the **green** light to the new conservation project, it will begin next year.

34.4
1 I want to see a contract **in black and white**, not just an informal agreement.
2 I wanted to apply for a visa, but a friend told me there **is a lot of / too much red tape**, so I've decided to forget it.
3 My new house has a big garden, but I **don't have / haven't got green fingers**, so I'll probably never do any gardening.
4 She was **caught red-handed** stealing food from the school kitchen.
5 He's always introducing **red herrings** into the discussion.

Unit 35

35.1
1 wide of the mark
2 take the plunge
3 lay/put your cards on the table
4 back to square one
5 when the chips are down
6 play ball

35.2
1 If you play your cards right, you should get an invitation to her party.
2 When the chips are down, you learn who your real friends are.
3 The ball is in their court, so we'll have to wait and see what they do.
4 If you sign the contract, others will soon follow suit.
5 On the spur of the moment we decided to go away for the weekend.
6 The children picked Mother some flowers off their own bat.
7 Going by train rather than bus or car would be your best bet.

35.3
1 Let's ask Pete for advice – he's usually **on the ball**.
2 The government always tries to **pass the buck** when there are economic problems, saying the previous regime is to blame.
3 I'd like you each to tell us why you have decided to do a creative writing course; Marie, would you **start the ball rolling**, please?
4 Applicants all have to agree to the same conditions for the interview in order to ensure **a level playing field**.
5 No one asked him to help – he did it **off his own bat**.
6 If you keep your things tidy, the others may **follow suit**.
7 It is still **on the cards** that I'll get a contract for the job.
8 He's been very frank and has **put his cards on the table**; now we'll have to do the same.
9 He claims he can speak fluent Japanese; let's **call his bluff** and invite him to dinner with our Japanese guests.

Unit 36

36.1
1 a dark horse
2 a party animal
3 a guinea pig
4 a cold fish

36.2
1 get/have/take the bit between your teeth
2 make a beeline for
3 a lone wolf
4 your bark is worse than your bite

5 chase your tail
6 make a (real) pig of yourself

36.3 1 Pat: No, he's a bit of **a lone wolf.**
2 Chris: Busy! It's ridiculous! I try to keep up with things, but I'm just **chasing my tail.**
3 Mike: Yes, he won't give up. He's really got **the bit between his teeth.**
4 Fiona: Yes, I **made a (real) pig of myself.** I feel so full now!
5 Eve: Oh, don't worry about him. His **bark is worse than his bite.**
6 Joe: Oh yeah, he always **makes a beeline** for the prettiest girl in the room.

36.4 1 Big Joe is quite harmless really, although he looks tough. He wouldn't **hurt** a **fly.**
2 I already know about Jill getting divorced. A **little bird** told me.
3 I hate making a speech to a big audience. I always get **butterflies** in my **stomach.**
4 It's a very unusual school. The pupils are **given** free **rein** to do just what they like.
5 I really got the travel **bug** after I went on a trekking holiday to Nepal. I can't wait to go away again.
6 I'd love to be a **fly** on the **wall** when Nigel tells the boss he's resigning.

Unit 37

37.1 1 There's **not (enough) room to swing a cat** at my house.
2 I'll let you know by **snail mail.**
3 Peter **has let the cat out of the bag.**
4 The economy is **going to the dogs.**
5 The office staff were **running round like headless chickens.**

37.2 1 put the cat among the pigeons
2 a can of worms
3 like water off a duck's back

37.3 1 b)   2 a)   3 c)

37.4 1 the bag   2 feelers   3 the law of the jungle

37.5 1 take the bull by the **horns**
(meaning: act decisively, and face a difficult or challenging situation in a confident way)
2 kill two birds with one **stone**
(meaning: produce two useful results by just doing one action)
3 at a snail's **pace**
(meaning: incredibly slowly)
4 like a bear with a sore **head**
(meaning: someone is behaving in a very bad-tempered or irritable way)
5 a **dog's** breakfast
(meaning: a mess; something that has been done very badly)

37.6 I was trying to finish my essay for my English class by the end of the week, but it all seemed to be going **at a snail's pace** and I was not very motivated. So I decided to **take the bull by the horns.** I stayed up until after midnight every day for four days and worked on my essay. I was tired in the mornings, and went round **like a bear with a sore head** all day, but, in the end I managed to **kill two birds with one stone**: I finished the essay and I read a number of important books I should have read weeks ago. My last essay was a bit of **a dog's breakfast,** but I'm hoping this one will get a better grade.

Unit 38

38.1 1 She was looking **daggers** at me last night. I wonder what I've done to upset her?
2 Her last remark was so hurtful, especially as I was already upset. I think she was just trying to **twist** the **knife** even further.
3 I really think you should **bite** the bullet, and go and speak to him.
4 She **stuck** to her **guns** and didn't sign the contract. So they've changed it.
5 You're **jumping** the gun. Wait till we know whose fault it was before you complain.
6 Freddy really puts the **knife** in sometimes. He is capable of saying such cruel things.

38.2 1 You're fighting a losing battle trying to persuade the teacher to tell you the exam questions before the exam takes place.
2 When it comes to the crunch, I'll be there to support you.
3 I'm my own worst enemy when it comes to trying to save money.
4 You'll be in the firing line in your new job.
5 I'd like to have a shot at bungee-jumping one day if I ever get the chance.
6 (If I were you, I'd / I think you should) hold fire before you send that letter.

38.3

TAURUS Someone you thought was a good friend will say something very hurtful today, and later on will *make it even worse / say something even more hurtful.* Stay calm and don't lose your temper.	**GEMINI** Two people you like and respect will quarrel today, and you'll be caught *in the middle / between the two of them.* Try to stay neutral, or you'll risk losing a good friend.	**CAPRICORN** Someone close to you will try to tell you what to do, but it's time you *acted independently / took control of your own life,* so don't be afraid to make your own decisions.	**VIRGO** You've always thought of yourself as a strong, determined person, but someone discovers *a weakness of yours / your weak point* and makes life difficult for you.

38.4 1 b)   2 c)   3 a)   4 c)

Unit 39

39.1 1 It's the best thing since sliced bread!
2 It provides the bread and butter.
3 I was left with a sour taste in my mouth!
4 He had egg on his face!
5 You can't have your cake and eat it.

39.2 1 bitter   2 whetted   3 fruit   4 flavour   5 date   6 cake
7 tooth   8 mouth

39.3 1 have a sweet tooth
2 be the best/greatest thing since sliced bread
3 pass / be past your sell-by date
4 have egg on your face
5 bear fruit
6 make your mouth water / whet your appetite

39.4 *Possible answers:*

1 **Piano teaching** is her bread and butter though she still hopes to succeed as an actress.
2 **The smell of fresh strawberries** always makes my mouth water.
3 **Geri Halliwell** seems to be flavour of the month in the pop music world at the moment.

4 Kate had egg on her face when **she failed to recognise the managing director of her company.**

5 For me **e-mail** is the best thing since sliced bread.

6 I hope that **all our work on this project** will bear fruit.

Unit 40

40.1
1 Airlines **drive** me round the **bend!** You can never get simple information from them when you phone them up.

2 I don't have any extreme views about anything. I'm quite **middle-of-the-road**.

3 I didn't like her at all, and I hope our **paths** never **cross** again, to be honest.

4 It's a good idea to change your job every few years. It's very easy to get stuck **in** a **rut** if you're not careful.

5 This video's **right** up your **street/alley**. It's all about how violins are made.

40.2
1 Well, it's been nice talking to you. Maybe **our paths will cross again somewhere**.

2 That TV programme about birds is **right up your street/alley**. You should watch it.

3 Jim is fairly **middle-of-the-road** when it comes to environmental issues.

4 The photocopier **drives me round the bend**. It always breaks down just when you need it most.

5 I gave up my job and went round the world. I felt I had **got stuck in a rut**.

40.3
1 False. It means they live in a remote/isolated place.

2 True.

3 True.

4 False. It means something is very difficult and problematic.

5 False. It means they are following a wrong or misguided idea or course of action.

40.4
1 It's time to hit the road.

2 The bus is the easiest way to get from A to B round here / in this/my area.

3 The Imperial Hotel has (really) gone downhill. Don't go there.

4 I think you're on the right track.

5 The new rock music festival has really put my/our town on the map.

6 I think my country is at a crossroads.

Unit 41

41.1
1 sitting on the fence

2 getting your foot in the door

3 getting out of bed on the wrong side

4 flying off the handle

5 putting someone in the picture

6 feeling at home

7 burning the candle at both ends

41.2
1 A decisive person will come down on one side or the other.

2 The student wants to work there in the future, and perhaps would like a full-time job in that company after graduating.

3 People often burn the candle at both ends before an exam when they are studying hard.

4 You're more likely to say that something important, something which has significant consequences, is brought home to you.

5 Probably pleased because imitation is said to be 'the sincerest form of flattery' – though in some circumstances people can be annoyed by being copied.

6 You are being honest because you are keeping them informed.

7 You feel irritable all day.
8 They are in an angry mood.

41.3 1 get / put me in the picture
2 make yourself at home
3 fly off the handle
4 as safe as houses

41.4 1 It will take some time before the impact of the new legislation **comes home to / is brought home to** the person in the street.
2 Sophie will make herself ill if she goes on **burning the candle at both ends**.
3 Before you take over the project, I'll **put you (fully) in the picture**.
4 The police think that DNA testing **will hold the key to** proving who the murderer must have been.
5 Jim **got out of bed on the wrong side this morning**.
6 The government can't **sit on the fence** for ever.
7 Rob **flies off the handle / hits the roof/ceiling** at the slightest provocation these days.
8 If you want to get fit, why don't you **take a leaf out of Katie's book** and join a gym?

41.5 *Possible sentences:*

Check your answers with your teacher or another good speaker of English if you are not sure whether they are correct or not.

What's the matter with Melanie? She seems to have got out of bed on the wrong side.
Please make yourself at home while I go and get ready.
My sister's burning the candle at both ends at the moment – she's got exams soon.
I wasn't at work last week. Can you put me in the picture, please?
I love being at my brother's. I really feel at home there.
Why don't you take a leaf out of Sandra's book and get a weekend job?

Unit 42

42.1 1 came   2 on   3 hit   4 find   5 kept

42.2 1 Is Anna Conda really a princess? – I don't know, but she's very upper-crust.
2 I guess he was delighted with the news? – Yes, he was over the moon.
3 So your new project failed after all? – Yes, it bit the dust.
4 Did your long talk with David help at all? – Well, it did help to clear the air a bit.
5 Did your dad enjoy his golfing holiday? – Yes, he was in his element.
6 Is Alfie a very romantic type of person? – No, he's very down-to-earth.

42.3 1 You could feel a sense of fear **in the air** when the planes came overhead.
2 It really is **a breath of fresh air** for us that the company has decided to move to London. We are all bored with working in a small town.
3 Sally **came (back) down to earth with a bang** when the bank manager told her she had spent all her money.
4 Things are **up in the air** at the moment. I'll let you know when a decision is made.

42.4 *Possible answers:*

Check your answers with your teacher or another good speaker of English if you are not sure whether they are correct or not.

1 My father was a very down-to-earth person. He always had a practical solution to problems. Sometimes I think our political leaders are living on another planet! They really do not know how ordinary people live, and what their day-to-day problems are.
2 I felt over the moon when I heard that one of my books was a best-seller.

3   An old friend I had not seen for 15 years was on a cycling holiday and she passed
    through the village where I live, and called in to say hello without any warning.
4   I'm in my element when I'm playing music on my guitar or on my fiddle (violin) with
    friends.

42.5 1   If you are **shaking like a leaf,** it means you are trembling because you are afraid or
              nervous. (Leaves often tremble in the breeze or wind.)
          2   I **slept like a log** means I slept very well/deeply. (A *log* is a very solid, heavy piece of wood.)
          3   If you **go with the flow,** you let events carry you along, without making any decisions
              yourself. (The *flow* here suggests a river flowing along and carrying things with it.)
          4   If it **goes against the grain** for you to say or do something, it means it is not in your
              character, or it is against your basic beliefs and principles to say/do it. (The *grain* means
              the natural lines you see in wood. If you want to cut wood with a saw, it is more
              difficult to cut it against the grain than along the grain.)

Unit 43

43.1 1   It could be both, but the phrase is more likely to be used idiomatically meaning an
              opportunity.
          2   Probably happy because it was easy.
          3   Yes, you are, because you won't be able to go back to how things were.
          4   Cheer them up because they are miserable.
          5   If you're overworked.
          6   To show you the ropes.
          7   They'll probably be annoyed with you – unless they also want change.
          8   Helping them.

43.2 1 same   2 plain   3 decks   4 sailing   5 push   6 doldrums   7 oar
          8 clear

43.3 1   change tack – take a different course of action
          2   know the ropes – be familiar with how things are done
          3   try a different tack – attempt to do something in a different way
          4   learn the ropes – get to know how to do things
          5   be a quivering wreck – be in a weak mental or physical condition
          6   steer a middle course – act in a way that is not extreme

43.4 1   Leave things as they are – it's better not to **put/stick your oar in / rock the boat.**
          2   Everything must seem strange at first, but you'll soon **learn the ropes.**
          3   Finish your course before you go travelling – there's no point in **burning your
              boats/bridges.**
          4   Parents usually try to **steer a middle course** between leniency and strictness.
          5   Sally's very miserable – do you know why she's **in the doldrums?**
          6   The new boy is bound to be feeling **(all) at sea** on his first day at school – perhaps you
              can help.
          7   Things are not working out – let's **change tack / try a different tack.**
          8   I hate job interviews – I'm always **a quivering/nervous wreck** before them.

Unit 44

44.1 1 D   2 A   3 C   4 B

44.2 1   B: Yes, it really **put/threw a spanner in the works.**
          2   B: Yes, he seems to be **back-pedalling.**

3 B: Yes, he absolutely **blew a fuse/gasket**.
4 B: Yes, everything seems to be just quietly **ticking over**.
5 B: Yes, I think we **got our wires/lines crossed**.
6 B: Yes, it's probably a good idea to **give her a buzz**.

44.3   1 in the pipeline
2 get into gear
3 a back-seat driver

44.4   1 It took us a long time to get into gear.
2 Brad is a back-seat driver.
3 There are plans in the pipeline for a new railway.

44.5   1 on   2 under   3 off   4 in   5 over   6 on

Unit 45

45.1   1 hands   2 thumbs   3 hand   4 finger   5 hand   6 thumb   7 fingers
8 fingers   9 finger   10 hands

45.2   1 I think it would be good if you got some **first-hand** experience of working in a poor
country before working for an aid organisation at home.
2 Jerry has **washed his hands (completely) of** the club committee. He was so disgusted
that he just quit, and never wants to see any of them again.
3 That new power station on the coast **sticks/stands out like a sore thumb**! You'd think
they would have built it to blend in with the landscape.
4 Have you ever **tried your hand at** water-skiing? My sister's got a boat if you would like
to try.
5 I always have to have the cookbook **to hand** when I'm trying out a new recipe.
6 I'm too busy to play football every week now, but I really should play occasionally, just
to **keep my hand in**.
7 She **got her fingers (badly) burnt** on the stock exchange. She bought shares in an
Internet company that went bankrupt.

45.3   1 Do you think you could **give** me a hand this weekend? I have to move some furniture to
our summer cottage.
2 If you're the sort of person who is prepared to **turn** your hand to anything, you'll be
able to earn a lot of money; people are always looking for willing workers.
3 I was very pleased when they told me my project had been given the **thumbs up**.
4 I decided to wash my hands **of** the whole idea and to have no involvement whatsoever
in it.
5 If you want to make a good impression at a business meeting, it is a good idea to have
all the facts and figures **at** your **fingertips**.
6 To build a horrible concrete bridge over such a beautiful river is terrible. It stands out
like a **sore** thumb!

Follow up
We said at the beginning of the unit that hands in idioms often refer to ownership, control,
acting and exercising skills. Idioms which follow those ideas include *to have something to
hand* (to have it near you, immediately available), *to be a dab hand at something* (to be
very good / very skilful at something). Fingers seem to touch things. Thumbs seem to be
something noticeable, visible, as a signal of something, e.g. *to thumb a lift* meaning to
hitch-hike. But remember, these are just general guidelines to meaning, and individual
idioms may suggest a different kind of meaning, e.g. *to be under someone's thumb*
meaning to be controlled by them.

Unit 46

46.1
1 get itchy feet – be restless / want to travel
2 find your feet – feel familiar with something
3 be under someone's feet – be constantly in the way
4 land/fall on your feet – be lucky/successful
5 get off on the wrong foot – start off in a bad way
6 be rushed off your feet – be very busy
7 get cold feet – regret a decision
8 stand on your own two feet – be independent
9 keep both feet on the ground – remain connected to the real world

46.2 *Possible answers:*

Check your answers with your teacher or another good speaker of English if you are not sure whether they are correct or not.

1 I usually get itchy feet when the summer holidays start, and long to go away and travel.
2 It took me a few weeks to find my feet in my new job.
3 The dog is always under my feet when I'm getting ready for work.
4 I landed on my feet when I met my friend Pat and he offered me a room in his house. It had been so difficult to find accommodation.
5 I got off on the wrong foot with my teacher and we've never liked each other since the first day.
6 I was rushed off my feet last week, but fortunately things are a bit quieter this week.
7 I often get cold feet after I've made a big decision.
8 I had to learn to stand on my own two feet when I left home and went to university.
9 If I became very rich and famous, I hope I'd always be able to keep both feet on the ground.

46.3
1 I said I would join Jim on the protest march, but then **got cold feet** and didn't go at all.
2 She was **rushed off her feet** in the shop last month, but she's pleased that the business is doing well.
3 He'll have to learn to **stand on his own two feet** now that he's at college and not living at home any more.
4 Mavis and I **got off on the wrong foot** when she first joined the company, but now we're working very well together.
5 I've **got itchy feet** these days. I'd love to go off on a backpacking holiday somewhere.

46.4
1 put your foot in it
2 follow in someone's footsteps
3 keep someone on their toes

46.5
1 True.
2 True.
3 False. They keep you busy / working with all your energy.
4 False. You follow the same course of action as them, for example, you take up the same profession as your mother/father.
5 True.

Unit 47

47.1

A bone of ....*contention*............................

The ....*bare*.................................... bones

```
        BONE
```

I have a bone ...*to pick with you*...

I can feel ...*it in my bones*...

47.2 1 I **have a bone to pick with you.**
2 This book will give you the **bare bones,** but it doesn't go into great detail.
3 I don't think we should allow the cost to become a **bone of contention (between us).**
4 There's going to be trouble at work. I can **feel it in my bones.**

47.3 1 c)   2 b)   3 b)   4 a)   5 c)   6 c)

47.4 *Possible answers:*

I think you should **keep Harold at arm's length,** as he can be a very difficult person.
I had to admit I was wrong. I **didn't really have a leg to stand on,** so it was pointless trying to defend my actions.

47.5 1 leg: the idiom means that something is very expensive
2 chance: if you *chance your arm,* you take a risk in order to get something you want

Unit 48

48.1 1 I **can't understand/accept** how much she's changed since she met Joel.
2 Mary will never **attract admiring gazes** in the way that her older sister does.
3 You'll **find it extremely funny** when you see Bill wearing a dinner jacket.
4 Dick hadn't had time to prepare a speech, but he spoke very well **without having made any preparations.**
5 If I were you, I'd **keep a low profile / be as inconspicuous as possible** until the situation improves.
6 Sam wants to use your saw to build a treehouse – you'd better **put a stop to that plan.**
7 My boss **reacted very angrily** just because I asked for an extra day off.
8 It was the first time that Joanna had talked about wanting to work abroad and her father blamed her new boyfriend for **giving her ideas.**

48.2 1 Mel **screamed her head off** when she saw a rat under the table.
2 When the pilot announced that the plane was having engine problems, all the passengers behaved calmly and no one **lost their head.**
3 I'm trying to get him to give up smoking, but I **am / have been banging my head against a brick wall.**
4 You'll easily pass your driving test as long as you **keep your head.**
5 I wish he wouldn't **snap my head off** when I ask him about his work.
6 Jack and Sue have not been getting on well for some time now, but Jack's rudeness to her last night **brought things to a head** and they had a blazing row.
7 The disagreement over pay **came to a head** at a meeting yesterday.

48.3 1 bite someone's head off
2 keep your head down

3 keep your head above water
4 be banging your head against a brick wall
5 turn heads

48.4 *Possible answers:*

Check your answers with your teacher or another good speaker of English if you are not sure whether they are correct or not.

1 I had my head bitten off by an ex-boss once. It wasn't, I think, because of anything serious that I had done, but was simply because he was having some problems at home at the time.
2 I'd find it hard to keep my head if I was in an emergency situation in an aeroplane.
3 Perhaps the last time I laughed my head off was watching the comedy TV quiz show *Have I got news for you.*
4 Someone tall, dark and handsome might turn my head in the street or someone wearing very striking clothes.
5 Various writers, political figures and pop stars have all, at different times, been criticised for putting ideas into young people's heads.
6 It would depend what its expectations were. It might be pleased that it was not making a loss; on the other hand, it might not be pleased that it was not making a significant profit.

Unit 49

49.1 1 face   2 throat(s)   3 shoulder   4 neck   5 throat   6 neck   7 chest
8 face   9 face   10 hair   11 face

49.2 1 You try to keep a straight face when you want to control your laughter.
2 You put a brave face on something when you try to hide your disappointment.
3 You can be said to be pulling your hair out when you get very upset about something.
4 You make a clean breast of something when you admit to doing something wrong.
5 You may make a face when you are not pleased about something.
6 You take something at face value when you accept it in a straightforward way.
7 You may be told to keep your hair on when you are showing your anger.
8 You give someone the cold shoulder when you deliberately ignore them.

49.3 1 Rose's father didn't **turn** a hair when she told him she was going to get married.
2 I wish my boss would let me get on with my work instead of breathing down **my** neck.
3 You should tell him directly how you feel rather than just giving him the cold **shoulder.**
4 Nina is very worried about her husband's illness, but she's putting **a** brave face on it.
5 Keep your hair **on**!
6 If you take what they say **at** face value, you'll soon get disappointed.
7 Having to do homework is such **a pain** in the neck!
8 I have to tell you a terrible secret. I'll go mad if I don't get it **off** my chest soon.

49.4 1 get it off your chest
2 ram something down someone's throat
3 put a brave face on something
4 tear/pull your hair out
5 breathe down someone's neck
6 give someone the cold shoulder

Unit 50

50.1 1 B: Don't worry, if it's just over the limit, they usually **turn a blind eye**.
2 B: I don't know. Let's wave and see if we can **catch her eye**.
3 B: No, not really, we just don't **see eye to eye**.
4 B: Yes, it's been **on the blink** for a while now.
5 B: Yes, I learnt a lot of things. It was a real **eye-opener**.
6 B: No, she didn't **bat an eyelid**.

50.2 1 eyes 2 eye 3 eyes 4 eyes 5 eyes

50.3 1 An accident can happen **in the blink of an eye**.
2 His behaviour at the meeting **raised a few eyebrows**.
3 You should always **have/keep one eye** on your chances of promotion when you take up a new job.
4 A very strange sight **caught my eye** as I was driving along the motorway yesterday.

50.4 Lines 1, 5, 6 and 11 use the word *eye* in its literal sense, meaning 'the organ we see with'. The rest of the lines use *eye* in idioms, many of which are on the left-hand page. But note the following:

keep an eye out for (lines 2 and 9): be careful and watch for something/someone
in your mind's eye (line 3): in your imagination
see someone (or something) out of the corner of your eye (line 12): see them without looking straight in their direction

If you do not know this last group of idioms, make a note of them in your Vocabulary notebook.

Unit 51

51.1 1 False. It means they can play without music.
2 True.
3 True.
4 False. It means they annoy or irritate you.
5 True.
6 False. It means people tell one another. The idiom is often used to contrast with reading about something or seeing an advertisement for something.

51.2 1 She said some very hurtful things to me, but I just **did not respond/react**, because I didn't want to show her I was upset.
2 I can't really advise you on how to behave at the interview. Just **respond to the situation / act according to your intuition**, and I'm sure you'll be great.
3 The government **says/claims it believes in** low taxes, but then puts up indirect taxes without people realising it.
4 We offered him a holiday at our house near the beach, but he **refused/rejected it**.
5 He said, 'Do you want to hear some gossip about Tom and Lily?' I said, 'Oh yes! Tell me. I'm **very eager/keen to hear**.'
6 I wish you wouldn't **interfere in** other people's affairs.
7 The table was piled high with **delicious-looking** desserts.

51.3 1 There's no point talking to her. Everything just **goes in** one ear and **out** the other.
2 I just **couldn't believe my ears** when they told me I had won first prize.
3 When I knew how bad the situation was I just **gritted** my teeth and decided to continue fighting.

4 The name of the village where he lives is on the **tip** of my tongue. Give me a few minutes and I'll remember it.

5 What she said is simply not true. She's lying **through** her **teeth**.

6 The sight of all those delicious pizzas is **making my mouth water**, but I'm on a diet, so I shouldn't really have any.

51.4   1 b)   2 c)   3 b)   4 c)

Unit 52

52.1 1 Don't lose heart! – Someone who is feeling discouraged.

2 Don't take it to heart! – Someone who is upset after being criticised.

3 You're a man after my own heart! – Someone with the same tastes.

4 Don't set your heart on it! – Someone who has a rather unrealistic ambition.

5 Learn it by heart! – Someone who has to give a speech.

6 You're breaking my heart! – A loved one who is causing you grief.

7 Your heart is in the right place! – A kind person who tries to do the right thing (but doesn't always succeed).

8 You can open your heart to me! – Someone with a secret to share.

52.2 1 My **heart missed/skipped a beat** when the handsome man smiled at me.

2 When we are on holiday, the children can build sandcastles **to their hearts' content** while we lie on the beach and read.

3 Jim used to support the Green Party, but he's **had a change of heart**.

4 If you ask Roy to help you, I'm sure he'll **put his heart and soul into it** and the job will be finished in no time.

5 It's not a good idea to **bare your heart/soul / pour your heart out / open your heart** to a journalist unless you want your secrets to become public knowledge.

6 Your dissertation is nearly finished, so don't **lose heart** now.

7 It **breaks my heart / makes my heart sink** to see my brother making such a fool of himself.

8 My **heart sank** when I realised that pay day was still a week away.

52.3 1 was determined to get

2 working with great energy and enthusiasm

3 have a frank interview

4 told him exactly how she felt

5 with increasing discomfort

6 telling him all her secret hopes

7 you certainly have very good intentions

8 we are similar people

9 Don't despair

10 took what he said very seriously

11 memorise it

52.4 1 He might set his heart on setting up his own guitar group, seeing a famous guitarist in concert, etc.

2 You do it a lot.

3 She is like you.

4 You are praising them a little, although you are also implying that you think their behaviour is not totally appropriate.

5 If your heart misses a beat, you might be all of these except sick.

6 She opens her heart to her best friend, her diary, etc.

7 She might have fallen in love with someone else and she might then cancel the wedding.
8 The break-up of a relationship might break a young lover's heart.

Unit 53

53.1 1 Getting him to agree to spend money is like getting blood out of a stone.
2 He's exhausted because he's been slogging his guts out.
3 I'm sure the doctor will set his mind at rest.
4 I've got that computer game on the brain.
5 He can still see her quite clearly in his mind's eye.
6 He tries not to think about it, but it's always at the back of his mind.
7 If you can't do it alone, you could try to pick his brains.
8 Crimes of passion are less horrific than murders which are cold-blooded.

53.2 1 brain   2 mind   3 gut   4 mind   5 guts   6 brains   7 blood
8 mind

53.3 1 The government are rather worried about **the brain drain**.
2 I like both shirts. I can't **make up my mind** which one to buy.
3 Don't think too long about the question. Just tell me your **gut feeling/reaction**.
4 Why do people enjoy films that are full of **blood and guts**?
5 Don't decide until you know all the facts. It's best to **have/keep an open mind** until then.
6 I know you must be worried, but I'm sure we can **put/set your mind at rest**.
7 I've had that awful song **on the brain** ever since hearing it on the radio this morning.
8 Getting him to tell me anything about his work is like **getting blood out of a stone**.

53.4 These seem to be the basic meanings of these parts of the body in idioms – although some of the idioms have moved quite a long way from these concepts and indeed blood in particular may have several different sets of associations for the English speaker.
mind – thinking
blood – emotion (though is also used in idioms with the physical meaning of blood)
brain – intelligence
guts – intestines or your insides

Unit 54

54.1 1 It almost certainly isn't tidy and your boss doesn't like this because he/she is always nagging you to tidy it up.
2 No, it's got worse because you've offended that person.
3 They do naughty things that they don't want the teacher to see.
4 They want you to do them a favour of some kind.
5 Yes, they are.
6 Revision is more important.

54.2 1 beyond   2 lorry   3 hand   4 leant/leaned/bent   5 stab   6 burner
7 door   8 see

54.3 1 Do you know the area well? – Like the back of my hand.
2 Was the test difficult? – I could have done it with my hands tied behind my back.
3 Where is the castle? – Somewhere in the back of beyond.
4 Where did they get the computer? – It fell off the back of a lorry.
5 How on earth did she get that position? – By the back door, I'm sure.
6 Do you like this hot weather? – I'll be glad to see the back of it.

7 Does your girlfriend like your motorbike? – She's always **on my back** about it.
8 How's your Japanese project going? – It's taking **a back seat** at the moment.

54.4 1 Jim **put/got May's back up** by telling her she was too young to go out with the others.
2 **You scratch my back and I'll scratch yours.**
3 Sue **leant/bent over backwards** to give her grandmother an enjoyable holiday.
4 The teacher **is always on my back** about my handwriting.
5 Let's **put any discussion of the merger on the back burner** until after next week's meeting.
6 My dream is to go off to a cottage **in the back of beyond** and work on a novel.
7 Joe went off to join the navy **without a backward glance.**
8 Quick! We can leave now **while Sasha's back is turned.**

Unit 55

55.1 1 My parents always go **to great lengths** to make any new friend of mine feel welcome if I bring them home.
2 You've come **a long way** since the last time we played tennis. You must have been practising hard.
3 Georgina and I go **back a long way.** I've known her since 1984.
4 My teacher at school always told me I would go **a long way,** but she was wrong; I'm stuck in a very boring job and don't earn much.
5 I'd be prepared to go **to any lengths** to get that job. I've never wanted anything so much in all my life.
6 It's time to take **a long, hard look** at our personal finances. I think we're spending too much.

55.2 *Possible answers:*

1 (You've done very well.) I think you'll go a long way.
2 My best friend (name) and I go back a long way.
3 The family I stayed with when I was learning (name of language) went to great lengths to make me feel at home.
4 You've come a long way since the last time I heard you play.
5 I think we should take a long, hard look at our plan to start a business.
6 I'd go to any lengths to persuade the owner to sell me that beautiful flat.

55.3 1 Yes, long time no see.
2 How long is a piece of string?
3 It's a long story.
4 All right, to cut a long story short, none of the members agreed with any of the committee's proposals.

55.4 1 a long-winded lecture
2 a long face
3 a long haul
4 a list as long as your arm

Unit 56

56.1 1 I hope I'm **in** line **for** a pay rise this year.
2 You must read **between** the lines of her letter to understand what she's saying.
3 I'd like to design a house **along/on** the lines of a place I read about.
4 I'll help with the play, but I draw the line **at** taking a speaking role.
5 There's a fine line **between** generosity and extravagance.

6 It's uncanny how we always seem to be thinking **along/on** the same lines.
7 You were quite **out of** line. Don't do it again!
8 When our house purchase is agreed, we'll sign **on** the dotted line.
9 It's time to draw a line **under** this sad occurrence and to make a fresh start.
10 Would you mind having a look at my essay plan and telling me whether you think I'm going **along/on** the right lines or not?

56.2   1 A: Jane considered that her previous relationship with Tim was now totally over.
     B: Jane would not consider starting a relationship with Tim.
2 A: David's actions were quite inappropriate.
     B: David's actions were appropriate.
3 A: Rebecca said she'd try to write to me.
     B: Rebecca said she'd try to think more deeply about what was meant by the words that had been written.
4 A: Accountancy is Jim's profession.
     B: Jim is likely to get the accountancy job at our company.

56.3   1 Drop me a line soon. – Of course, I will.
2 You're absolutely out of line. – I'm sorry.
3 I'm in line for promotion. – Congratulations.
4 What's Tony's line of work? – He's in computer programming.
5 Shall we draw a line under our past problems? – That's fine by me.
6 Nick doesn't dare step out of line. – Why ever not?
7 I draw the line at going on strike. – So do I.
8 Was my talk along the right lines? – It was great.

56.4   1 Please **drop me a line** as often as you can.
2 What's Natasha's **line of work**?
3 What Paul did was totally **out of line**.
4 My dream is to open a school **along the lines of** the one I attended myself as a child.
5 **(In some ways) there is a very fine/thin line between** genius **and** insanity.
6 **There's a fine/thin line between doing enough exercise and doing too much. Where would you draw the line?**
7 Let's now try to **draw a line under** our previous disagreements.
8 Marcus **is in line for** a new company car this year.
9 We'd like to visit you in Australia, but the **bottom line** is that we just can't afford it.

56.5   *Possible sentences:*

Check your answers with your teacher or another good speaker of English if you are not sure whether they are correct or not.

My colleague isn't speaking to me – I think I said something out of line.
I asked Isobel to drop me a line while she was away.
The bottom line is that we must get rid of hooliganism from football.
I work for an insurance company. What's your line of work?
Reading between the lines, I think my mum's pleased my brother has left home.
I read through the document before I signed on the dotted line.

Unit 57

57.1   1 B: Yes, he's been **out of action** for a while now.
2 B: Yes, I agree. She should learn to **act her age**.
3 B: Yes, she's **all talk and no action**.

4 B: Yes, it's time **he got his act together**.
5 B: Yes, it's a very delicate **balancing act**.

57.2

¹T	O	²G	E	T	³H	E	R
		O			I		
		A			V		
⁴P	U	T		⁵G	E	T	

57.3
1 He was stealing a car, and the police caught him **in the act (just as he was getting into it)**.
2 I was out of the team for three weeks with a knee problem, but now **I'm back in action (again)**.
3 I think it's time we **followed/took a different course of action**.
4 The film industry should **clean up its act** and stop making violent films.
5 Everyone wants **to get in on the act / get a slice/piece of the action** now that we are making a lot of money.
6 Our office is **a hive of activity** these days as we prepare for the launch of our new products.

Unit 58

58.1 1 good   2 bad   3 better   4 best   5 worst, worst   6 best
7 best, bad   8 bad, worse

58.2
1 Sarah always has to go one better than everyone else.
2 Conditions seem to be going from bad to worse.
3 The weather was bad, but we tried to make the best of a bad job.
4 I nearly told her the truth, but I thought better of it.
5 As Mark is very ambitious, he will never settle for second best.
6 Rose tried to learn to ski, but soon gave it up as a bad job.
7 If the worst comes to the worst, we can always ask Dad for a loan.
8 Whatever happens, happens for the best.

58.3
1 No, he isn't.
2 The boy might, for example, be rude to the important visitors.
3 They are trying to have a bigger and more impressive car.
4 He's broken his leg.
5 He might find he can enjoy the sympathy of his friends and the attentions of the nurses as well as the chance to relax and watch TV.

58.4 *Possible answers:*

Check your answers with your teacher or another good speaker of English if you are not sure whether they are correct or not.

I wanted to tell my boss what I thought of him, but fortunately I thought better of it.
I did a course in teaching English because I thought it would stand me in good stead if I needed to work when I was abroad.
I didn't really want to leave the school I had taught in for years, but it certainly all turned out for the best.
I admire the way my friend decided to make the best of a bad job when she was made to take early retirement – she decided to take up painting and also began to write the novel she had always been planning.

The situation wasn't easy in January, but it has certainly gone from bad to worse throughout the year.
Anna has been in a bad way ever since her children grew up and left home.

Unit 59

59.1
1 The Minister cleverly cut the ground **from under** her opponents' feet by announcing new tax cuts.
2 He got **in on** the ground floor with e-commerce and became a millionaire when it took off.
3 Good hotels are thin **on** the ground in the smaller cities; you have to go to the capital to get hotels of international standard.
4 The project has got **off** the ground quicker and more smoothly than we expected.
5 Part-time work suits me **down to** the ground at the moment as I'm trying to study at the same time.

59.2
1 I'm afraid **good cafés are thin on the ground** in the town centre.
2 Working from home **suits me down to the ground** as I can look after our small child at the same time.
3 If you join our company now, I promise **you are getting in on the ground floor** of some really exciting developments.
4 Reducing the price now will **cut the ground from under the feet of** our competitors, because they will not be able to do the same.
5 It's a good idea, but I don't know if it will ever **get off the ground**.

59.3
1 She **held/stood her ground** and had a meeting with the boss to tell her everything.
2 We **have a lot of common ground**, so we need to discuss how we can work together.
3 I think **you are on dangerous ground if you** raise the subject of longer holidays at the staff meeting.
4 English Language schools **are thick on the ground** in the capital city.
5 The idea that public transport is better for the environment is **gaining ground**.

59.4 *Possible answers:*
1 They do not appear in public and hide from the media.
2 So embarrassed you wish you could disappear / were invisible.
3 They refuse to change their position or opinion in a dispute/argument.
4 To shift your ground.
5 (My) stamping/stomping ground. It means a place where you spend a lot of time.
6 It means that they have probably been to that country and made useful contacts for you or informed people about your company, so that it will be easier for you to launch your product.

Unit 60

60.1

	animal	right adjective	example sentence
1	bat	blind	I'm as blind as a bat without my glasses.
2	ox	strong	My brother is as strong as an ox.
3	bee	busy	I was as busy as a bee all last week.
4	eel	slippery	She's as slippery as an eel. You'll never get a direct answer from her.
5	bird	free	I felt as free as a bird when I left university.
6	fox	sly	He's as sly as a fox. Don't trust him. He'll find a way of getting what he wants.

60.2
1 I don't mind carrying this box. It's **as light as a feather**. The other one was **as heavy as lead**.
2 If I were you, I would avoid that restaurant **like the plague**. The food is awful.
3 Millie never misses anything you do in the office. She **has eyes like a hawk**.
4 I felt **like a fish out of water** with my electric guitar among all those classical musicians.
5 There are hotels **as far as the eye can see** all along the coast.
6 She got up late and came down to breakfast looking **like something the cat brought/dragged in**.

60.3
1 a bear 2 a bull 3 a bat

60.4
1 He was very bad-tempered, like **a bear with a sore head**.
2 Her comments were like **a red rag to a bull**.
3 He ran off like **a bat out of hell**.

60.5
1 greased 2 sieve 3 plain 4 ugly

60.6
1 as flat as a pancake, e.g. *The landscape is as flat as a pancake.*
2 as daft as a brush (*daft* means silly; used of people)
3 as good as gold (*good* here refers to someone's behaviour)
4 as bold as brass (*bold* here means cheeky/without any inhibitions)
5 as dry as a bone, e.g. *I must water my plant. The soil's as dry as a bone.*

Phonetic symbols

Vowel sounds

Symbol	Examples		
/iː/	sleep	me	
/i/	happy	recipe	
/ɪ/	pin	dinner	
/ʊ/	foot	could	pull
/uː/	do	shoe	through
/e/	red	head	said
/ə/	arrive	father	colour
/ɜː/	turn	bird	work
/ɔː/	sort	thought	walk
/æ/	cat	black	
/ʌ/	sun	enough	wonder
/ɒ/	got	watch	sock
/ɑː/	part	heart	laugh
/eɪ/	name	late	aim
/aɪ/	my	idea	time
/ɔɪ/	boy	noise	
/eə/	pair	where	bear
/ɪə/	hear	beer	
/əʊ/	go	home	show
/aʊ/	out	cow	
/ʊə/	pure	poor	

Consonant sounds

Symbol	Examples		
/p/	put		
/b/	book		
/t/	take		
/d/	dog		
/k/	car	kick	
/g/	go	guarantee	
/tʃ/	catch	church	
/dʒ/	age	lounge	
/f/	for	cough	
/v/	love	vehicle	
/θ/	thick	path	
/ð/	this	mother	
/s/	since	rice	
/z/	zoo	houses	
/ʃ/	shop	sugar	machine
/ʒ/	pleasure	usual	vision
/h/	hear	hotel	
/m/	make		
/n/	name	now	
/ŋ/	bring		
/l/	look	while	
/r/	road		
/j/	young		
/w/	wear		

Index

blood and guts 53
be after sb's **blood** 3
be out for **blood** 3
blue **blood** 34
get **blood** out of a stone 53
in cold **blood** 53
new **blood** 20
sb's **blood** is up 3
blow a fuse/gasket 3, 44
blow hot and cold 33
blow sth out of (all) proportion 14
see how / which way the wind is **blowing** 33
blue blood 34
blue-collar 34
between the devil and the deep **blue** sea 33
once in a **blue** moon 32
out of the **blue** i, 42
until you are **blue** in the face 34
call sb's **bluff** 35
be in the same **boat** 43
miss the **boat** 43
push the **boat** out 43
rock the **boat** 43
burn your **boats**/bridges 38, 43
as **bold** as brass 60
a **bone** of contention 47
be as dry as a **bone** i, 60
have a **bone** to pick with sb 47
I (can) feel it in my **bones** ii, 47
the bare **bones** 47
take a leaf out of sb's **book** 41
be in sb's good **books** 22
burn the candle at **both** ends 41
the best of **both** worlds 58
at the **bottom** of the (career) ladder 25
be/hit rock **bottom** 42
get to the **bottom** of 8
the **bottom** line 56
be duty **bound** to do sth 18
by/in leaps and **bounds** 26
a **brain** drain 53
have sth on the **brain** 53
pick sb's **brains** 53
rack your **brains** 30
put the **brakes** on 44
as bold as **brass** 60
put a **brave** face on sth 49
sb's **bread** and butter 39
the best/greatest thing since sliced **bread** 39
be/live on the **breadline** 24
break sb's heart 52
a dog's **breakfast** 37
make a clean **breast** of it 49
a **breath** of fresh air 42
in the same **breath** 27
take your **breath** away 21
breathe down sb's neck 49
be banging/hitting your head against a **brick** wall ii, 48
come up against a **brick** wall 7

burn your **bridges**/boats 38, 43
bring a lump to your throat 14
bring sth home to sb 41
bring sth to a head 48
bring sth to light 8
be on the **brink** of sth ii
be **brought**/called to account 10
look like something the cat **brought**/dragged in 60
be as daft as a **brush** 60
pass the **buck** i, 35
kick the **bucket** 1
not **budge**/give an inch 10, 23
the travel **bug** 36
be like a red rag to a **bull** 60
take the **bull** by the horns 37
bite the **bullet** 38
come (back) down to earth with a **bump**/bang/ jolt ii
burn the candle at both ends 41
burn your boats/bridges 38, 43
be on the back **burner** 54
get/have your fingers **burned**/burnt 45
be as **busy** as a bee 60
sb's bread and **butter** 39
have **butterflies** in your stomach 36
give sb a **buzz** 44
be a piece of **cake** 17
have your **cake** and eat it 39
the icing on the **cake** 39
call it a day 32
call sb's bluff 35
call the shots 38
be at sb's beck and **call** 9
not have a minute to **call** your own 32
be **called**/brought to account 10
cool, **calm** and collected i, 21
a **can** of worms 10, 37
carry the **can** 9
can't for the life of me 4
burn the **candle** at both ends 41
be as easy as taking **candy** from a baby 17
be on the **cards** 35
lay/put your **cards** on the table 35
play your **cards** right 35
the **cards** are stacked against you 19
take **care** of the pence/pennies 29
career ladder 25
at the bottom of the (**career**) ladder 25
at the top of the (**career**) ladder 25
climb to the top of the **career** ladder 25
carry the can 9
a basket **case** 1
cast aspersions on 12
cast/run your eye over 50
let the **cat** out of the bag ii, 37
look like something the **cat** brought/dragged in 60
not (enough) room to swing a **cat** 37
put/send the **cat** among the pigeons i, 3, 37

While the **cat's** away, the mice will play. 29
catch sb in the act 57
catch sb red-handed 34
catch sb's eye 50
caught in the middle 23
be **caught** in the crossfire 38
be **caught** napping 16
hit the **ceiling**/roof 41
left, right and **centre** 26
chance your arm 19, 47
not have the ghost of a **chance** 6
change hands 45
change tack 43
a **change** of heart 52
chase your tail 36
get it off your **chest** 49
run round like a headless **chicken** 37
be **child's** play 17
a **chink** in your armour 38
have a **chip** on your shoulder 47
when the **chips** are down 35
a vicious **circle** 10
go round in **circles** 10
clean up your act 57
make a **clean** breast of it 49
clear the air 42
clear the decks 43
loud and **clear** 28
steer **clear** of 43
climb to the top of the career ladder 25
work against the **clock** 32
go/run/work like **clockwork** 32
pop your **clogs** 1
be too **close** for comfort 16
sail **close** to the wind 43
be on **cloud** nine 2
not have a **clue** 4
clutch at straws 7
the other side of the **coin** 10
to **coin** a phrase 27
cold-blooded 53
a **cold** fish 36
blow hot and **cold** 33
get **cold** feet 46
give sb the **cold** shoulder 47, 49
in **cold** blood 53
pour **cold** water on sth 33
cool, calm and **collected** i, 21
come to light 8
come (back) down to earth with a bang/bump/
  jolt ii, 42
come a long way 55
come down on one side or the other 41
come home to you 41
come to a head 48
come to terms with 14
come up against a brick wall 7
come/spring to mind 30
the shape of things to **come** 31
if push **comes** to shove 18

if the worst **comes** to the worst 58
if/when it **comes** to the crunch 38
be too **close** for comfort 16
see sth **coming** (a mile off) 19
commit sth to memory 30
common ground 59
a foregone **conclusion** 19
the pros and **cons** i, 10
to your heart's **content** 52
a bone of **contention** 47
too many **cooks** 29
cool, calm and collected i, 21
see sth out of the **corner** of your eye 50
politically **correct** 20
cost (sb) an arm and a leg 47
follow/take a **course** of action 57
steer a middle **course** 43
the ball is in your **court** 35
at the **crack** of dawn 32
not be all it's **cracked** up to be 13
by hook or by **crook** i, 17
cross your fingers 45
cross your mind 30
at **cross**-purposes 22
sb's paths **cross** 40
get your lines/wires **crossed** 44
keep your fingers **crossed** 45
be caught in the **crossfire** 38
at a **crossroads** 40
when it comes to the **crunch** 38
a shoulder to **cry** on 47
be a far **cry** from sth 23
It's no good / There's no point **crying** over spilt
  milk. 29
as **cunning**/sly as a fox 60
cut a long story short i, 55
cut the ground from under sb's feet 59
cut things fine 16
have your work **cut** out 25
be a **dab** hand 45
be as **daft** as a brush 60
look **daggers** at 38
be pushing up (the) **daisies** ii
put a **dampener**/damper on 2
on **dangerous** ground 59
a **dark** horse 36
be in the **dark** 42
keep sb in the **dark** 42
be past / pass your sell-by **date** 39
at the crack of **dawn** 32
An apple a **day** keeps the doctor away. ii
at the end of the **day** 31
call it a **day** 32
make your **day** 2, 21
frighten/scare the (living) **daylights** out of ii
have seen better **days** 31
it's early **days** (yet) 31
a **dead** end 40
be a **dead** loss 13
would not be seen **dead** 18

go with the flow 42
go/get beyond a joke 26
go/get from A to B 40
go/work like a dream 6
go/run/work like clockwork 32
be on the go 25
have a go at 17
let yourself go 14
make a go of 6
not go amiss 18
act the goat/fool i, 57
be in the lap of the gods 19
your mind goes blank 30
be as good as gold 60
like gold dust 12
It's no good / There's no point crying over spilt
    milk. 29
be as good as gold 60
be in sb's good books 22
give as good as you get 12
stand sb in good stead 58
airs and graces 20
go against the grain 42
take sb/sth for granted 19
sour grapes 2
hear sth on/through the grapevine 5
the grass is always greener 29
grate/get on sb's nerves 12
like greased lightning 60
the greatest/best thing since sliced bread 39
green belt 34
be green with envy 34
give sth the green light 34
have green fingers 34, 45
the grass is always greener 29
a grey area 34
grin and bear it 2
have an axe to grind 38
get to grips with 8
grit your teeth 51
ground-breaking 12
be thick/thin on the ground 59
common ground 59
cut the ground from under sb's feet 59
fall on stony ground 33
gain ground 59
get (sth) off the ground 59
get in on the ground floor 59
give ground 59
go to ground 59
have/keep both/your feet on the ground 46
hold/stand your ground ii, 59
on dangerous ground 59
prepare the ground 59
run to ground 33
sb's stamping/stomping ground 59
shift your ground 59
suit sb down to the ground 59
the middle ground 23
wish the ground would swallow you up 59

Absence makes the heart grow fonder. 29
no prizes for guessing sth 19
a guinea pig 36
jump the gun 38
stick to your guns 38
a gut feeling/reaction 53
a misery guts 2
blood and guts 53
slog/sweat/work your guts out 53
have had it up to here 3
Keep your hair on! 49
not turn a hair 49
pull/tear your hair out 49
six of one and half a dozen of the other 11
never/not do anything/things by halves 13
give sb a hand 45
a bird in the hand 29
be a dab hand 45
could do sth with one hand/arm tied behind
    your back 54
first hand 45
get out of hand 45
give sb a free hand 45
keep your hand in 45
know sth like the back of your hand 54
live (from) hand to mouth 51
on the one hand 10
on the other hand 10
the left hand doesn't know what the right hand
    is doing i
to hand 45
try your hand at sth 45
turn your hand to sth 45
fly off the handle 41
Many hands make light work. 29
change hands 45
have your hands full 25, 45
take the law into your own hands 9
take your life into your hands 16
wash your hands of sb/sth 45
your life is in sb's hands 16
hang by a thread 16
hang/be in the balance 14
a question mark (hanging) over 28
hard/hot on the heels of sth 46
be a hard/tough act to follow 12
give sb a hard/rough/tough time 12, 14
take a long, hard look at sth 55
a long haul 55
have a bash 17
have a bone to pick with sb 47
have a chip on your shoulder 47
have a familiar ring (to it) 4
have a go at 17
have a lot of time for sb 31
have a lot to answer for 13
have a mind of its own 53
have a screw loose 1
have a shot at 38
have a soft spot for sb 22

have a sweet tooth 39
have a word in sb's ear 51
have all the makings of 13
have an axe to grind 38
have butterflies in your stomach 36
have egg on your face 39
have eyes like a hawk 60
have green fingers 34, 45
have had it up to here 3
have it in for sb 22
have it out with sb 22
have itchy feet 1
have mixed feelings 21
have sb over a barrel 7
have second thoughts i, 5
have seen better days 31
have sth on the brain 53
have the edge over 13
have your cake and eat it 39
have your fill of 21
have your hands full 25, 45
have your heart set on sth 52
have your work cut out 25
have/get itchy feet 1, 46
have/get your fingers burned/burnt 45
have/get/take the bit between your teeth 36
have/keep an open mind 53
have/keep one eye on 50
have/keep both/your feet on the ground 46
have/throw a fit 3
not have a clue 4
not have a leg to stand on 47
not have the faintest idea 4
not have the foggiest (idea) 4
not have the ghost of a chance 6
have eyes like a hawk 60
be headhunted 25
be banging/hitting your head against a brick
    wall ii, 48
be like a bear with a sore head 37, 60
bite sb's head off 48
bring sth to a head 48
come to a head 48
get your head (a)round 48
keep your head 48
keep your head above water 48
keep your head down 48
knock sth on the head 48
laugh your head off 48
lose your head 48
need sth like you need a hole in the head 18
not be right in the head 1
off the top of your head 48
put ideas into sb's head 48
scream your head off 48
shout your head off 48
run round like a headless chicken 37
turn heads 48
hear sth on/through the grapevine 5
Absence makes the heart grow fonder. 29

a change of heart 52
a man/woman after your own heart 52
bare your heart/soul 52
break sb's heart 52
have your heart set on sth 52
know/learn sth off by heart 52
lose heart 52
open your heart 52
pour your heart out 52
put your heart and soul into sth 52
sb's heart is in the right place 52
sb's heart is in their mouth 51
sb's heart misses/skips a beat 52
sb's heart sinks 52
set your heart on sth 52
take sth to heart 52
to your heart's content 52
heart-to-heart 52
in the heat of the moment 33
be in seventh heaven 2
heavy-going 17
as heavy as lead 60
dig your heels in 46
drag your heels/feet 26, 46
hard/hot on the heels of sth 46
like a bat out of hell 60
have had it up to here 3
a red herring 34
a hidden agenda 9
a high-flyer 20
hit sb where it hurts (most) ii
hit the big time 6
hit the ceiling/roof 41
hit the road 40
hit/be rock bottom 42
not know what hit me 21
be hitting/banging your head against a brick
    wall ii, 48
a hive of activity 57
hold fire 38
hold the key to sth 41
hold your ground ii
hold/keep sb at arm's length 47
hold/stand your ground 59
get (hold of) the wrong end of the stick 4
put sth on hold 25
be left holding the baby 7
a black hole 34
dig yourself into a hole 7
need sth like you need a hole in the head 18
be/feel at home 41
bring sth home to sb 41
come home to you 41
make yourself at home 41
by hook or by crook i, 17
get/let sb off the hook 9
take the bull by the horns 37
a dark horse 36
not look a gift horse in the mouth ii
hot/hard on the heels of sth 46

be in **hot** water 33
blow **hot** and cold 33
strike while the iron is **hot** 15
get on like a **house** on fire 22
be as safe as **houses** 41
people who live in glass **houses** 29
wouldn't **hurt** a fly 36
hit sb where it **hurts** (most) ii
the **icing** on the cake 39
not have the faintest **idea** 4
not have the foggiest (**idea**) 4
put **ideas** into sb's head 48
if need be 18
be a figment of your **imagination** 5
from time **immemorial** ii
in a nutshell 10
in cold blood 53
in keeping with sth 18
in the bag 8
be **in** line for sth 56
be **in** the air 42
be **in** the dark 42
be **in** the doldrums 43
be **in** the red 34
be **in** your element 42
be/get/stay **in** touch with sb 22
have it **in** for sb 22
keep **in** touch with sb 22
keep sb **in** the picture 41
put sb **in** the picture 41
not budge/give an **inch** 10, 23
add insult to **injury** 12
the **ins** and outs 5
know sth **inside** out 4
fade/pale into **insignificance** 14
add **insult** to injury 12
strike while the **iron** is hot 15
get/have **itchy** feet 1, 46
give sth up as a bad **job** 58
make the best of a bad **job** 58
jog sb's memory 30
be no **joke** 27
come (back) down to earth with a **jolt**/bang/
   bump ii, 42
jump for **joy** 2, 21
against your better **judgement** 58
jump for joy 2, 21
jump in the deep end 33
jump the gun 38
jump/get/leap on the bandwagon 13
the law of the **jungle** 37
Just my luck! 19
keep a lid on sth 14
keep a low profile 20
keep a straight face 49
keep an eye on 50
keep an eye out for sb/sth 50
keep an open mind 53
keep in touch with sb 22
keep sb in the dark 42

keep sb in the picture 41
keep sb on their toes 46
keep sb/sth at bay 22
keep track 26
keep up appearances 20
keep your fingers crossed 45
Keep your hair on! 49
keep your hand in 45
keep your head 48
keep your head above water 48
keep your head down 48
keep yourself to yourself 22
keep/bear in mind 30
keep/have an open mind 53
keep/have one eye on 50
keep/have both/your feet on the ground 46
keep/hold sb at arm's length 47
can't **keep** your eyes off 50
in **keeping** with sth 18
hold the **key** to sth 41
kick the bucket 1
get a (real) **kick** out of sth 2
do sth for **kicks** 2
kill two birds with one stone i, ii, 37
make a **killing** 24
not take **kindly** to sth 21
on a **knife**-edge 16
put/stick the **knife** in ii, 38
twist the **knife** 38
knock sth on the head 48
tie yourself (up) in **knots** ii, 10
know sth inside out 4
know sth like the back of your hand 54
know the ropes 43
know where you stand 5
know your stuff 4
know/learn sth off by heart 52
not **know** the meaning of the word 28
not **know** what hit me 21
not **know** where to put yourself 21
not **know** which way to turn 21
at the bottom of the (career) **ladder** 25
at the top of the (career) **ladder** 25
career **ladder** 25
climb to the top of the career **ladder** 25
land/fall on your feet 46
find out how the **land** lies 42
take a stroll/trip down memory **lane** 30
be in the **lap** of the gods 19
in the **lap** of luxury 24
loom **large** 23
be **larger** than life 23
it's the **last** straw 29
laugh your head off 48
Don't make me **laugh.** 11
a **laughing** stock 13
be no **laughing** matter 27
become a **law** unto yourself 9
lay down the **law** 9
take the **law** into your own hands 9

the **law** of the jungle 37
lay/put your cards on the table 35
lead sb astray 16
as heavy as **lead** 60
one thing **leads** to another 15
shake like a **leaf** 42
take a **leaf** out of sb's book 41
lean/bend over backwards 54
leap/get/jump on the bandwagon 13
by/in **leaps** and bounds 26
learn the ropes 43
learn your lesson 5
learn/know sth off by heart 52
leave a lot to be desired 13
leave a sour taste in the mouth 39
leave sb in the lurch 14
leave sb to their own devices 9
leave well alone 16
leave your mark 6
I can take it or **leave** it. 11
left, right and centre 26
be **left** holding the baby 7
the **left** hand doesn't know what the right hand
   is doing i
cost (sb) an arm and a **leg** 47
not have a **leg** to stand on 47
pull sb's **leg** 47
hold/keep sb at arm's **length** 47
go to any/great **lengths** 55
the **lesser** of two evils 15
learn your **lesson** 5
teach sb a **lesson** 5
let off steam 44
let the cat out of the bag ii, 37
let yourself go 14
let/get sb off the hook 9
a **level** playing field 35
keep a **lid** on sth 14
lie through your teeth i, 51
a pack of **lies** 27
find out how the land **lies** 42
a fact of **life** 7
be larger than **life** 23
can't for the **life** of me 4
Get a **life!** 11
Such is **life.** 11
take your **life** into your hands 16
That's **life.** 11
It's/That's the story of my **life.** 11
the facts of **life** 7
This is the **life!** 11
your **life** is in sb's hands 16
once in a **lifetime** 32
not **lift** a finger 45
thumb a **lift** 45
light at the end of the tunnel 8
be all sweetness and **light** 12
be as **light** as a feather 60
bring sth to **light** 8
come to **light** 8

give sth the green **light** 34
make **light** of 27
Many hands make **light** work. 29
shed/throw **light** on 8
like greased **lightning** 60
like gold dust 12
A **likely** story. 27
be out on a **limb** 16
go out on a **limb** 16
line of work 56
a fine/thin **line** 56
be in **line** for sth 56
be in the firing **line** 38
be out of **line** 56
draw a **line** under sth 56
draw the **line** (at sth) 56
drop sb a **line** 56
sign on the dotted **line** 56
step out of **line** 56
the bottom **line** 56
toe the **line** 46
along the **lines** of sth 56
along/on the right **lines** 56
along/on the same **lines** 56
get your **lines/**wires crossed 44
read between the **lines** 56
lingua franca 28
pay **lip** service to 51
My **lips** are sealed. 51
a **list** as long as your arm 55
A **little** bird told me. 36
live (from) hand to mouth 51
live on another planet 42
live/be on the breadline 24
never **live** sth down 15
people who **live** in glass houses 29
you haven't **lived** 11
in/within **living** memory 30, 31
be a **load/**weight off your mind 53
be as easy as falling off a **log** 17
sleep like a **log** 42
be at **loggerheads** i, 22
a **lone** wolf 36
a **long** face 55
a **long** haul 55
a list as **long** as your arm 55
come a **long** way 55
cut a **long** story short i, 55
go a **long** way 55
go back a **long** way 55
How **long** is a piece of string? 55
in the **long** run 31
in the **long/**medium/short term 31
It's a **long** story. 55
Long time no see. 55
long-winded 55
take a **long,** hard look at sth 55
look daggers at 38
look like death warmed up 1
look like something the cat brought/dragged
   in 60

spend **money** like water 24
flavour of the **month** 39
be over the **moon** 2, 42
once in a blue **moon** 32
The **more** the merrier. 11
make the **most** of 14
go through the **motions** 17
by word of **mouth** 51
foaming at the **mouth** 51
leave a sour taste in the **mouth** 39
live (from) hand to **mouth** 51
make sb's **mouth** water 39, 51
mouth-watering 51
not look a gift horse in the **mouth** ii
sb's heart is in their **mouth** 51
get a **move** on 26
face the **music** 7
make a **name** for yourself 20
you **name** it 11
be caught **napping** 16
a **narrow** escape 16
a **necessary** evil 16
be a pain in the **neck** 49
breathe down sb's **neck** 49
if **need** be 18
need sth like you **need** a hole in the head 18
neither here nor there 11
get/grate on sb's **nerves** 12
a **nervous**/quivering wreck 43
never live sth down 15
new blood 20
in the **nick** of time 31
nine times out of ten 32
be on cloud **nine** 2
in **no** time at all 32
be second to **none** 12
neither here **nor** there 11
be as plain as the **nose** on your face 60
get right up sb's **nose** 51
No such luck! 11, 19
No way! 11
pay through the **nose** for sth i, 24
poke/stick your **nose** into 51
turn your **nose** up 51
be **not** on 15
There's **nothing** to it. 11
think **nothing** of 14
in the middle of **nowhere** 23
pluck a **number** out of the air 33
do your **nut** 3
in a **nutshell** 10
be as **nutty** as a fruitcake 1
put/stick your **oar** in 43
a drop in the **ocean** 33
the **odd** one out 20
against (all) (the) **odds** ii, 19
odds and ends i
be **off** the beaten track 40
be **off** your rocker 1
be **off** your trolley 1

go **off** the deep end 3
off and on 32
off the top of your head 48
off your own bat 35
off-colour 1
off-the-cuff 27
on and **off** 32
on the **off**-chance 19
be **on** about 27
be **on** edge 21
be **on** sb's back 54
be **on** the ball 35
be **on** the cards 35
be **on** the go 25
be **on** the mend 1
be **on** the right track 40
be **on** the run 26
be **on** the threshold of sth 31
be **on** the wrong track 40
be not **on** 15
off and **on** 32
on a knife-edge 16
on and off 32
on paper 25
on the big/expensive, etc. side 13
on the blink 50
on the face of it 49
on the one hand 10
on the other hand 10, 45
on the spot 26
to be **on** the safe side 8
once and for all 32
once in a blue moon 32
once in a lifetime 32
be **one** sandwich short of a picnic 1
come down on **one** side or the other 41
could do sth with **one** arm/hand tied behind
    your back 54
Don't put all your eggs in **one** basket. 29
go **one** better 58
go back to square **one** 35
go in **one** ear and out the other 51
have/keep **one** eye on 50
kill two birds with **one** stone i, ii, 37
on the **one** hand 10
one thing leads to another 15
one way or another 15
six of **one** and half a dozen of the other 11
the odd **one** out 20
open sb's eyes to sth 50
open your heart 52
have/keep an **open** mind 53
with your eyes **open** 50
be a matter of **opinion** 28
be a tall **order** 28
on the **other** hand 10
six of one and half a dozen of the **other** 11
the **other** side of the coin 10
out of the blue i, 42
out-of-date 31

be **out** for blood 3
be **out** of action 57
be **out** of line 56
be **out** of sorts 2
be **out** of this world 12
be **out** of touch with 4
be **out** of your depth 33
be **out** of your element 42
be **out** on a limb 16
get **out** of hand 45
go **out** of your way to do sth 17
go **out** on a limb 16
go all **out** 17
have it **out** with sb 22
out-and-**out** 12
Out of sight, **out** of mind. 30
the odd one **out** 20
the ins and **outs** 5
be **over** the moon 2, 42
be **over** the top 15
do your **own** thing 18
have a mind of its **own** 53
be as strong as an **ox** 60
at a snail's **pace** 37
a **pack** of lies 27
put **paid** to 24
be a **pain** in the neck 49
pale/fade into insignificance 14
be as flat as a **pancake** 60
panic stations 16
on **paper** 25
a **party** animal 36
pass your sell-by date 39
pass the buck i, 35
be **past** your sell-by date 39
sb's **paths** cross 40
give you **pause** for thought ii
pay lip service to 51
pay the price for 24
pay through the nose for sth i, 24
There's no **peace**/rest for the wicked! ii
take care of the **pence**/pennies 29
people who live in glass houses 29
fall off your **perch** 1
to coin a **phrase** 27
pick sb's brains 53
pick up the bill/tab ii, 24
pick up the pieces 8
have a bone to **pick** with sb 47
take your **pick** 18
be one sandwich short of a **picnic** 1
get the **picture** 41
keep sb in the **picture** 41
put sb in the **picture** 41
a **piece**/slice of the action 57
be a **piece** of cake 17
give sb a **piece** of your mind 3
How long is a **piece** of string? 55
pick up the pieces 8
a guinea **pig** 36

make a real **pig** of yourself 36
put/send the cat among the **pigeons** i, 3, 37
a bitter **pill** (to swallow) 1
sugar the **pill** 1
a **pillar** of society 20
be in the **pipeline** 44
fever **pitch** 26
all over the **place** 26
fall into **place** 8
sb's heart in the right **place** 52
go **places** 6
avoid sth like the **plague** 60
be **plain** sailing 43
be as **plain** as the nose on your face 60
live on another **planet** 42
all work and no **play** 29
be child's **play** 17
play ball 35
play devil's advocate 13
play it by ear 51
play with fire 33
play your cards right 35
While the cat's away, the mice will **play.** 29
a level **playing** field 35
pluck a number out of the air 33
take the **plunge** 35
There's no **point** / It's no good crying over spilt milk. 29
a sore **point**/spot 1
be beside the **point** 28
miss the **point** 28
poke fun at 12
poke/stick your nose into 51
I wouldn't touch sb/sth with a barge **pole.** 18
politically correct 20
go to the **polls** 9
pop your clogs 1
take **pot** luck 19
pour cold water on sth 33
pour your heart out 52
the answer to sb's **prayers** 8
prepare the ground 59
under false **pretences** 13
at a (considerable) **price** 24
pay the price for 24
the fine/small **print** 28
no **prizes** for guessing sth 19
keep a low **profile** 20
blow sth out of (all) **proportion** 14
the **pros** and cons i, 10
pull out (all) the stops 25
pull sb's leg 47
pull your finger out 17
pull your weight 17
pull/make a face 49
pull/tear your hair out 49
push the boat out 43
push your luck 19
at a **push** 17
if **push** comes to shove 18

take a back **seat** 54
second best 58
be **second** to none 12
have **second** thoughts i, 5
as far as the eye can **see** 60
be glad/happy/pleased/not sorry to **see** the back
    of sth 54
Long time no **see.** 55
see eye to eye 50
see how / which way the wind is blowing 33
see sth coming (a mile off) 19
see sth out of the corner of your eye 50
see/spot sth a mile off 23
would not be **seen** dead 18
be past / pass your **sell**-by date 39
send/drive sb round the bend/twist i, ii, 3, 40
send/put the cat among the pigeons i, 3, 37
pay lip **service** to 51
have your heart **set** on sth 52
not **set** the world on fire 33
set alarm bells ringing 16
set your heart on sth 52
set/put sb's mind at rest 53
set/put the record straight 5
be in **seventh** heaven 2
shake like a leaf 42
the **shape** of things to come 31
all **shapes** and sizes 23
shed/throw light on 8
shift your ground 59
take a **shine** to sb 22
be in sb's **shoes** 15
step into sb's **shoes** 25
talk **shop** 25
be one sandwich **short** of a picnic 1
cut a long story **short** i, 55
in the **short**/medium/long term 31
give it a **shot**/whirl 8
have a **shot** at 38
call the **shots** 38
a **shoulder** to cry on 47
give sb the cold **shoulder** 47, 49
have a chip on your **shoulder** 47
stand **shoulder** to **shoulder** 47
shout your head off 48
if push comes to **shove** 18
show sb the ropes 43
be **sick** and tired 21
come down on one **side** or the other 41
get out of bed on the wrong **side** 41
on the big/expensive, etc. **side** 13
the other **side** of the coin 10
to be on the safe **side** 8
have a memory like a **sieve** 60
lose **sight** of 5
Out of **sight**, out of mind. 30
be a **sign** of the times 31
sign on the dotted line 56
be as ugly as **sin** 60
sb's heart **sinks** 52

sit on the fence 41
six of one and half a dozen of the other 11
all shapes and **sizes** 23
by the **skin** of your teeth 16, 51
sb's heart **skips**/misses a beat 52
sleep like a log 42
a **slice**/piece of the action 57
the best/greatest thing since **sliced** bread 39
a **slime** ball ii
a **slip** of the tongue 27
slip your mind 30
be as **slippery** as an eel 60
slog/sweat/work your guts out 53
as **sly**/cunning as a fox 60
a **small** fortune 23, 24
in **small** doses 23
It's a **small** world. 11
lose a **small** fortune 24
make a **small** fortune 24
small talk 27
the **small**/fine print 28
There's no **smoke** without fire. 33
go up in **smoke** 33
at a **snail's** pace 37
snail mail 37
be **snowed** under 25
a pillar of **society** 20
have a **soft** spot for sb 22
a **sore** point/spot 1
be like a bear with a **sore** head 37, 60
stand/stick out like a **sore** thumb 45
be out of **sorts** 2
bare your **soul**/heart 52
put your heart and **soul** into sth 52
safe and **sound** i, 16
leave a **sour** taste in the mouth 39
sour grapes 2
put/throw a **spanner** in the works 44
go **spare** 3
Actions **speak** louder than words. 29
speak your mind 28
not be on **speaking** terms 3
spend money like water 24
It's no good / There's no point crying over **spilt**
    milk. 29
a **spin** doctor 9
a sore **spot**/point 1
have a soft **spot** for sb 22
on the **spot** 26
spot/see sth a mile off 23
spread like wildfire 33
spread yourself too thin 7
the word **spread** 26
spring/come to mind 30
on the **spur** of the moment 35
go back to **square** one 35
stab sb in the back 54
the cards are **stacked** against you 19
sb's **stamping**/stomping ground 59
know where you **stand** 5

be at the end of your **tether** 21
Thanks a million! 11
That's life. 11
then and there 32
there and then 32
There's nothing to it. 11
be **thick** on the ground 59
Blood is **thicker** than water. 29
a **thin**/fine line 56
be **thin** on the ground 59
spread yourself too **thin** 7
do your own **thing** 18
make a big **thing** of 23
one **thing** leads to another 15
the best/greatest **thing** since sliced bread 39
never/not do **things**/anything by halves 13
the shape of **things** to come 31
think better of sth 58
think big 23
think nothing of 14
This is the life! 11
a train of **thought** 30
give sb food for **thought** 5
give you pause for **thought** ii
have second **thoughts** i, 5
hang by a **thread** 16
be on the **threshold** of sth 31
be **thrilled** to bits 2, 21
be at each other's **throat** 49
bring a lump to your **throat** 14
ram sth down sb's **throat** 49
throw sb in the deep end 33
throw the baby out with the bathwater 13
throw/have a fit 3
throw/put a spanner in the works 44
throw/shed light on 8
a rule of **thumb** 45
be under sb's **thumb** 45
give sth the **thumbs** down/up 45
stand/stick out like a sore **thumb** 45
thumb a lift 45
tick over 44
the **tide** turns 33
tie up loose ends 8
tie yourself (up) in knots ii, 10
could do sth with one arm/hand **tied** behind
    your back 54
tighten your belt 24
How **time** flies! 11
be only a matter of **time** 31
before your **time** 31
for the **time** being 31
from **time** immemorial ii
give sb a hard/rough/tough **time** 12, 14
have a lot of **time** for sb 31
hit the big **time** 6
in a **time** warp 31
in no **time** at all 32
in the nick of **time** 31
Long **time** no see. 55

make up for lost **time** 31
stand the test of **time** 31
from **time** to **time** 32
be a sign of the **times** 31
nine **times** out of ten 32
(be) on the **tip** of your tongue 30, 51
be sick and **tired** 21
to hand 45
toe the line 46
keep sb on their **toes** 46
toffee-nosed 20
get your act **together** 57
put two and two **together** 4
as if there was/were no **tomorrow** 31
like there's no **tomorrow** 31
a slip of the **tongue** 27
(be) on the tip of your **tongue** 30, 51
bite your **tongue** 51
too many cooks 29
have a sweet **tooth** 39
at the **top** of sb's/the agenda 15
at the **top** of the (career) ladder 25
be on **top** of the world 2, 21
be over the **top** 15
climb to the **top** of the career ladder 25
off the **top** of your head 48
be **touch**-and-go 19
be out of **touch** with 4
be/get/stay in **touch** with sb 22
I wouldn't **touch** sb/sth with a barge pole. 18
be a **tough**/hard act to follow 12
give sb a **tough**/hard/rough time 12, 14
be off the beaten **track** 40
be on the right **track** 40
be on the wrong **track** 40
keep **track** 26
a **train** of thought 30
the **travel** bug 36
do the **trick** 6
take a **trip**/stroll down memory lane 30
be off your **trolley** 1
be asking for **trouble**/it 12
(not) ring **true** 27
try a different tack 43
try your hand at sth 45
light at the end of the **tunnel** 8
not **turn** a hair 49
not know which way to **turn** 21
turn a blind eye 50
turn heads 48
turn your hand to sth 45
turn your nose up 51
when/while sb's back is **turned** 54
the tide **turns** 33
drive/send sb round the **twist**/bend i, ii, 3, 40
twist sb's arm 47
twist the knife 38
two-time sb 22
kill **two** birds with one stone i, ii, 37
stand on your own **two** feet 46

the lesser of **two** evils 15
put **two** and **two** together 4
be as **ugly** as sin 60
be **under** sb's thumb 45
be **under** your feet 46
go **under** your own steam 44
an **unknown** quantity 23
up-and-coming 20, 25
an **uphill** battle/fight/struggle 40
be (right) **up** your alley/street 40
be **up** in arms 38
be **up** in the air 42
make it **up** to sb 22
on your **way up** 20
upper-crust 42
take sth at face **value** 49
a **vicious** circle 10
sb/sth is a **victim** of their/its own success 6
be **walking**/floating on air 2
a fly on the **wall** 36
be banging/hitting your head against a brick
    wall ii, 48
come up against a brick **wall** 7
drive sb up the **wall** 3
wave a magic **wand** 8
for **want** of a better word 27
look like death **warmed** up 1
in a time **warp** 31
wash your hands of sb/sth 45
be (like) **water** off a duck's back i, 37
be in deep **water** 33
be in hot **water** 33
be like a fish out of **water** 60
Blood is thicker than **water.** 29
keep your head above **water** 48
make sb's mouth **water** 39, 51
pour cold **water** on sth 33
spend money like **water** 24
wave a magic wand 8
be on the same **wavelength** 44
make **waves** 33
be in a bad **way** 58
come a long **way** 55
get your own **way** 9
go a long **way** 55
go back a long **way** 55
go out of your **way** to do sth 17
No **way!** 11
not know which **way** to turn 21
one **way** or another 15
rub sb up the wrong **way** 3, 22
see how/which **way** the wind is blowing 33
be/feel under the **weather** 1
be a **weight**/load off your mind 53
pull your **weight** 17
leave **well** alone 16
well-heeled 24
well-off 24

well-to-do i, 24
when the chips are down 35
know **where** you stand 5
not know **where** to put yourself 21
whet your appetite 39
(not) be worth your **while** 18
give it a **whirl**/shot 8
in black and **white** 34
white-collar 34
There's no peace/rest for the **wicked!** ii
be **wide** of the mark 35
spread like **wildfire** 33
get **wind** of sth 33
sail close to the **wind** 43
see how / which way the **wind** is blowing 33
get your **wires**/lines crossed 44
wish the ground would swallow you up 59
be at your **wits'** end 3
a lone **wolf** 36
a **woman**/man after your own heart 52
by **word** of mouth 51
for want of a better **word** 27
get a **word** in edgeways 28
have a **word** in sb's ear 51
in a **word** 27
not know the meaning of the **word** 28
the **word** spread 26
word for word 28
Actions speak louder than **words.** 29
be lost for **words** 27
all **work** and no play 29
be up to your ears/eyes (in **work**) 25
have your **work** cut out 25
line of **work** 56
Many hands make light **work.** 29
work against the clock 32
work like magic 6
work/go like a dream 6
work/go/run like clockwork 32
work/slog/sweat your guts out 53
put/throw a spanner in the **works** 44
be on top of the **world** 2, 21
be out of this **world** 12
It's a small **world.** 11
not be the end of the **world** 2
not set the **world** on fire 33
the best of both **worlds** 58
a can of **worms** 10, 37
go from bad to **worse** 58
sb's bark is **worse** than their bite 36
be your own **worst** enemy 38
if the **worst** comes to the **worst** 58
(not) be **worth** your while 18
wouldn't dream of 14
a nervous/quivering **wreck** 43
be on the **wrong** track 40
get (hold of) the **wrong** end of the stick 4
get out of bed on the **wrong** side 41
get/start off on the **wrong** foot 46

rub sb up the **wrong** way 3, 22
from/since the **year** dot 31
keep **yourself** to **yourself** 22